CW01677166

EX LIBRIS

Paula Diamandi

Boston, Massachusetts

January 1981

Illustrated Dictionary of Fabrics

Illustrated Dictionary of Fabrics

Martin Hardingham

STUDIO VISTA

A Studio Vista book published by
Cassell & Collier Macmillan Publishers Ltd,
35 Red Lion Square, London WC1R 4SG
and at Sydney, Auckland, Toronto, Johannesburg,
an affiliate of
Macmillan Publishing Co., Inc.,
New York

Copyright © Martin Hardingham 1978
First published in 1978

All rights reserved. No part of this
publication may be reproduced, stored in
any retrieval system, or transmitted in any
form or by any means, electronic, mechanical,
photocopying or otherwise,
without the prior permission in writing of
the Publishers.

Designed and produced by George Rainbird Ltd,
36 Park Street, London W1Y 4DE

Editors: Mary Anne Sanders and Fiona Roxburgh
Design: Youé and Spooner Ltd
Picture Research: Tom Graves
Photographs: Dave Bradfield
Diagrams: Phil Green
Production: Jane Collins and Bridget Walsh

ISBN: 0 289 70847 8

Set by Tradespools, Frome, Somerset, England
Printed by Butler and Tanner Ltd, Frome, Somerset, England

Frontispiece: Voile with satin stripes

Contents

Gilbert Deblois,

At his Shop oppoſite School-Street, near the Old South Meeting-Houſe, BOSTON,

Imports from LONDON, BRISTOL, and SCOTLAND,

And Sells at the very loweſt Rates for Ready Money only,

ALL ſorts Engliſh, India & Scotch Goods, with moſt ſorts of Hard Ware,

viz. Plain and ſtrip'd Duffil Shag, Rugs, Blankets, Cotton Counterpins, Flannels, Baizes, Ratteens, German Serges, Kerſeys, Bearſkins, Bath Beavers Beaver Coating, Whitneys, ſcarlet, crimſon, and all other colour'd Broad Cloths, Duroys, Sagathees, Fuſtians, Cotton Thickſets, dyed Jeans, Hair Pluſhes, Cotton Velvets, worſted knit Breeches Patterns, flower'd Drawboys of all Colours, Damaſcus, &c. &c. with all ſorts Shalloons, Buttons, Twiſt, &c. to ſuit.—Double and twiſted Camblets, Callamancoes, Tammies, plain and ſtriped Camblets, Poplin, colour'd Crapes, Silverets, Grazets, Brolioes, figur'd Pruſſians, ſilk and cotton Luteſtrings, with every other kind neweſt faſhion plain & figur'd Stuffs.—A large Aſſortment of Callicoes, Chints, Copperplate Furniture for Beds.—Beſt Engliſh ſilk Damaſks, Ducapes Grograms, plain and flower'd Luteſtrings, Mantua Silks, Capuchin Silks, plain and flower'd Sattins for Hatts and Cloaks, of all Colours, with ſuitable Trimmings.—A great Aſſortment of Mens, Womens and Childrens Hoſe, Mens worſted and ſilk Caps, Mens, Womens and Childrens Gloves and Mitts of all kinds, faſhionable Engliſh made Bonnets, Hats, Cloaks, Scarffs, &c. A beautiful Aſſortment of Ribbons, plain and flower'd Gauze, Catgut, all kinds of Silk, Cotton and Linnen Handkerchiefs, Fans, Head and Breaſt Flowers, Feathers, Turbans and Tippets, Necklaces, &c. all Widths of Mancheſter Checks, Iriſh Linnens, Cambricks, Lawns, &c. &c. Table Linnen, &c. Mens and Boys Hats, beſt London Wool and Cotton Cards, Engliſh and German Steel, Powder, Shot, London Pewter, French Flints, Nails, Bar and Sheet Lead, Tin'd Plates, Window Glaſs, with a Variety of Braziery, Ironmongery, Cutlary and other ſmall Wares.——Choice Bohea and Hyſon Tea, warranted good, Pepper and other Spices, Looking-Glaſſes, a large Collection of genteel China, Engliſh and German Flutes, Violins, and beſt Roman Strings, &c. &c.

☞ The above Goods will be ſold very Cheap, but no Abatement made on the Prices aſked.

18th-century broadside describing imported European and Indian fabrics into America

Introduction

This catalog contains a comprehensive collection of names and descriptions of fabrics we wear and use in our homes, as well as some used for industrial purposes. This is a reference book for people who use fabrics of all kinds and it is not intended that it should advise the expert. It shows in the simplest terms origins and true descriptions of fabrics which are known today. Some of these names are well known and others less common. The illustrations throughout show for what purpose the fabrics were originally used, for what purpose they have been used or what purpose they could be used. Sometimes it is possible to illustrate the fabric itself but it is not possible or even desirable to do this in every case because there are many cloths which look identical to each other, particularly in black and white.

For convenience, and in some way to give the book a degree of historical progression, the catalog is divided into sections dealing with the most significant fiber groups: wool and hair, cotton, silk, other plant fibers and finally man-made and mineral fibers. The term man-made is now used to describe the whole range of chemical fibers which at one time were referred to as synthetic or artificial. Since the early days of man-made fibers they have taken on their own character and are now not only used as substitutes, but are used to make fabrics for which no other natural fiber could ever be used.

One of the obvious problems we have today is deciding if it is better to buy the natural fiber cloth, the natural and man-made fiber mixture or the 100 per cent man-made fiber cloth. Usually man-made fiber fabrics are less expensive but this need not necessarily be the only reason you choose a particular cloth or garment. Drip-dry, wash-and-wear, easycare are familiar terms we use today. Until recent years these terms would only be used where man-made fibers were used in combination with natural fibers or by themselves. However, synthetic resins are now applied to natural fibers making them easier to wash or clean. The more fibers and finishes there are the more confusing it becomes and the more difficult it is to choose.

Increasingly it is the responsibility of the fiber producer, the fabric manufacturer and the garment maker to give the consumer accurate information regarding the fiber content and finish of a piece of cloth or a garment with explicit instructions on how to wash or clean it. There are many useful books which set out to help the consumer choose the right fabric for the right job but there are few, which give a description of a fabric and identify it with a specific name. This information is necessary because of the incredible differences of terminology used throughout the textile industry. Not only are these differences found between countries but also between producers within the same country. The term denim for instance is the name of a cloth, which in recent years, has been very popular all over the world and jeans, which are made of denim are the mode of dress for millions of people. Traditionally, however, denim is a fabric which was used for working garments only and is part of the American tradition, so although the fashion for wearing this fabric might decrease it will continue to be used as an ideal cloth for working clothes. Denim is a cotton cloth and it got its name from Nîmes, in France, where it was originally made. It has a specific look, feel and is traditionally blue. Now we see drip dry denim, different colored denim, printed denim and knitted denim which, in the true sense of the word, is not denim at all—and this can become very confusing.

This book provides the basis of a different language—the language of textiles—needed to identify fabrics more accurately. A thorough description of each fabric type is included along with the sources of the fabric and fiber names, an important and revealing addition. Usually the names come from one of the following four main sources: country of origin; process by which the fabric is made or finished; material content; use. However, clever names are continually being invented for fibers and fabrics, so there are many exceptions to the above sources. A textile manufacturer is free to borrow parts of the names of different fabrics and combine them into a new one. A fabric might be a combination of the fiber name and the original fabric name. A slight change of one syllable in the name of a fiber or fabric can create a new name and in the process add to the confusion. Or a fabric can be named after the manufacturer's wife, girlfriend, best customer, popular personality of the day or an animal.

So complex and numerous are the various possible combinations of fiber, construction and finish of fabrics that it would be impossible to list them all in one book and in any case the list would be out of date very soon. This book contains a list of fibers and fabrics which are current and can be identified by their original name. If throughout the course of time the fiber content changes or a new finish to the fabric is added the name of the fabric should remain the same. Poplin, for instance was originally made of pure cotton. It could have been made of the best quality Sea Island Cotton or Egyptian, American or Indian cotton. Poplin can also be made from any number of combinations of cotton and man-made fibers such as cotton and polyester. Polyester fiber is added for easy care, but the fabric looks the same, handles slightly differently, perhaps costs a little less but is still called poplin.

We are usually attracted to a fabric by its look and then by its feel. We first see its color, pattern and texture and then we handle the fabric to see if we like it or not. Color likes and dislikes are determined by social or cultural background, climate, age, superstition or fashion. This catalog is limited to descriptions of color and handle and only experience will help in formulating a sense of color and a feel for quality. There are many ways to describe pattern starting with simple terms like linear, checked, dotted, spotted, floral, ethnic, paisley, William Morris, art nouveau, arabesque, Tudor, half drop, ogee, large small, allover and so on. As long as designers design fabrics the patterns will be ever changing. Fabric texture is much less varied and less likely to change radically. One of the senses we seldom use when identifying fabric is that of smell. Wool for instance, particularly when it is being washed, has a distinctive smell different from any other fiber. The burning test for the identification of fibers is based on smell. When yarn or cloth is scorched or burnt it has its own odor and quite often this can be helpful in finding out the unknown fiber content of a fabric. A table in the 'Textile Terms' section shows this in more detail.

No judgments have been made about the use of certain fabrics for specific purposes. Apart from those which have an obvious industrial use, the merits and demerits of each fabric are a matter of personal taste and the mode of the moment determines whether to acclaim or deride the rags of the trade. The examples of the fabrics illustrated and the pictures of the fabrics in use have been selected to show the character of the cloth and not the aesthetic quality. A fabric used in one way today may be used in a completely new way tomorrow.

Wool

The History of Wool

Our word wool comes from the Old English *wull.* The Latin was *lana*, and this is the origin of the word for wool in six of the important European languages, often encountered on garment labels:

Greek—lenos	French—laine
Italian—lana	Portugese—lá
Spanish—lana	German—Wolle

Wool, which is the hair of the sheep, has been used as a textile fiber in clothing for the past 6000 years. Over the long history of the domestication of the sheep it has primarily been reared for its meat. There are many references to sheep, lambs and wool in the Bible and other early accounts are found in the writings of Herodotus (484–425 BC), Ovid (43 BC–AD 18) and Pliny (AD 23–79). The Romans considered the rearing of sheep and weaving woolen cloth a very important industry and in AD 80 they started wool weaving in Britain and later brought sheep to Spain. The climate in Spain was ideal for rearing sheep and in the province of Tanaconensis the Merino sheep was developed by crossing the Tarentine with the Laodicean from Asia Minor. The Merino sheep was highly prized and protected and only the wealthy owned Merino sheep. Although they could not be exported a special gift of Merino sheep was given to the king of France who kept them on his farm at Rambouillet.

Toward the end of the tenth century wool was already a fast growing export from England. By the eleventh century the Flemish weavers whom William the Conqueror had allowed to settle in England began to develop the craft of weaving. In 1080 the first weaver's guild was formed and in 1155 King Henry II granted a charter to establish the Worshipful Company of Weavers which has today the privilege of being the oldest of all Livery Companies in the City of London. This charter meant there could be greater supervision over the standards of clothmaking. As parent guild, the Company of Weavers also controlled the branches of the craft at that time which later became the independent guilds of Woolmen, Clothworkers, Dyers Mercers and Drapers. At that time a superior quality woolen cloth was being made in the village of Worstead near Norwich in the eastern part of England known as East Anglia. Today we use the word worsted to describe a wool yarn which has been combed and the short fibers removed to give a smooth, light and sometimes lustrous yarn.

The Domesday Book which was started in 1080, says a lot about sheep rearing and the production of wool but little is said about clothmaking. It was not until the fourteenth century, in fact, that the weaving industry began to flourish. A further influx of Flemish weavers were driven to England following an embargo enforced by King Edward III on the export of wool to Flanders. As the textile industry began to flourish in England with the immigration of the Huguenots in 1685 the first domesticated sheep landed in North America. Such were the restrictions on the export of wool and woolen yarn from England that the early colonists were forced to build their own woolen industry. In 1656 the Massachusetts General Court ordered each family to spin yarn:

> To assess each family for one or more spinners or fractional part that everyone thus assessed, do after this present year, 1656, spin thirty weeks every year a

pound per week of lining cotton wooling and so proportinaltely for halfte or quarter spinners under penalty of twelve pence for each pound short.

By 1768 even George Washington is said to have been making an average of a yard of cloth a day in his house at Mount Vernon.

Until this period all clothmaking processes had been done by hand but now was the time of inventions which were to revolutionize the textile industry: James Hargreaves invented the Spinning Jenny in 1764; Richard Arkwright invented the Water Frame Spinning Machine in 1769; Samuel Crompton invented the Spinning Mule in 1779; James Watt invented the steam engine which was applied to textile production in 1785. After this period the woolen industry in America and Europe developed rapidly and mechanical processes throughout the whole woolen industry replaced what had been until then a hand craft.

The so called Woolen Movement was started in Britain in 1870 by Gustav Jaeger, founder of the Jaeger Company known today for woolen cloth and clothing. He promoted the idea of a 'woolen health culture' where wool, if worn for clothing, should never be dyed. Among its distinguished followers were the British writers Oscar Wilde and George Bernard Shaw. Shaw took the cult very seriously and ordered a complete suit in natural undyed woolen stockinette. In the United States Mrs Amelia Bloomer introduced the fashion of woolen knickerbockers which were to be worn by females for cycling and playing games. The authoritative British medical journal, the *Lancet*, attacked this fashion in 1879 by saying these garments were unhealthy.

(opposite above) Medieval French stained glass window depicting the four stages of cloth finishing
(above) Mule spinning in Yorkshire, England

Wool Production

Although sheep are now reared in practically every country in the world for the production of wool, the main countries are Australia, New Zealand, South Africa and South America. The most internationally well known sheep is the Merino of Australia which came originally from Spain. Some of the sheep from Scotland such as the Cheviot and Shetland have become well known

by fabrics named after them. Today there is a world production of over 1,500,000,000 kilogrammes of clean wool per year from a population of over 925,000,000 sheep. Each breed of sheep produces a variety of types of wool which can be divided into five main groups:

1 Coarse kempy wool from hill and mountain sheep—Shetland, Herdwick, Scottish Blackface, Cheviot, Welsh Mountain, Swaledale, Lonk, Spaelsau.
2 Lustrous and semi-lustrous long wool from pure-bred sheep—Lincoln, Leicester, Border Leicester, Wensleydale, Romney Marsh or Kent, Cotswold, Devon Longwool, Dartmoor.
3 Short and medium Down wools from pure-bred sheep—Oxford, Dorset Down, Southdown, Suffolk, Hampshire, Devon Closewool, Shropshire, Clun Forest, Ryeland, Kerry Hill, Poll Dorset, Dorset Horn.
4 Fine soft short wool from pure-bred sheep—Merino, Rambouillet.
5 Crossbred wools from crossbred and halfbred sheep—Corriedale (Lincoln and Merino in New Zealand), Columbia (Lincoln and Rambouillet in the United States), Targhee (Lincoln and Rambouillet in the United States).

(left) Arab woman hand spinning with a spindle
(below left) Romney Marsh ram
(below—left to right) Welsh mountain yew with crossbred lambs; Blackface with crossbred lamb; Lincoln longwool; Border Leicester rams

(above)
The International Wool Secretariat Woolmark for pure new wool

The fleece of the sheep opened out flat to show the various types of wool

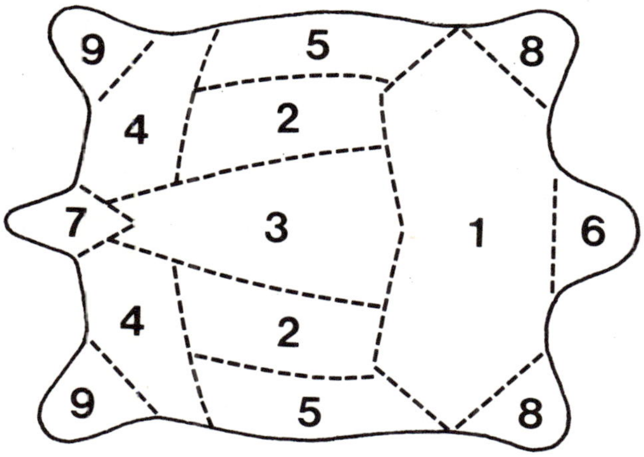

1 Shoulders—best quality
2 Sides—not as fine or regular as 3
3 Back—not so dense and less strong than 1
4 Haunches—coarse and long
5 Belly—fine and short
6 Neck—fine and short and slightly irregular
7 Tail—coarse and kempy
8 Forelegs—short and poor quality
9 Hind legs—coarse and strong

Cheviot sheep in Roxburgh, Scotland

Wool, which is very similar to the hair on the human head, is made up of small sections or scales which allow the fiber to bend without breaking. This gives wool a very special springy quality. So far no man-made fiber has yet been able to imitate this quality.

Producing a piece of woolen fabric is a lengthy process. The following simple chart shows the complete story from sheep to cloth:

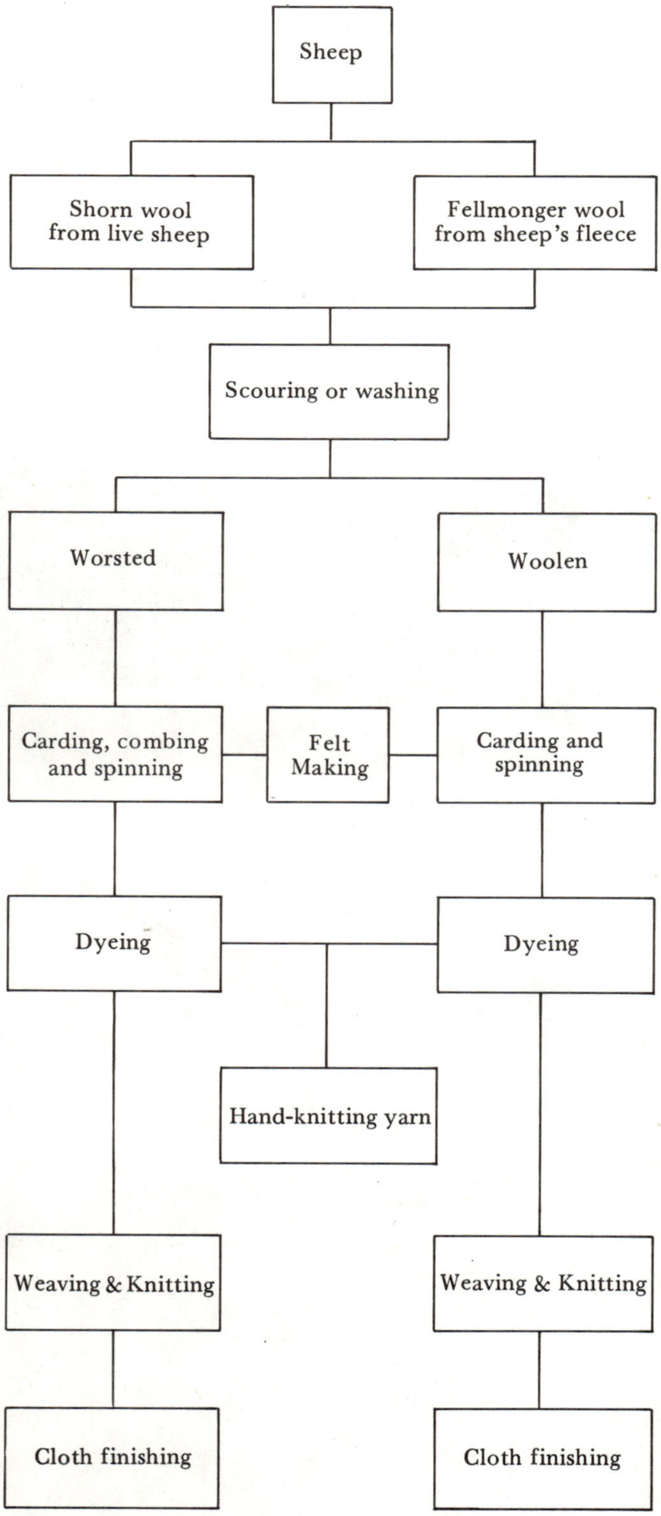

Wool is usually shorn off the sheep's back on the farm but where sheep are also farmed for meat the sheep is first killed and the fleece is processed by the fellmonger who pulls the wool from the skin. The wool fiber is then processed by the spinner to make yarn and during this process the wool is first sorted into various grades and scoured or washed. The clean dry wool is then carded to remove any vegetable matter and to mix the fibers thoroughly together, at the same time straightening the fibers ready for spinning. When preparing wool for worsted spinning the carded wool is combed to remove all the short fibers and parallel them to produce a smooth sliver which is then wound into a top ready for spinning. Before the final spinning process can take place the sliver is drawn out still further into a roving and then finally reduced in thickness and a twist inserted into the yarn. Two yarns may be twisted together to make 2-ply yarns or three to make 3-ply yarns and so on. It is possible to sheer a sheep, spin, dye, knit and finish a sweater in less than five hours.

One of the most amazing characteristics of woven or knitted woolen cloth is that it shrinks. This peculiar

property is technically called felting, fulling or milling. Felt is made by pummelling wool fibers together into a permanent entanglement. A good quality suiting is always well shrunk to give body to the cloth. For several hundreds of years the tailors in London have always had their cloth finished with a special process called London shrinking which at one time was carried out on the common land of Bermondsey in London. The cloth was sent down from the mills of Scotland and Yorkshire and rolled out on the grassland of the common. It was then left out over night to allow the dew to fall on it and the following day was walked (*waulked*) on to felt or mill the fabric. It was then pressed with heavy hot irons. Similar processes are still carried on today, no longer in London, with mechanical substitutions. A shrink resistant finish which prevents felting is now being applied to some woolen knitting yarns. Unless this special finish has been used on woolen garments or fabrics dry cleaning is recommended. Some knitted woolen garments can be washed with care.

Wool has many outstanding features which no other fiber can impersonate. It is absorbent (it can absorb 30 per cent of its weight without feeling damp), it dries slowly, is naturally water repellent, resilient and springy, strong when dry, weaker and more elastic when wet, flameproof and an excellent insulator. (On sheep it forms a natural insulator keeping the body heat even.) Sometimes it is difficult to identify wool or other animal fibers with the naked eye but a simple burning test can be used for identification: Wool melts first of all then burns steadily with a sizzle, finally disintegrating into a crumbly black deposit. There is a faint smell of ammonia while the wool is burning. Animal hair begins to decompose at 266°F (130°C), scorches at 399°F (204°C) and chars at 572°F (300°C). Drying woolen cloth in direct heat should be avoided. It will cause a harsh handle and will yellow. Prolonged exposure to sunlight will make wool harsh to handle, yellow and lose strength.

The United States Wool Products Labeling Act of 1941 stipulates the following definitions:

1 **Wool** means the fiber from the fleeces of the sheep or lamb or hair of the Angora or Cashmere goat (and may include the so-called speciality fibers from the hair of the camel, alpaca, llama and vicuna) which has never been reclaimed from any woven or felted wool product.
2 **Reprocessed wool** means the resulting fiber when wool has been woven or felted into a wool product which,

Bactrian camels

wit [illegible] any way by the ulti [illegible] been made into a fibr [illegible]

3 Re-[illegible] per when wool or rep [illegible] oven, knitted or felte [illegible] fter having been usec [illegible] ner, subsequently has [illegible]

The I [illegible] oolmark symbol signifie [illegible] only of pure new wool.

Oth [illegible] hich are used in textiles [illegible] uxury fibers and many of the animals are found in South America: alpaca, angora goat (mohair), angora rabbit, beaver, camel, cow, cashmere goat, chinchilla, deer, fox, goat, guanaco, hare, kangaroo, llama, muskrat, nutria, opossum, rabbit, raccoon, vicuna, yak, weasel, and sometimes dogs and cats. The hair from these animals is generally much softer than that of the sheep but more often much warmer to wear. Many of these animals are now protected species and use of this hair has been restricted.

Albatross
This is a fine, lightweight soft fabric woven in plain weave from worsted yarn. The twist of the yarns give it a characteristic crêpe feel and crinkled appearance. Traditionally, this cloth is piece-dyed usually in pale colours and used in sheer dresses, blouses and children's wear. This fabric returns into fashion periodically but has never been over popular. The name also applies to a plain woven, soft Egyptian cotton cloth, having a nap face. Many varieties of this cloth have been made and are known as: Satin Moss, Vienna, Snowflake (using a flecked yarn) and Llama Croise.

Albert Cloth
This is a double cloth construction woven to produce a double-faced fabric from different coloured, good quality woolen yarns. Sometimes it is made with a different check or stripe design on either face. Albert Cloth is a heavy, warm overcoating used by the best tailors who have often added to the garment, according to fashion, a distinctive velvet collar. Albert Twill is made of cotton in a 1 × 3 twill weave.

Alpaca
Alpaca is the name of an animal and is also the name given to certain fabrics. The alpaca, a member of the camel family and closely related to the llama, is found chiefly in Peru round Lake Titicaca. The colour of the fleece varies from white or reddish brown to black having a very fine and silky soft sheen. The suri, a breed of alpaca, produces an even finer quality fiber. Alpaca fabric is soft, warm and hairy. Cumbri is a cloth made of alpaca wool in Peru and Bolivia. Sometimes the yarn is spun into very fine threads and woven with silk or wool to produce dress cloths and luxurious men's jacket cloths. Alpaca wool is also spun by hand in Peru and used as a knitting yarn from which sweaters, ponchos, socks and hats are made. Alpaca fabric should be dry cleaned. Hand knitted garments should be washed very carefully in light suds or dry cleaned.

Andalusians
This is the term given to a variety of fancy woven, worsted dress fabrics made in England. Originally made from the finest Spanish merino wool, the name is taken from an area in southwestern Spain where this cloth was first produced. Andalusian wool is also the term used in England for a fine worsted knitting yarn. The yarn is fine and soft and is used for socks and stockings. It is similar to a Shetland knitting yarn but 2-ply instead of 4-ply.

(top) Alpaca and baby

(centre) Alpaca fabrics
(below) Andalusian

(top) Angora rabbit

(centre) Knitted and woven Astrakhan
(below) Karakul farming in the U.S.S.R.

Angora

The angora rabbit is a rodent and produces the finest of all hair. It is a very fine, fluffy and silky fiber commonly known as angora wool. Most angora rabbits are found in Turkey and Asia minor, and the best angora wools come from France, Italy and Japan. This hair is usually used in knitting yarn either by itself or combined with a fine woolen thread for strength. Angora is usually dyed in pale colours although the most popular shade is white. It is mainly used for sweaters and baby clothes. It is the softest of all wools.

Armure

At one time this cloth used to be woven only in silk and cotton but it is now best known as a wool used in dresses, coats and furnishings. *Armure* is a French term meaning small pattern and is a special weave resembling chain armor. The weave produces a pebbled ribbed effect on the face of the cloth. The name is also given to various types of metallic fabrics for evening wear. *Armure royale* is an all-worsted cloth. Silk armures resemble barathea and ottoman cloths.

Astrakhan

Real astrakhan is the name given to a second grade karakul (caracul) lambskin from sheep reared in Astrakhan, the Russian province bordering the Caspian Sea. It has longer hair and has a more open curl than the first grade of Karakul skin known as Persian lamb. It is usually brown. The lustrous, uneven, curled surface of astrakhan has been imitated in a heavy woven cloth made of wool, usually mohair, and is used in coats and hats, and trimmings. A knitted astrakhan is also made.

Baize

Baize is a loosely woven cloth, felted with a long nap on both sides, usually dyed green or red. The term baize was used in the early seventeenth century to specify a flannel-like cloth woven in the eastern counties of England. The name bay (pl. bayes), from the old French *baie*, a brownish red color, was used to describe the cloth which was originally made in several weights, the lightest being used for clothing. In the past it has also been used for table covers, lining cutlery drawers and gardener's aprons. *Bayetta* is the Spanish name for this fabric and the Navajo indians used strips of imported red *bayetta* to weave into their rugs. Brazilian baize is dyed orange by dye obtained from Brazil wood.

Bannockburn

Bannockburn tweed or suiting gets its name from a cloth woven originally in the historic Scottish town of that name made famous by the great Scottish victory over the English in 1314. The fabric is made in 2-and-2 twill weave from marled cheviot woolen spun yarns, prepared by twisting together two different colors and then woven to produce a mottled effect. Sometimes these 2-ply yarns are woven alternately with single yarns. These cloths are now made in the borders of Scotland and sometimes have fine silk stripes woven in the warp to add sparkle and relieve the all-over pattern. This cloth is ideal for jackets, suits and even lightweight overcoats.

Barathea

The name barathea, originally a registered trademark for an armure cloth made with a silk warp and worsted weft, and used for neckties and cravats, has become synonymous with a type of soft woven fabric with a broken twill effect. This fabric is now usually woven with worsted yarns throughout and is recognized by the twill hopsack weave which gives it a characteristic pebbled appearance. This cloth is commonly dyed black or dark blue, and used for suitings.

Beaver Cloth

This is a heavily milled and raised woolen overcoating cloth made from soft, fine grade wools, to imitate the fur of the beaver. Traditionally this cloth is made with a 4-end satin weave and is shrunk considerably, making it solid and firm. The longer nap of this fabric gives a softer feel than other cloths in the same group such as melton, kersey and broadcloth. This type of fabric is used for hats, uniforms and overcoats. A cheaper version is made with a cotton warp. A cloth called beaverteen made entirely of cotton in a broken twill weave with a short nap on both sides, has been produced and used in sportswear and as a tough trousering. The short, soft inner fur fibers of the beaver were used at one time in the production of top hats or beaver hats. This has now been replaced by silk. The Romans used the fur of the beaver in making very luxurious fabrics; these were known as *castoreae* from which the French have taken the name *castorine* for a coating made of beaver hair.

Bedford Cord

Originally this fabric was known as a cord broadcloth and was made in Britain by Flemish weavers during the reign of Edward III. Later in the fifteenth century it was adopted by the Duke of Bedford for his troops' uniforms. Since then this strong, worsted cloth has been used extensively for riding breeches and uniforms. It is usually dyed in solid shades ranging from ecru to brown. It is now made with man-made fibers, cotton, worsted or mixtures of all three. The Bedford cord weave gives this cloth its outstanding character by producing ribs or cords lengthwise or warpwise in the piece of cloth, similar to corduroy. Depending on the type and size of

(below) Eton boy in a top hat in 1934

(below) Bedford cord

yarn used, this weave, with all its modification, is used to produce other fabrics such as London cord, a heavy broad rib, all cotton cloth or the finest pique. The French make a similar fabric to Bedford cord, calling it *côte de cheval* while the term *diable fuerte* is the term used by the South Americans. Crocodile cloth is a Jacquard woven Bedford cord.

Championship game of snooker at Thurston Hall, London, 1938

Billiard Cloth

This fabric requires great skill to make and uses the finest merino wools. The cloth is usually woven in plain weave or 2-and-1 twill with great precision, then heavily milled and cropped producing a fabric which is perfectly smooth, soft and waterproof, capable of resisting the dampest atmosphere. Billiard cloth is traditionally dyed bright green and, as the name describes, is used for covering billiard table tops. An all cotton billiard cloth is now made but is less durable. During the nineteenth century, billiard cloth was exported from Britain to India where the green dye was extracted, and re-used to dye yarns for Kashmir shawls.

Small sample of Witney blanket cloth

Blanket

The name blanket comes from the old French word *blankete* which was derived from *blanc* meaning white. *Blankete* was an undyed woolen cloth chiefly used as a warm heavy bed covering. Blanket cloth, or blanketing from which blankets are made, is also used as a coating fabric. Acrylic fibres are now also commonly used to weave blanket cloth. The cloth is made with a 2-and-2 common twill weave, then raised or brushed with teasles to produce a deep dense nap on both sides. Some blankets are woven with a cellular or honeycomb weave and remain unbrushed.

There are many traditional types of blanket, most famous is the Witney produced in the town of that name near Oxford, England. The Mexican, South American and Navajo Indian blankets (*See* Navajo blanket, p31) are woven by hand using a plain tapestry weave, covering the warp threads completely with a heavy woolen weft. Moqui Indians weave an all-wool blanket in plain weave usually in black, blue and brown stripes. Blanket is also used in textile mill terminology to describe a sample length of cloth usually with a variety of different patterns and colorings in one piece.

Striped blazer at Henley-on-Thames, England, 1931

Blazer Cloths

The blazer is a jacket worn to identify a person who belongs to a particular club, school or college. The French word *blason* means a coat of arms (sometimes a badge is worn on the outside chest pocket) and to blazon literally means to inscribe with colors. Hence blazer cloths are made in a variety of solid colors and stripes, usually woven with a 5-end satin weave in worsted yarns. There have been many variations made and imitation blazer cloths are sometimes made with a plain weave, using wool, cotton or man-made fibers. These cloths are usually heavily milled, and can be used for lightweight jackets or suits.

Captain Cook's chart of Botany Bay, New South Wales, Australia

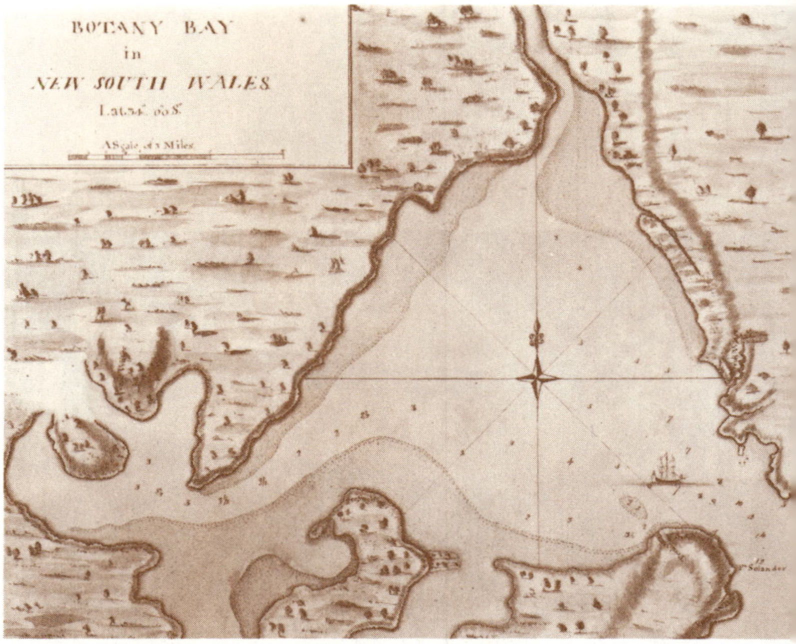

Botany

The term botany was originally applied to the fine, wavy wool from the Merino sheep grown near Botany Bay on the eastern coast of Australia. This is now always referred to as merino wool and it is only during processing—i.e., spinning, weaving and knitting—and in the final product when the term botany is used. The merino wool produces the best quality botany fabrics and garments recognized by the very soft but firm handle created by the fine, long woolen fibers, which makes botany wool important in the production of high quality worsted suitings.

Broadcloth

There are basically two very dissimilar fabrics called broadcloth—one of cotton, or cotton with man-made fibers or silk, the other of wool or wool with man-made fibers. Each has a very different weave and finish to the other. Wool broadcloth, made from merino wool, is a fine open woven 2-and-1 twill weave (sometimes plain weave) fabric which has been milled to give a uniform, slightly felted but lustrous appearance. The face of the cloth is smooth, velvety and quite dense making it suitable for well-tailored suits where the garment needs to hang well. It is in the same group of cloths as beaver cloth, kersey, and melton. The term broadcloth has also been used to describe a garment worn by the Clergy. (*See also* Broadcloth p51.)

(below)
The late Duke of Windso
when Prince of Wales,
wearing an Indian chief'
buckskin jacket

Buckskin

Buckskin is the skin of the male fallow deer although sometimes in the United States, it is the skin of a ram. The yellow-grey skin, denuded of its fur or wool, was used to make breeches worn by the American soldiers in the Revolutionary War. Buckskin cloth, a rugged durable material, is made to emulate real buckskin and used for making riding breeches. Made with an 8-end satin weave, it is then raised, heavily milled and then cropped, resulting in a firm smooth finish. It is then usually piece-dyed creamy white.

Bunting

The Old English word *bontin* meant 'to sift' and from this comes the dialectic expression 'to bunt': to sift meal or flour. A plain, open weave, woolen cloth was made and stretched across the bunt or sieve. This cloth was known as bunting. By coincidence, it seems, the German word *bunt* means strong bright colors which are also characteristic of bunting. The German for colored fabric is *buntgewebe*. Both these terms could be linked but both describe the present-day plain woven, crossbred, woolen cloth called bunting which is usually dyed in basic armoral colors—red, blue, yellow, white and black—with the addition of green and orange, and used as flags or banners as patriotic decorations. Bunting is known as *etamine* in France. Apart from its traditional use it is a cloth which could be used for furnishings and apparel.

(right) Street bunting for the Jubilee celebrations of Queen Elizabeth II, London, 1977

Cadet Cloth

As the name of this fabric indicates it is a cloth which is made especially for overcoats worn by cadets as part of their uniforms in public and private institutions, and military schools such as the United States Military Academy at West Point. It is a heavy woolen fabric with a nap finish, durable and a rather boardy feel. It is constructed as a double cloth, usually in 2-and-2 twill on both sides, heavily milled and cropped to give a very compact fabric capable of keeping out the wind and rain. It is usually made in dark blue, grey, grey-blue and blue-white.

Camel Hair

Camel hair comes from the Bactrian or two-humped camel found in all parts of Asia from Turkey to China and as far up as the north of Siberia. The extremely soft, lustrous hair is selected from the shorter hair nearest the camel's skin. The best quality comes from the camels in Mongolia from which the finest fabrics are made. It is usually used in its undyed natural color, varying from light tan to dark brown. A good quality camel fabric is one-and-a-half times as warm as a comparable woolen fabric of similar weight. Camel coats were popularized by the polo-playing fraternity of Westbury, Long Island and soon the fabric used for these coats was to become known as polo cloth. Many so-called camel cloths are made with a high proportion of merino wool or even a mixture of cashmere and wool and some are made of wool alone. A luxurious fabric called camlet originated in India where it was woven in satin weave from camel hair. This was later imitated by the Dutch and English using worsted yarns made from soft lustrous wools. This fabric became known as camleteen or camletine.

The coarse, tough outer hair of the Bactrian camel and the hair of the single-humped Dromedary is used for weaving native tent cloths, blankets, floor rugs and for making ropes. It is interesting to note that contrary to popular belief camel hair is never used for making artist's brushes.

(above) United States army cadet wearing a greatcoat made of cadet cloth

(right) Camel hair coat

Cashmere

Although it is hair and not wool, cashmere is more like wool than any other animal hair. It comes from the Himalayan goat found in Tibet, Kashmir, Iran, Iraq and Southwest China. This hair is sometimes referred to as *pashmina* which is Persian for woolen. There are many local cashmere fabrics woven from pashmina yarns and these are collectively known as jamawars. The most expensive of these is chaporast. The hair is used in its natural undyed state, either black, brown, grey or white. This luxuriously soft hair is plucked from the inner hair of the goat producing between 3 to 5 ounces each of valuable fiber annually. It is so expensive now that wool is usually blended with it when yarns are spun for weaving and knitting. The term cashmere has been indiscriminately used to describe cloths containing either a small percentage of the hair or none at all. Imitation cashmere fabrics sometimes are produced, even using cotton and wool. Kashmir shawls are handwoven in the North Indian province of that name (*See also* paisley, p32).

Cavalry Twill

This is a strong, durable cloth made with a distinctive 63° diagonal weave construction, recognizable by its ribs in groups of two. Cavalry twill is also known as elastique or tricotine in the United States. The weave varies slightly with the weight of the fabric but the characteristic diagonal is always retained, although the ribs do not appear on the reverse side. In many ways, because of the cloth structure, it resembles a knitted fabric at times. It is woven from tightly twisted worsted or woolen yarns. It is commonly dyed in natural colors usually fawn, brown or sometimes black. British army officers during the 1914–18 War in Europe wore riding breeches made from this fabric. It is for this reason that it is called cavalry twill. Since then it has become a popular material from which to make jackets, trousers, breeches and uniforms.

(below) Cavalry twill

Challis

This cloth (also spelt challie, chalys, challi) was originally woven from silk and wool. The name comes from an Anglo-Indian expression *shalee* meaning soft. Now the best quality is usually woven from 100 per cent wool in plain weave. Sometimes cheaper versions are produced, using cotton or man-made fibers. Often printed, this popular fabric in the United States has the desirable qualities of being firm, but not closely woven, lightweight, soft, resilient to crushing and drapes well. These features make it an excellent fabric for dresses, shirts, scarves and ties. Challis, first woven in England in about 1830, is known in France as *etamine glacée*.

(right)
Officers of the 18th Hussars in Germany, December 1918, wearing cavalry twill riding breeches

(below) Cheviot fabrics

Cheviot

Cheviot fabrics get their name from the wool originally used to weave them. The wool is from the cheviot sheep found not only in the Cheviot Hills, dividing Scotland and England, but also in the United States, Australia, Canada and New Zealand. No longer are cheviot fabrics made from 100 per cent pure cheviot wool. The original character of the rough rugged tweed remains in spite of the use of other wools and even man-made fibers. The natural crispness of the cheviot wool contributes greatly to the feel or handle of the cloth making it a most acceptable, hardwearing material for men's jackets, suits and coats. Its tweedy appearance is accentuated by the slightly harsh handle and use of traditional twill or herringbone weaves.

Chinchilla

The chinchilla is a small rodent about the size of a large squirrel, found in Peru and Chile. Its coat is pearl grey and very soft. As a luxury fiber in fabrics, it is always used blended with other wools. Present day chinchilla cloth does not in anyway resemble the pelt of the animal. Usually it is produced by combining a cotton warp and woolen weft in a tightly-woven, twill double cloth. The face of the cloth is brushed up or raised and the surface is rubbed with a circular motion producing small tufts, nubs or knobs. This fabric is often used in making livery, uniforms or coats.

Corkscrew Cloth

The term corkscrew is misleading when describing this type of cloth. Although an attempt was made in the design of this woolen dress fabric to simulate a corkscrew by using a special weave, the result is not convincing. There are a variety of different types of corkscrew weaves, all of which are twill ribs with the warp showing more on the face of the cloth. Some cloths are made with yarns having a corkscrew or spiral structure. These types of fabric are also called corkscrew cloths.

Covert Cloth

The word covert comes from the French word *couvrir* meaning to cover. The term covert cloth literally means a covering or protective material. Originally this cloth was made entirely of wool or wool and silk but now man-made fibers are frequently used alone or blended with wool. It is a lightweight, smooth cloth usually constructed with a closely set 2-fold warp and single yarn weft in a twill weave, sometimes making a completely waterproof fabric. Often a combination of two single threads of different color or tones of the same color are twisted together to form what is called a marled effect in the warp yarns, a distinguishing feature of the cloth. The weft is usually dyed black. Covert cloth is commonly used as a lightweight coating.

(left) Gentleman in a covert coat

Crossbred

Crossbred fabrics are woven from crossbred wools. Crossbred wools come from sheep of mixed breeds. These sheep were originally crossed to evolve a profitable business in mutton and lamb but the farmers soon realized that the wool was just as valuable. New Zealand is the largest producer of crossbred sheep; the most famous being Corriedale. The other main producing countries are Argentina, South Africa and Australia. Crossbred wool is used a great deal in the production of knitting yarns. Woven crossbred fabrics vary in construction and type but all contain crossbred wool which is particularly strong, shiny and hardwearing. Much crossbred wool is used in the manufacture of upholstery fabrics but it is chiefly a material for use in jacket and coating cloths.

Delaine

Delaine is French for 'of wool' and the term is derived from *mousseline delaine* which literally means wool muslin. Today the term delaine implies a lightweight woolen fabric in plain weave, soft and drapable, usually printed directly on to the cloth or sometimes on the warp only. The best quality delaines are produced from high grade merino wool and are used as dress fabrics. Cotton delaines are made as imitations and are generally known as delainettes.

Doeskin

The fabric takes its name from doeskin, a soft finished leather made from the hide of the female deer. Real doeskin is now rarely seen although sheepskin is often given a chamois finish and sold as doeskin. The fabric is made to resemble doeskin and is constructed from good quality botany wool closely set in the warp to give a smooth finish on the face of the fabric. Usually woven with 5-end satin, the effect of the weave is not clearly visible due to the closeness of the warp threads. The cloth is then shrunk and finished with a fine nap producing a firm, soft fabric with a slightly lustrous finish and is used for suitings and coatings.

Duffel

Duffel is a small town south of Antwerp in Belgium and it was here that this fabric was first made. The term is used for a woolen cloth woven in 2-and-2 twill weave, heavily milled and raised with a dense nap on both sides. Best wools need not be used for this type of fabric. It is a very heavy cloth and made famous in the 1939–45 World War when used extensively to produce bulky weatherproof hooded coats, known as duffel coats, for sailors. Other types of this fabric, such as down and flushing are produced, duffel being the lowest quality. The term duffel is also applied to a low grade blanket and a duffel bag is the name given to a cylindrical canvas bag with a draw string at one end, originally used by sailors to carry their blankets and clothes.

Duffel coats worn by British Navy personnel in World War II

Elastique

This is a sturdy cloth made with a distinctive 63° diagonal weave and recognizable by its ribs in groups of two. Elastique is the American term given to cavalry twill and tricotine. The weave varies slightly with the weight of the fabric but the characteristic diagonal is always retained. This diagonal does not appear on the reverse side of the cloth which sometimes has a nap finish. In many ways, because of the structure of the cloth, it resembles a knitted fabric. It is usually woven from tightly twisted worsted or woolen yarns. Because of its strength and resistance to abrasion it is an ideal fabric for riding breeches. It is a popular material from which jackets, trousers and uniforms are made. It is commonly dyed in natural colors ranging from fawn to black.

Etamine

The French word *étamine* means sieve and the fabric known by that name was used for sifting. Etamine comes from the old French word *estamine* from which many cloth names have derived such as estame, a knitted worsted fabric made in France, estamet, and estamene. Although originally made of wool, etamine fabric is also made from coarse cotton or linen. It is a fabric similar to bunting which had a similar usage originally and was also known as tammy. *Etamine glacée* is a French term for challis. *Etamine à bluteau* was a fabric made specifically for flour sifting and *etamine à voile* was a fine worsted muslin, either white or dyed black, and used for church vestments.

Flannel

The name is derived from the Welsh term *gwlanan*, the Welsh for wool being *gwlan*. It is traditionally a soft woolen cloth loosely woven, usually in plain weaves, made originally for underclothing and also worn by women as a red petticoat as part of the traditional Welsh costume. The Welsh coal miners used to wear long, tailed shirts made of Welsh flannel. Nowadays there is considerable variance in the weight and texture of this cloth, some woven with a twill weave, napped on both sides such as West of England flannel, Shaker flannel, kasha cloth, suede flannel, domet, Oxford flannel. Although usually woven in plain colors, some flannel is striped. It is a fabric commonly used for trousers, jackets, (including blazers), and sportswear. Cricket trousers are commonly known as flannels or whites.

(left) English cricketer John Snow sporting cricket flannels

Fleece Fabrics

The fleece is the complete crop of wool shorn from a living sheep in one go. The first clip of the sheep is termed lambswool, subsequent clips are fleece wools. Many different types of fleece fabrics have been produced to impersonate a sheep's fleece, and these can be knitted or woven in wool, cotton or man-made fibers. They can be heavy and they can be lightweight but in each case the common factor is that they are made by introducing and firmly fixing untwisted wads of fiber into a flexible backing cloth to create tufts. In some cases it may also mean that a fabric has been heavily raised with wire brushes, cropped and steamed to produce a very dense nap. Fleece fabrics make good insulators and are ideal for lining winter garments or making overcoats.

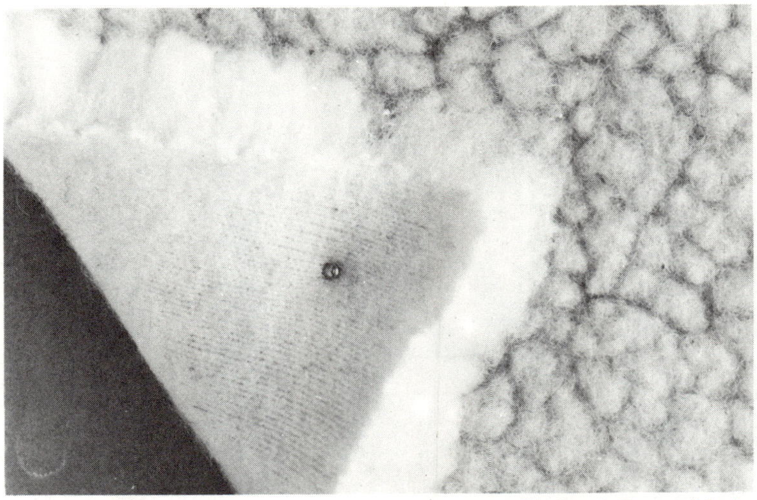

Knitted fleece fabric

Frieze

Frieze is a heavy wool coating known to have been made in Ireland in the fourteenth century, probably of French origin. It is a hard fabric woven in either common or irregular twill and so heavily felted as to make it impossible to separate one thread from another after cutting the cloth. The rough nap on the face of the cloth completely hides the woven structure. Irish frieze is used for making the traditional overcoat, a Cotha Mhor, and is both durable and waterproof. Cloth of a similar type was also made elsewhere in Britain in the fourteenth century: in England it was called falding, mentioned in Chaucer, and in Scotland it was called kelt. Both of these are seldom heard of now.

19th-century Irish farmer in his Cota Mor

Frisé

Friser is the French verb 'to curl' and from this word frisé fabric gets its name. It is a warp-looped pile fabric made in a similar way to terry towelling or astrakhan cloth but much more closely woven. Traditionally the loops of this fabric are made of wool or mohair although now cotton or man-made fibers are sometimes used. This fabric makes an excellent upholstery cloth as the loops of the pile are resilient and hardwearing.

Gabardine

The term gabardine comes from the Medieval Spanish word *gabardina* meaning protection against the elements. A Hebrew cloak worn by Shylock in Shakespeare's *Merchant of Venice* was called a gaberdine. Thus the word is used to describe a garment as well as a fabric. The best gabardine cloth is made from worsted wool although cotton and man-made fibers are also used. The fabric is recognized by the steep twill which forms a fine wale on the face of the cloth but is not evident on the back. Woven very tightly, it gives a smooth uniform finish, making the cloth water repellent and hardwearing. There is also a warp-faced fabric called gabercord which is of different construction to gabardine. Both are ideal for rain-wear and suits.

Orthodox Jew in a contemporary version of the gaberdine

Glenurquhart check

(below) Haircloth interlining

(bottom) John McGregor weaving Harris tweed

Glen Checks and Gun Club Checks

Glenchecks, or glenplaids as they are sometimes known in the United States, are synonymous with Scottish district checks. These bold, distinctive woolen checks were made in the Highlands of Scotland, and originally designed for the livery of big landowners. The northern Highlands of Scotland are divided by the Great Glen (Scottish for valley) between Inverness and Fort William. Castle Urquhart looks over Loch Ness which is the longest waterway in the Glen, and it is here that the most famous glencheck originates: The Glenurquhart. Other glenchecks include: Mar, Carnegie, Glenfeshie, Ing, Ardtornish, Guisachan, Russell, Kinlochewe, Minmore, Coigach, Dacre, Seaforth, Strathspey, Lochmore, Gairloch, Glenmorrison, Hay or Dupplin, Brooke, Kintail, Arndilly, Wyvis, Fannich, Scotsguard, Small Glenurquhart, Carnousie, Strathmashie, Horse Guards, Welsh Guards, Bateson, Glencoe, Benmore Forest, Gordon Highlanders Tweed, King's Own Scottish Borderers, Dalhousie.

Haircloth

This cloth is usually woven with a strong well-twisted cotton or linen warp with a horse hair, goat hair or coarse camel hair weft. The cloth, sometimes known as baline, is stiff and springy. Traditionally used for coat interlinings, it is now superseded by less expensive bonded fiber fabrics with similar characteristics. The sleek black finish of a haircloth when horsehair is used on the face of the cloth makes it hardwearing and ideal for upholstering dining chairs. This is practically obsolete now but still used when renovating antique furniture. An all woolen haircloth is made from wool waste and some calf hair. Finished with a well raised nap, this cloth is used for rough blankets. Cilice was a Roman term for haircloth woven in Cilicia. This was woven from goat hair and often made into shirts worn by monks while doing penance.

Harris Tweed

The best known of all tweeds is Harris tweed which comes from the Isle of Harris and Lewis on the west coast of Scotland. It is made entirely from tough Scottish wools, the yarn being spun centrally in the main island towns and then distributed to the outlying croft weavers. Harris tweed is woven on Hattersley domestic peddle looms using simple weaves, either plain or twill. The cloth is collected from the crofts and centrally finished in the towns, usually to a width of 27–28 inches, known as narrow width fabric. Until the later part of the nineteenth century, Harris tweed was handwoven and used only by the islanders. In 1909 the Harris Tweed Association was formed and the familiar orb mark was registered as its trademark. Similar tweeds, such as Hebridean cloth and blighty tweed have been made but no other tweed unless it has been woven on the Isles of Harris and Lewis can be called Harris tweed. It is strong, wears well and is ideal for jackets, suits, coats and upholstery.

Homespun

Homespun refers to a fabric which was traditionally hand woven from handspun yarns. These cloths are made now on power looms from machine spun yarns, impersonating the look of the original cloths. The yarn is irregular and spun from coarse kempy wools, woven usually in plain weave, giving an all over simple rough tweedy effect with a spongy handle. Homespun cloths are popular for jackets and coats because of their hardwearing qualities.

Irish Tweed

Ireland has for hundreds of years been a producer of woolen cloths. Since before the twelth century, Irish hand weavers have made friezes, serges and tweed type fabrics. Ireland is now famous for woolen cloths which come under the heading of tweed. Donegal tweed, originally woven on handlooms in County Donegal, is probably the best known and most easily recognized. Usually made in plain weave, the warp is solid color, the weft a similar yarn containing contrasting colored neps or spots giving an overall speckled effect to the cloth. Similar to Donegal is Connemara tweed. This tends to be brighter in color. Blarney tweed is yet another fabric with the same characteristics. Irish tweed is used for jackets, suits, coats and furnishings.

Jacob Tweed

This tweed is made from the wool of the piebald, or spotted, four-horned Jacob sheep about which many romantic stories have been written. The fleece of this sheep contains a variety of shades of wool from very dark brown to off-white and is very kempy. The wool, which is comparable to cheviot in quality, gives a crisp handle to the tweed making it hard wearing and suitable for jackets as well as furnishings.

It is thought that the Jacob sheep is descended from Palestinian flocks which travelled along the North African coast into Spain. The Spanish Armada, shipwrecked in the Hebrides in 1588 had taken the sheep on board as live meat. Small flocks of Jacob sheep are now found all over the British Isles and rearing them has become a popular hobby.

Irish tweeds

Jacob sheep and lambs

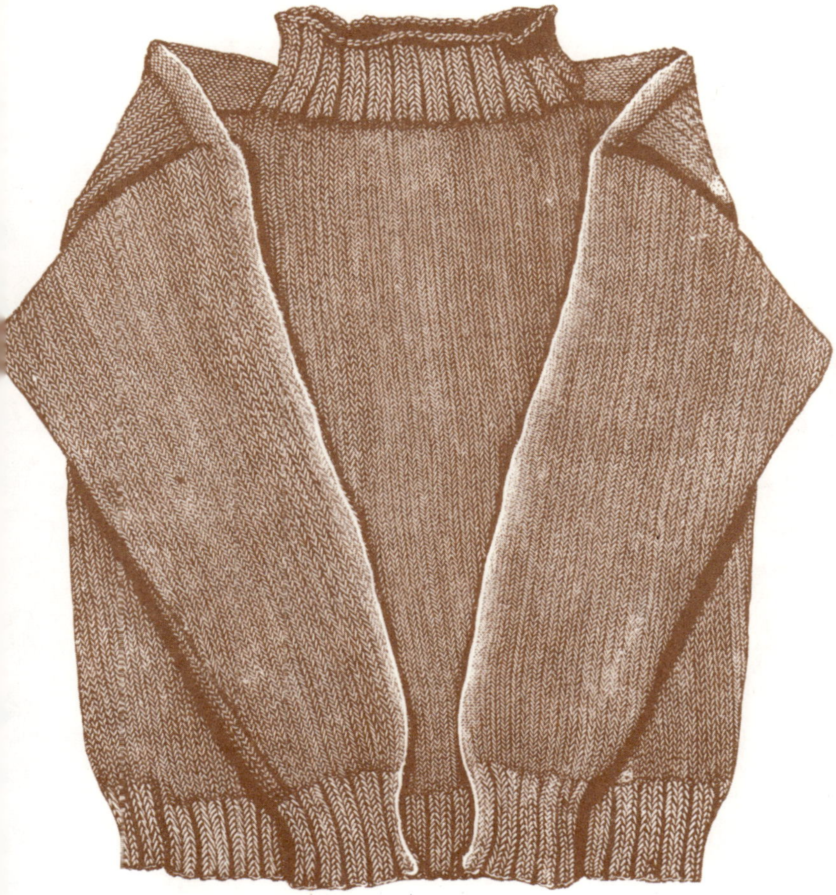

(above) Hand-knitted fisherman's jersey

Jersey

Jersey is used to describe a knitted garment or a knitted fabric. In America the jersey garment is called a sweater, or sometimes a pullover. Jerseys are usually made of wool and the origin of the word comes from Jersey, the largest of the Channel Islands between Britain and France.

Jersey fabric (single or double jersey) is the term given to fine gauge, machine-knitted fabric which stretches because of its structure. Manufactured in great quantity it usually has a smooth, fine surface made from worsted wool, cotton, silk or man-made fiber yarns. It is extremely versatile and can be used for dresses, skirts and jackets. Laminated to other materials, it becomes a cloth which can be tailored. The well known British Edwardian actress, Lillie Langtry, was the daughter of the Dean of Jersey. She adopted the fashion of wearing a long tight jersey garment with her long tight skirt and became known as Jersey Lily.

Kersey

Kersey or carsey is a woolen fabric which gets its name from the village of Kersey in Suffolk, England, where it was originally made. The cloth has been known since the fourteenth century but since then many variations have been woven. Normally a kersey is a heavy milled woolen fabric with a short lustrous nap obscuring the twill weave from which it is made. It is similar to a melton cloth although kersey is heavier and more lustrous. Pilot cloth and navy cloth have a finish similar to kersey. Some kerseys are very fine, including cloths like kerseymere, made from the best quality wool, or kooroon, a cloth used in northern India made of goat or camel hair. These cloths have many uses from overcoats to military uniforms.

Lincoln Green

Lincoln is the county city of Lincolnshire in England from where the Lincoln longwool sheep originates. As well as being the largest breed of sheep, it produces a fine quality wool which is the longest, most lustrous and strongest of all British wools. A stout woolen cloth was once made by the weavers in that area many years ago, and dyed green. This was commonly known as Lincoln green and used by archers, foresters and huntsmen. The legendary Robin Hood wore Lincoln green and the jacket lapels of the dress uniforms of the Sherwood Foresters regiment are of Lincoln green.

(left) The legendary Robin Hood dancing with Friar Tuck as imagined by a Victorian illustrator

Loden

The term loden comes from the old German word *Loda* meaning hair cloth traditionally woven in the Tyrol mountain area of Austria. Loden cloth is a sturdy fabric which has been made in the same way for almost a thousand years. At one time it was made only of sheep's wool but now it is made of a blend of Australian wool, alpaca, mohair and camel hair. Once the cloth has been woven it is shrunk by about a third of its original width in the loom, then raised, sheared and finally brushed. The traditional colors are black, red and white although now green has become the most popular color from which the well-known Loden coats are made.

(below)
Mackinaw coats from an American clothing catalog, 1906. The model on the left sold for $2.75

Mackinaw Cloth

The Straights of Mackinac join Lake Huron with Lake Michigan in the United States. It was here that stores were distributed to Indians from the town of Mackinaw in Michigan. These supplies included blankets and coats for the cold northern winters. These double breasted coats became known as mackinaws, made from cloth which was checked on one side and plain on the other. It is a double cloth with twill weaves both face and back, heavily milled and brushed to withstand the wind and snow. It was very fashionable in the United States in about 1915, and has retained its popularity with miners, lumberjacks, cowpunchers and fishermen.

Melton

The name Melton comes from Melton Mowbray in Leicestershire, England, an area famous for fox hunting. Melton is a thick, well-milled fabric with a nap which has been closely sheared to give a smooth surface. Normally woven with a twill weave in wool, less expensive Melton has cotton warp and woolen weft. It is always dyed in solid colors and has become one of the most commonly used woolen cloths for overcoats, uniforms and riding habits. Melton is one of the same group of fabrics as kersey, boxcloth, admiralty cloth and espagnolette. Meltonette is a lighter weight cloth similar to Melton and used for women's suits and coats.

(right) Engraving of a huntsman in a Melton hunting coat

(above) Mohair cloths

(above) Cut (right) and uncut (left) moquette upholstery fabrics

Mohair

The hair from the angora goat is called mohair. Angora goats are found in Turkey, South Africa and the south-western United States. Mohair is the most commonly known and widely used luxury animal fiber. It is recognized by its long, lustrous, hairy and soft quality. Mohair fabric comes in many forms. When spun to fine counts and combined with silk or woolen warps it makes very smooth cloth suitable for men's suits. Twisted into loops, and then brushed, it has a very hairy appearance and is used in weaving scarves and knee-rugs or as a knitting yarn. Mohair, as with many other smooth, long hair wools, does not mat when washed.

Moquette

Moquette is French for tufted cloth and it is made with a warp-looped pile similar to Brussels carpet, frisé or velvet. The pile loops remain uncut although sometimes tufts are cut to create contrasting pattern areas of dense velvet pile against the lustre of the loop. Although commonly produced in one color, it is now possible to obtain multi-color moquette. Usually made with wool or mohair pile with a cotton backing, many of these fabrics are now made in man-made fibers. It is an excellent upholstery cloth and occasionally used for luggage.

Navajo Blanket

In 1540 the Spaniards brought sheep to Mexico and the native Indians began to weave woolen cloth and blankets. The Navajo Indians adopted the art of weaving from the captured Pueblo women and acquired sheep by raiding Pueblo flocks. By 1780 Navajo Indians were known to be weaving blankets and woolen cloth, and the tradition has continued to flourish. Their blankets, which developed considerably from those of the Pueblo, are woven into colorful geometric designs. In the early days, the deep red yarn frequently used was obtained by unravelling strips of imported English red baize or *bayeta* (Spanish) and laboriously hand twisting it into thicker threads. Later an American flannel was used but was more orange-red in color. The blankets, which are double-sided, are so closely woven with a plain tapestry weave as to be water-proof.

Nun's Veiling

Nun's veiling is a light, flimsy, good quality worsted cloth made in plain weave. It is soft to the touch, has a slight crêpe appearance and drapes well. Manufactured in its natural undyed state, it is also dyed in plain colors and black. A similar fabric, convent cloth, is made with a silk warp and worsted weft. Nun's veiling, as the name describes, is used for religious clothing. In recent years it has become popular as a print cloth and is now widely used for dresses and shirts. With age this fabric develops a slight luster due to the type of wool and the high twist of the yarn used.

(left) Navajo rug weaver in Arizona

Paisley

Between 1805 and the early 1870s, shawls were woven and printed in Paisley, a town near Glasgow, in Scotland, with designs based on the pine motif. The pine motif, which later became known as the paisley pattern, originated in Kashmir, India, where for centuries it has been the basic design source for all the elaborately decorated shawls, handwoven from Pashmina wool. (*See* cashmere, p22.) The original Kashmir motif was based on the pine cone, although the so-called pine motif is, however, more directly identifiable with the cashew fruit and seed pod which has been a symbol of fertility for thousands of years. The cashmere shawls or jamawars were highly valued as far back as Roman times, and were traded throughout their Empire. They were introduced into France and then England by way of Napoleon's officers who brought them back from their Egyptian campaign. This started the vogue for shawls in Europe, and the cheaper reproduction of the precious cashmere shawls began in Lyons, Norwich and Edinburgh, but it did not take long before the expertise of the Paisley weavers took over the sole production of shawls. The Paisley pattern which was originally woven and then printed, is used nowadays in all manner of fabrics, and has become a classic design motif.

Pattu

The Hindi word *pattu* means a narrow homespun woolen cloth of which there are other local spellings of the same word such as *puttoo* and *pattoo*. The word puttee stems from this and is a narrow piece of woolen cloth used by soldiers to spiral round their lower legs. *Patti* is also the word for bandage. Pattu fabric is made in Northern India from the hair of the Kabul goat. It usually consists of several narrow widths of cloth sewn together to make pieces about 2 to 3 yards wide which are then used as blankets. There are various pattu cloths including: *pattu chet*, a printed cloth; *pattu abshar*, a striped cloth; *pattu pashmini*, a shawl or blanket (*See* cashmere, p22) and pattu kundrang, a fine cloth made with camel hair which is then embroidered and made into dressing gowns and loose robes.

Piano Cloth

Piano cloth is a fabric made in Gloucestershire, England for the sole purpose of covering piano hammers. This cloth is closely woven from fine undyed woolen yarns and then heavily milled, raised and cropped giving it the appearance of felt. It is so heavily milled that it is impossible to unravel the weave and is dense yet resilient enough to withstand the continual hammering on piano wire. Piano cloth is always red in colour but unlike most other woolen cloths the dye is applied by rollers. This process is called padding. Although the dye is pressed into the fabric, under pressure of the rollers, it still leaves the center woven structure undyed.

(above)
Section of a Paisley shawl showing the pine motif

(left)
East African cashew fruit and seed pod

An advertisement for Fox's puttees, 1900

(above) 17th-century broadsheet showing Highlanders in plaids
(below) Plush fabric

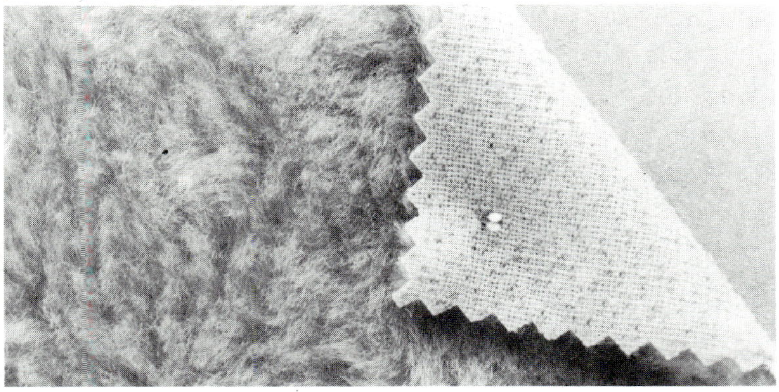

The Season's Novelty. "THE TUMBLING BEAR," fitted with best clockwork and covered with brown plush. After being wound, and placed upon its back, the bear rolls over, draws itself up until it stands upon its head, falls over upon its back again, and repeats the performance. Very laughable. Price 7/3. Postage 6d.

Plaid

In the USA the term plaid infers a large pattern consisting of similar multi-colored stripes crossing each other at right angles and is used mistakenly to describe tartan. In fact, a plaid is not a pattern but a piece of tartan woolen cloth two yards wide and 4–6 yards long used as part of the older form of Highland dress. The plaid was pleated so that the width was adjusted to the girth of the wearer. It was secured by a leather belt and pinned on the left shoulder with a large brooch. This was known as the belted plaid. Conveniently, the plaid could be used as a cloak by day and a blanket by night. The Highland kilt (30 inches wide and between seven and eight yards long) is a development from the belted plaid. Today, a modified form of plaid can be worn with the kilt by a Highlander. (*See also* Tartan, p36.)

Plush

The term plush is taken from the French *peluche* meaning shaggy or hairy. The fabric is an exaggerated form of velvet with a deeper and less dense pile. It is usually woven in wool or mohair although some is made with cotton and often now with man-made fibers. Springy resilient fiber such as wool is used so that the pile will stand erect. Ideal for coats, lining and furnishing fabric, plush is also used extensively in making soft toys. Teddy-bear cloth is, for instance, a type of plush fabric which is manufactured, as the name describes, for that sole purpose. Knitted plush is also made and used for linings.

Ratiné

Ratiné fabric was first made in Italy in the seventeenth century but is a French term to describe a rough, woven woolen cloth. One of the basic characteristics of a ratiné cloth is the spiral yarn (*See* Textile Terms), sometimes with nubs or knotty texture, used in the manufacture. The term ratiné also applies to the type of yarn used which can be knitted as well as woven. When woven, this yarn is thick and widely spaced in the warp to produce a spongy bulky fabric. It is used as an overcoating when slightly twilled, but can also be used for furnishing fabrics. Cotton ratiné fabrics are also made using gimp yarns which are smaller than the woolen spiral and usually used in the weft instead of the warp.

Saxony

Saxony fabric gets its name from the area, now situated in the northern part of West Germany, where it was first woven from local wool. It is now woven in other countries from high quality, soft, botany, worsted yarns. It was originally woven in Germany as an overcoating but now saxony fabric includes lighter cloth, with a tweed effect, suitable for jackets and suits. The cloth is made in many weights and qualities but all have the common characteristics of being soft and hardwearing.

(left) Saxony fabrics

Sealskin

Sealskin fabric is a woven or knitted pile cloth made to imitate real seal fur. In line with other pile fabrics which are made to imitate their natural and real originals they are usually lighter in weight and can be cut more economically. Sealskin fabric can be made in several ways but is most commonly woven with a cotton back and mohair pile. The pile can also be of tussah silk and cheaper varieties are made of cowhair or man-made fibers. The fabric is dyed black to match the real skin and can be used for coats and hats.

Serge

Serge is one of the oldest fabric names. The word, derived from the Latin *serica*, implies that it was once a silk fabric. The term is used today more often than not to describe a hardwearing, worsted cloth made with a 2 up and 2 down twill weave. It usually has a smooth face although it tends to shine with wear due to the hand twist in the yarn and the compact weave structure. It does, however, hold its crease well. There are many names given to Serge including the following: French serge—a good quality fabric, excellent for tailoring; storm serge—a heavier quality using coarser yarns and French back serge—a menswear cloth, almost twice the weight of French serge (sometimes the French call this type of cloth *canourge* or *ponchery*). Imperial serge is a lightweight coating sometimes known as perpetuana and navy serge is a very strong, well-made cloth used for US Navy uniforms, sometimes known as navy cloth. A very fine quality serge made in the twelfth century was known as say or saye.

British sailor in serge

Shepherd check

Sharkskin

As the name implies, this fabric is constructed to resemble the skin of a shark. Sharkskin fabric is a worsted cloth made with a very fine twill weave often using two different colored yarns arranged alternately in the warp and alternately in the weft. This gives a small step pattern, although check and stripes are sometimes made. It is used for suiting. There is a second sharkskin fabric made of acetate or sometimes cotton, which in no way resembles the worsted type, being made in plain weave or basket weave, giving the fabric a crisp feel. This type of cloth is used for sportswear and women's wear.

Shepherd Check

A shepherd check cloth is traditionally a woolen cloth woven in Scotland and worn as a plaid or cloak by shepherds in the Highlands. The pattern of the shepherd check is usually made in 2-up and 2-down twill weave and in equal, quarter-inch, blue-and-white checks of no special number of threads per check (although a pattern of 6-and-6 is commonly used so that it will not be confused with a dogtooth or houndstooth check, which are both made with 4-and-4). The blue was replaced by the more familiar black, and this simple check pattern is now used by itself or as the basis of all glen checks, Scottish district checks, and gun club checks, in many types of cloth from woven woolen tweed, to double jersey Jacquard.

Shetland

The Shetland Islands are just over a hundred miles north of the most northern tip of the mainland of Scotland. The sheep which live on these barren isles produce some of the finest quality British wool used in woven fabrics or knitting. The wool is a mixture of coarse and soft, fine fibers giving any end product its characteristic feel, softer than its appearance suggests. Many imitations have been made in recent years using inferior or mixed wools but still the best quality is genuine Shetland. It is considered to be the warmest of all sheep's wool. Unlike most sheep, shetlands are not all white but vary in color from skeila (brown grey) to moorit (dark reddy brown).

Shetland fabric is a soft tweed made wholly, or partly, with Shetland wool and used for jackets or suits.

Tartan

Traditional, authentic tartan cloths are usually made of wool in twill weave. The word tartan is of French derivation and is a cloth woven with stripes of different colors crossing each other at right angles. Sometimes the term is confused with plaid (*See* Plaid, p33) or check. Originally tartans were made of local wool dyed with vegetable dyes but modern tartans are now chemically dyed and the colors are much brighter. The color is, nevertheless, always solid in the yarn unlike the mixed color in Harris and Shetland tweeds. The setts (number of threads per color in each warp and each weft stripe) must be very accurate in order to make an authentic tartan cloth. Each tartan belongs to a Highland clan or 'family', and all Scottish regiments have their own tartans, some of which have been adopted from the Scottish families who first raised the regiments. All highland Scottish soldiers wear tartan kilts, all lowland Scottish soldiers wear tartan trews (trousers). The earliest mention of tartan occurred in 1538 when the French wife of King James V, mother of Mary Queen of Scots, purchased 'three ells [a Scottish measure still used] of Heland Tartane'.

The following is a list of the most well-known clan tartans: Anderson, Armstrong, Barclay, Brodie of Brodie, Bruce, Buchanan, Cameron, Campbell, Carnegie, Chisholm, Colquhoun, Crawfurd, Cumin, Cunningham, Dalzell, Davidson, Douglas, Drummond, Dunbar, Dundas, Elliot, Erskine, Farquharson, Ferguson, Forbes, Fraser, Gordon, Graham, Grant, Gunn, Hay, Henderson, Home, Innes, Johnston, Keith, Kennedy, Kerr, Lamont, Leslie, Lindsay, Livingston, Logan, MacAlister, MacArthur, MacAulay, MacCallum, MacDonald, MacDonell, MacDougall, MacDuff, MacEwen, Macfarlane, Macfie, MacGillivray, MacGregor, MacInnes, Macintyre, Mackay, Mackenzie, Mackinlay, Mackinnon, Mackintosh, MacLachlan, MacLaren, Maclaine, Maclean, Macleod, Macmillan, Macnab, MacNaughton, MacNeil of Barr, McNeill of Colonsay, Macpherson, Macquarrie, Macqueen, Macrae, Matheson, Maxwell, Menzies, Montgomerie, Morrison, Munro, Murray of Atholl, Nicholson, Ogilvie, Ramsay, Robertson, Rose, Ross, Ruthven, Scott, Seton, Sinclair, Skene, Stewart, Sutherland, Urquhart, Wallace, Wemyss.

Scottish tartans: (top) Dress Stewart; (centre) MacIvor; (above) MacHardy

Tattersall

Tattersall is the term given to a heavy but lightly milled woolen cloth, similar to kersey, made in bold, brightly colored checks. The cloth is used for jackets, suits and overcoats. The term tattersall comes from the bloodstock auction company in London of that name, who deal in racehorses. It is supposed that the bold checked horse-blankets appealed to the horse dealers and that they had coats made for themselves from them.

Tattersall check suiting

Tropical Cloths

Tropical cloths or suitings come in this section because of the fact that so many, but not all, are made with worsted yarns. Tropical cloth is such a broad term that it extends over each fiber section in this book. Many tropical cloths are mixed fiber fabrics which include: wool and polyester fiber; cotton and polyester fiber; cotton and mohair; linen and polyester or cotton; linen and polyester fiber by themselves. Tropical cloths must be light, smooth and preferably easy to maintain. Any clothing used in hot weather needs more frequent washing or cleaning.

Tweed

Tweed is a term given to a long list of medium weight, rough woolen fabrics made with a 2-up and 2-down twill weave. They can be solid colors, mixtures, stripes, or checks but all must traditionally be made of wool. The word tweed came about by accident by the slip of a London cloth merchant's pen in about 1840 when referring to a consignment of tweel cloth woven in the Borders of Scotland in a twill weave. Coincidentally much of the cloth was, and is still, woven in mills along the banks of the River Tweed.

Tweed has a variety of uses including jackets, suits, skirts, overcoats, hats and caps. Some of the most well-known tweeds are: Bannockburn, Bute, Connemara, Craiganputtach, Donegal, Gala (Galashiels), Glengarry, Harris, Hebridean, Homespun, Irish, Knickerbocker, Linton, Lovat, Manx, Shetland, Thornproof.

Vicuna

The vicuna is the smallest of the llama and alpaca family and lives in the Peruvian Andes between Lake Titicaca and the coast. This small animal has the distinguishing feature of having an apron of long white hair which falls from the front of his lower neck down between his fore-legs. The rest of his fleece is a warm brown color. The Vicuna is a wild animal and it is necessary to hunt and kill this small creature to obtain its rare hair, of which only the finer hair is used. Since 1921, the Peruvian Government has tried to protect the vicuna from extinction with strict conservation laws. The export of the fleece is now restricted. The hair or wool is the softest and warmest of all animal fibers. It is used in knitting and weaving in its natural colors, although the luxurious coatings which have become almost non-existent now, are made from fleece which has been dyed black. A woolen fabric similar to this black coating has been made without any vicuna wool yet it is still called a vicuna fabric.

(left)
A tropical suit

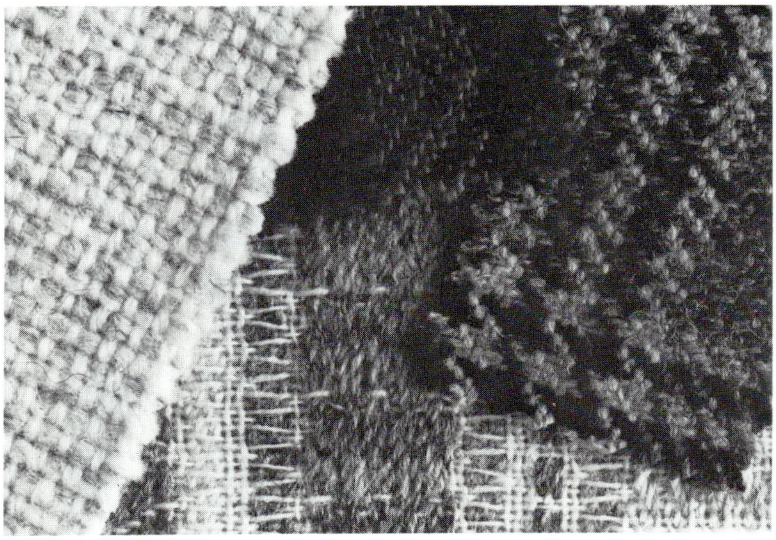

(centre) A variety of tweed cloths
(right) A pair of vicunas

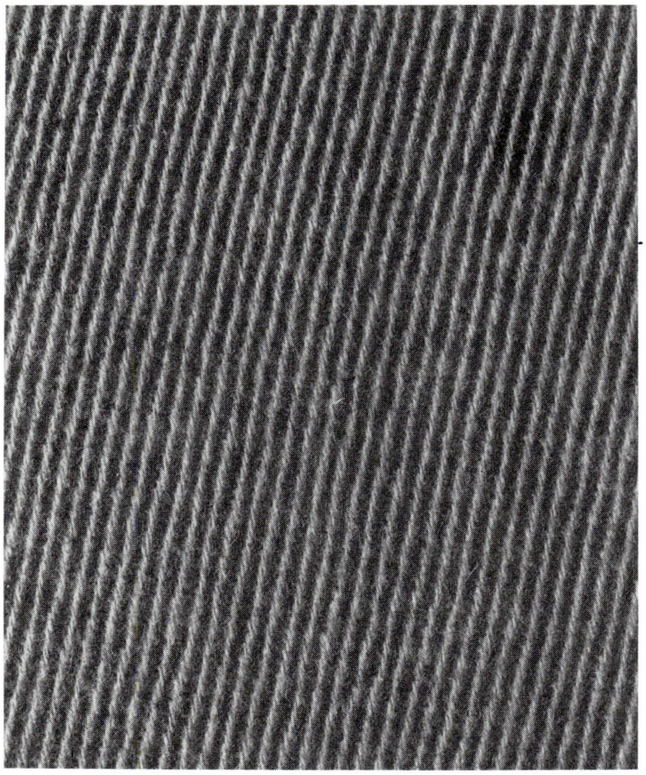

Viyella

This fabric name is the registered proprietary brand name for a twill woven cloth made from 55 per cent wool and 45 per cent cotton. It has the appearance of a very fine flannel and has become synonymous with cloths of similar type now manufactured by other companies. Viyella gets its name from Via Gellia, pronounced locally as Vijella, a road linking the villages of Cromford and Bonsall in Derbyshire, England. It was there that William Hollins and Company developed the fast yarns to make Viyella cloth. The name Viyella was registered as a trademark in 1894. This fabric is most suitable for shirts, dresses, nightwear, and is available in solid colors, checks, stripes and is also printed. Viyella is sometimes confused with Clydella, made by the same company (*See* Clydella p56).

Whipcord

Although of the same family of cloths, whipcord has a slightly steeper twill rib than cavalry twill, elastique, tricotine, gabardine or gabercord. The cord of whipcord. unlike most of these other fabrics, is emphasized by the warp threads on the face of the cloth as with gabercord. The yarn used for this cloth is slightly bulkier than in other types, making it a heavier fabric altogether and more suitable for overcoats. This rugged and hardwearing fabric is also known as artillery cloth and is used for uniforms, horseriding clothes and suits. A cotton whipcord of similar construction is also made usually with a nap finish on the back of the fabric.

Zibeline

Zibeline is the pelt of a Siberian sable and the fabric gets its name from this soft, silky fur. The fabric is meant to look like the fur, and does not use any of the fur in its manufacture. The cloth is made from lustrous, crossbred worsted yarns woven in satin weave, raised with a fine nap on one side, cropped and then steamed to develop the even velvety appearance of the cloth. The fabric is usually dyed black and a faint striping effect caused by the construction can be seen through the nap. It is more lustrous than broadcloth and is used for coats and jackets. Another name for zibeline is ripple cloth.

(left) Whipcord

Cotton

The History of Cotton

The Sanskrit for cotton was *kapaski* but the word cotton comes from the old Arabic *qutun*. Every language has its own word for cotton:

France—coton
Italy—cotone
Spain—algodón
Germany—Baumwolle
Egypt—quoton
Greece—vamvax
India—pucu
China—hoa mein
Japan—momen
Persia—poombeh
Thailand—tonfaa
Mongolia—kohung

Cotton has been used in making textiles for the past 5000 years although there is evidence that the cotton plant grew in India and the Tehanan Valley in Mexico over 7000 years ago. Cotton fabrics were discovered beneath the ruins of the city of Mohenjodaro in the Indus valley in India about 3000 BC. In about 2500 BC cotton cloths, made during the pre-Inca civilization, were found in Peru. The Bible refers to cotton many times and it is thought that the word *kapas*, which is used in the book of Esther, means cotton. It is also thought that Joseph's coat was probably made of cotton.

The Greek historian Herodotus wrote in 445 BC after returning from India: 'There are trees growing wild the fruit of which is a wool exceeding in beauty and goodness that of sheep'. The Romans were known to have used cotton awnings for the Apollonaris games in 63 BC but it was much later that any quantity of cotton was brought to other countries. In AD 77 Pliny reported in his *Historiae Naturalis* that the cotton shrub was growing in upper Egypt and that, 'There is nothing to be prefered to those stuffs for softness and whiteness; beautiful garments are made from them for the priests of Egypt'. Between AD 100 and 200 the Greeks began to grow cotton and from the yarn they spun they made hair nets. At the turn of the tenth century the Moors introduced cotton into Spain and by the thirteenth century a flourishing industry in Barcelona was established for the production of cotton sailcloth.

Cotton fiber was already known in England in the early thirteenth century, being mentioned in the Wardrobe Act of 1212 during the reign of King John, who in 1215 signed the Magna Carta, but no one in England at that time had ever seen how cotton grew. Sir John Mandeville, returning from his explorations of India in 1350, reported: 'There grew there a wonderful tree which bore tiny lambs on the endes of its branches. These branches were so pliable that they bent down to allow the lambs to feed when they are hungrie.' The confusion between plant and animal exists in present day languages. The German word *baumwolle* literally means tree-wool. The English term cotton wool refers to a processed cotton fiber which is used for surgical swabs and make-up. The American term for this is simply cotton.

(top) The Barometz, from Duret's *Histoire de Plantes*, Paris, 1605
(above) The Lamb Tree, from Mandeville's *Voiage and Travaile*, London, 1725

(opposite) Cotton roving ready for spinning

2
Platts

(opposite) Cotton spinning

When Christopher Columbus sailed westward to discover new trade routes to Asia he found cotton growing in Watlings Island, the most easterly island of the Bahama Islands in the West Indies. This was reported in his journal of 12th October 1492. It was then only a matter of a few years before Spanish settlers planted cotton in Florida. Not until 1607 was cotton first planted in North America for commercial purposes.

The wool industry in England began to feel the effects of cotton exports from America by the late seventeenth century and in 1700 laws were passed prohibiting the use of cotton. The British Parliament passed an act in 1721 saying that anyone caught wearing cotton would be fined £5.00 which was a lot of money in those days. By 1730 the first cotton yarn was spun by machine in England and it would seem that by then the law of 1721 was lifted. By 1790 from an annual production of 1,500,000 pounds of cotton in America almost 200,000 pounds was exported to England. In 1733 a most important piece of equipment was invented by John Kay called the flying shuttle. Until then the weaving process had been done entirely by hand but this new invention speeded up the process much to the anger of many handloom weavers who thought that this revolutionary gadget would put them out of work.

In 1793 a young American named Eli Whitney invented a piece of equipment which he called a saw gin which was later to be known as the cotton gin. The purpose of this machine was to separate the cotton fiber from the seeds. As a result the cotton growing industry developed rapidly in the southern states of America which inevitably led to an increase in slave labour and by 1810 there were over 1 million slaves working in the cotton fields. Within 50 years, as the industry developed, the slave population increased to over 4 million.

The cotton-growing industry thrived in America at the beginning of the nineteenth century and the cotton weaving industry in Lancashire, England, was developing rapidly although every ounce of cotton converted into cloth on the looms in Lancashire had to be imported from either America, Egypt, Sudan or India. America on the other hand produced a surplus of cotton fiber in excess of its own needs. 'King Cotton' was a common expression in America as it grew to be the largest producer of cotton in the world although other countries grow cottons which are of the finest quality while others grow coarse cheaper varieties.

(above and below) Whitney's cotton gin

Cotton Production

There are three basic types of cotton fiber and each type can be converted into specific end uses. The quality of cotton fiber is determined by its length (staple), fineness, uniformity, maturity, color and cleanliness. Cotton is classified into three main groups:

1 Fine, high lustre fiber with $1\frac{1}{4}$–$2\frac{1}{2}$ in (3–6.5 cm) long staple. This is the best quality cotton:
Sea Island (grown in the West Indies, Central America and Mexico), Egyptian, Sudanese, Peruvian, American Pima, East African.

2 Medium, $\frac{3}{4}$–$1\frac{1}{4}$ in (2–3 cm) long staple:
American Upland (the bulk of United States production).

3 Short, coarse, dull $\frac{1}{2}$–$\frac{3}{4}$ in (1–2 cm) long staple:
Indian, Chinese.

Cotton is a soft fluffy vegetable fiber which grows from the seed pod of the cotton flower. Most varieties produce white fiber but some cotton is naturally brown. The combination of seed pod and cotton fiber is called a cotton boll and varies in size between that of a golf ball and a tennis ball depending on the variety. The cotton plant, known by its

(above) Cotton boll

(below left) Cotton harvesting in the U.S.A.

(below right) Cotton ready for spinning

(opposite) Packages of cotton yarn ready for weaving

OEB

Latin name *gossypium*, grows in sub-tropical humid conditions and varies in height between $2\frac{1}{2}$–5 ft (.8–1.5 m) according to type. All cotton plants are annuals except for a Brazilian type which is perennial and grows between 8–12 ft (2.5–3.5 m) high.

Each cotton fiber is a tube of almost pure cellulose. The tubular layered structure of cotton fiber allows it to absorb and release moisture rapidly. Not only is this an advantage when wearing cotton fabrics or using cotton towelling but it also means that dyes and bleach can be readily absorbed into cotton. Raw cotton fibers possess a natural wax coating which repels water, consequently the absorption in this state is relatively low. The natural waxes and oils are removed by washing and the cotton then has excellent absorption properties. Increased moisture content increases the strength of cotton but reduces its elasticity.

Cotton fiber is converted into finished thread or yarn through the following processes:

Picking The cotton bales arrive at the textile mill for spinning and must be opened and blended. The picker is a machine which then removes all the seeds and heavy impurities and produces a roll cotton fiber known as a lap.

Carding The roll of lap is then passed through a machine which disentangles the fibers and produces a thin web which is then made into a roll about half an inch thick.

Combing The finest quality yarns are produced with combed cotton. This process eliminates all the short fibers and forms yet another sliver of smooth strong fiber. The short fibers, called noils, are not wasted and are usually spun into cheaper yarns.

Drawing Several slivers are drawn out and combined into one sliver about the same size as the original.

Roving This sliver is then drawn out still further into a finer strand and a twist put into it.

Spinning The drawing out process continues and more twist is put into the yarn. It is during this process that the size of the yarn is determined. A single yarn can then be doubled together with another to make what is known as a two-fold yarn.

The yarn is now ready for weaving or knitting. If required the yarn or the cloth can be mercerized which is done by treating the cotton with caustic soda. This process adds strength, luster and more absorbent qualities to the yarn.

Cotton soils and crushes easily but it can be washed without injury as the use of boiling water and soap or detergent do not materially affect it. For this reason cotton is considered to be the most hygenic fiber. Cotton fabrics can easily be laundered at home or commercially. Although fabrics containing 100 per cent cotton are considered to be the most comfortable Cotton Incorporated of America have introduced a trade mark known as natural blend which is the preferred level of cotton and polyester blending below which the comfort factor is decreased. The composition of the blend for woven cloth is 65 per cent cotton and 35 per cent polyester; for knitted cloths, 70 per cent cotton and 30 per cent polyester.

(opposite) Cotton-cloth finishing

Symbol used by
Cotton International in Europe

Symbol used by
Cotton International Incorporated in the U.S.A.

Airplane Cloth

Early airplanes were constructed of wood and cloth. The cloth was a plain woven cotton or linen fabric stretched over the wings and fuselage of the airplane framework, then pained with cellulose acetate lacquer to stretch it. This treatment added strength and made it weatherproof. Unfortunately it was very combustible. This fabric is still made but seldom used for covering airplanes except perhaps model ones or repairing museum pieces. It is a closely woven fine mercerized cotton or linen fabric made with the minimum number of faults and blemishes. It is now often used for sportswear, shirts, uniforms and light luggage.

(above) Airplane, about 1910

Atlas

Although the term atlas is used in Europe to describe a 5- or 8-end, satin-weave, silk or cotton fabric, (*See* satin, p89) the word is more commonly used in knitting. Atlas is a warp knitted cotton fabric with a $\frac{3}{8}$–$\frac{3}{4}$ inch striped effect on the reverse side of the cloth. A double atlas is ladder-proof, a single atlas is not. This cloth is used primarily for glove making. (*See also* Atlas silk, p80.)

Awning Cloth

This fabric is also known as awning stripe, awning duck, Austrian cloth or Austrian shade cloth. It is a heavy, closely-woven cotton cloth. Although usually woven in colored warp stripes from dyed yarns, a plain fabric is often printed with stripes or other motifs. This fabric can be made more durable by giving it finishes which make it resistant to mildew, fire and water. This type of fabric has a multitude of uses from awnings to beach umbrellas, hammocks, tents and outdoor furniture.

(left) An advertisement showing awning cloth

Balbriggan

Balbriggan is named after the small coastal town a few miles north of Dublin in Ireland where this fabric was first made. It is a lightweight single weft knitted cotton fabric often lightly napped on one side. The name Balbriggan was eventually given to underwear made from the cloth. This knitted fabric is inherently elastic but will soon run into holes if one of the stitches is broken. It can be used for lightweight sweaters and gloves as well as underwear.

(right) Awning cloth

Racing balloons in Belgium, 1963

Balloon Fabric

This is a finely-woven cotton cloth in plain weave with equal breaking strength in the warp and the weft. It is usually impregnated with rubber, then vulcanized making it waterproof. It was originally intended to be used for airships like the Zeppelin used in World War I and the silver barrage balloons used extensively in Britain during World War II. The fabric was laminated into a three-ply cloth, the outer fabric running longitudinally, the center cut diagonally and placed on the bias and the back cloth placed transversely to the outer. This laminated construction reduced the risk of tearing if the balloon was pierced. Today most fabrics used in the manufacture of modern airships and balloons are polyurethane-coated nylon, and balloon fabric is used mainly for apparel. As a single-proofed cloth, it is used for rainwear, and unproofed it is often used as downproof interlinings for cushions.

Similar fabrics are airship cloth and airship envelope cloth—lightweight, coated fabrics which are gas-proof.

Bandanna

The Hindi word *bandhana* means knot, bind or tie and is used to describe the Indian process of producing a spotted fabric by resist dyeing. The word comes from the Sanskrit *bandh*, meaning to tie fabric ready to be dyed. This fabric and its western mass produced counterpart is known as bandanna. Plangi is similar. The spots are produced by skillfully hand-binding small areas of a fine cotton cloth according to a set pattern with thread to resist the dye. Once the binding thread has been removed after dyeing the cloth is ironed flat and used for saris, dresses and scarves. Mass produced bandanna fabric is printed with a regular pattern of white dots usually on a ground of red, blue, yellow, brown or black. This fabric is most commonly used as handkerchief or dress cloth.

Basket Cloth

Basket cloth is a coarse fabric using heavy mercerized cotton yarns and a 2-, 3- or 4-thread matt, hopsack or basket weave. The cloth is stable but not tightly woven. It is usually used as an embroidery cloth. There are many varieties of basket embroidery cloths each having its own trade name. (*See* Needlework Fabrics, p142.)

(above) Goodyear balloon over Edinburgh, 1977
(left) Bandanna handkerchief
(far left) Hand-dyed Indian bandanna fabric

Batiste
Batiste was named after the Frenchman Baptiste of Cambrai in the thirteenth century. Originally made in linen it is now more commonly woven with mercerized cotton yarns. It is also woven in silk or wool. This is a lightweight cloth in plain weave with a lustrous finish. It is a very fine quality cloth using long, staple combed cotton. Traditionally produced in its undyed natural state it is now bleached white or dyed and ideal for handkerchiefs, dresses and shirts. A heavy quality batiste is also made for foundation garments. Tamise cloth is another name for batiste.

Bird's Eye
Many fabrics are called bird's eye or contain so-called bird's eye patterns. The fine bird's eye cloth is an all-cotton dobby woven fabric with a distinctive diamond-shape pattern having a small dot in the center of each diamond. This cloth is constructed with loosely-spun, short, staple cotton yarns making it soft and absorbent. The most common usage of this fabric is for diapers (nappies) and is referred to as diaper cloth. It might be interesting to note here that the word diaper comes from the French word *diasper* meaning a figured cloth and also from the Greek word *diaspros* meaning pure white. This fabric is also ideal for towels. Bird's eye worsted cloths are used for suitings.

A fabric known as bulbuldrasum or bulbulchasm, which literally means nightingales' eyes, is woven in India. This cloth is made in cotton with a small diamond pattern in the weave.

Book Cloth
Book cloth is also known as bookbinder's cloth, bookbinding holland or binder's cloth and was formerly known as chagin. There are many qualities and weights produced from a variety of base cloths like sheeting, print cloth, osnaburg or fine duck. The cotton base cloth is usually heavily sized, 'starched and clayed' or treated with pyroxylin to make it washable or waterproof, then passed through heavy rollers producing a very flat, smooth-surfaced, stiff fabric. Color is applied by dyeing the base cloth in the normal way or applied to the surface of the cloth after the stiffening treatment. The fabric can also be embossed through special rollers and as the name indicates, its prime use is for binding books.

Book cloth

Broadcloth

There are two dissimilar fabrics called broadcloth. One is of cotton, or cotton with man-made fibers or silk, the other of wool or wool and man-made fibers. Each has a very different weave and finish to the other. Originally the term referred to a fabric made on a loom wider than 27 inches (68 cm). When introduced into the United States in the 1920s from Great Britain, the British name poplin was not used because it had connotations with a heavier cloth. So the term broadcloth, for no other reason was used. The main feature of cotton broadcloth is that it has a fine ribbed effect across the cloth. These ribs are produced by the compact warp crossed by two or more tightly woven weft threads. The cotton is mercerized and the cloth is usually sanforized with a soft lustrous finish. Broadcloth is similar to poplin and is widely used for shirts and dresses. Also called Fuji. (*See also* Broadcloth, wool, p20.)

Broderie Anglaise

Broderie Anglaise

This term, which literally means English embroidery, is given to a type of cotton fabric which is embroidered with a design to form a button hole stitch outline, the centers of which are then cut away. Broderie Anglaise is made in white cotton fabric and embroidered with white cotton threads. If colored thread or fabric is used the cloth is then called eyelet. Sometimes it is also known as Madeira work.

Buckram

Buckram comes from the early English word *bokeram* derived from the French *boquerant* describing a particular fabric from Bukhara in South Russia. This fabric is made of cotton, sometimes linen, and is traditionally stiffened with flour paste, china clay and glue size. Usually buckram is a two cloth laminate; a loose plain-woven fabric using heavier cotton yarns combined with a more closely woven cloth using finer yarns. Sometimes buckram is made as a single cloth, and stiffened by the same method. The use of buckram, as a stiffening cloth for hats and interlining for garments to give them shape and form has somewhat been superseded by bonded fiber fabrics but it is still used in millinery, lampshade making and bookbinding.

Bump cloth

Bump Cloth

Bump cloth is a heavy, coarse plain-woven fabric made with a low-quality, medium-sized cotton warp and a heavy, low-quality, bump yarn weft. The term bump is used in the raw cotton market and means a hard lump in the bales of cotton. Bump yarns are made from waste cotton material collected after better quality yarns have been spun. This fabric is used primarily for cleaning cloths.

Calico

Calico was the name given to all types of cotton cloth coming from the small town of Kozhikode, known as Calicut, on the south west coast of India. In the United States it has been generally adopted as a term used in the retail trade to describe an inexpensive, printed, cotton plain-weave cloth where the print hardly shows on the back of the fabric. In Britain the term which dates back to the seventeenth century is used to describe a plain-woven cotton cloth made of carded cotton which has retained small dark flecks or spots normally taken out in further spinning processes and bleaching. This cloth is known as unbleached calico. Other cotton fabrics such as cambric, percale, chintz and muslin are sometimes sold as calico. The printed calicos have a starched finish which disappears when washed. This cloth has a variety of uses from dresses to furnishings. Traditional rag dolls are still made of calico.

Printed calico doll

Candlewick

Candlewick is a soft, heavy cotton string or yarn used literally for making candle wicks. Until the turn of the twentieth century it was sewn by hand into heavy cotton fabric forming the candlewick into loops. The loops were then cut to produce fluffy tufts which added considerably to its weight and insulation. The tufts were introduced individually into the fabric and spaced out to form linear, three-dimensional patterns. It was originally a hand craft of the southern states of the USA. It is also called kraft brown muslin sheeting. Candlewick fabric is now mass produced on tufting machines and has retained its popularity as a cloth used in making bedspreads and bathroom mats. It can be washed easily and needs no ironing.

Candlewick fabric

Canton Flannel

This cloth was originally made in Canton, China. It is a strong and absorbant cotton cloth made with a basic common twill weave using a soft, loosely spun weft. The fabric is finished with a long soft nap on the face. It has been used as an inexpensive substitute for wool flannel and often used in glove manufacture, sometimes for sleeping garments. It is sometimes known as swansdown or swanskin.

Cantoon

Cantoon is a name which derives from Canton in China. It is a heavy, diagonal, irregular twilled fabric similar to fustian. This all cotton cloth has a distinct cord effect on the face and smooth satin effect on the back. It is lightly napped on the back. This is not a very common fabric but it is used for riding and sports clothing. A plain-weave cotton cloth woven in China is also known as cantoon. This fabric is dyed purple or blue, has a starched crisp feel and is used as mummy cloth.

Sails made of canvas

Canvas

Canvas has become the generic term to describe many types of heavy, closely-woven cotton and linen fabrics. The name canvas comes from the Early English word *canevas* which derives from the Latin for hemp: *cannabis*. It was from hemp and flax that early, heavy closely-woven fabrics were made for tents and sails. Canvas fabrics are now usually made from cotton and flax. The following list includes some of the most commonly known canvas fabrics:

Artist's canvas A cotton or flax fabric which is stretched onto wooden frames and primed for oil painting. Sometimes this canvas is referred to as ticking and kit-cat canvas.

Embroidery canvas There are many canvas-type cloths and loosely woven stiff cloths used for embroidery and needlework: Berlin canvas, Java canvas bincarette or ada canvas—a basket weave cloth; hardanger, panama canvas—a hopsack or matt weave; penelope canvas—a loosely woven stiff fabric in a two-and-one weave. (*See* p142.)

Prelate canvas A canvas made for sails. The cloth is treated with tar, oil or varnish. It is known also as prelas and was used extensively as sail cloth in the French navy.

The use of man-made fibers has now superseded cotton and linen in the manufacture of fabric or canvas suitable for sails or tents. The term canvas-man is used to describe the man who erects and dismantles circus tents.

Casement

There are many variations of casement cloth. Casement has become the generic term given to types of cloth often used in the United States, and becoming popular in other countries, to hang at windows, more specifically casement windows. It is intended to ensure privacy when the curtains are drawn but at the same time retaining the maximum amount of light coming into the room. The cloth is usually heavier than net or lace curtaining and therefore can afford to be more decorative. Casement curtain fabric has in the past and is sometimes still made of cotton but is now more likely to be made of man-made fibers or fiberglass which are inherently flameproof. This type of fabric is either woven or *raschel* knitted (*See* knitting, p138).

Cellular

Cellular fabrics are usually made of all cotton. The main advantages of the combination of the open cloth structure and natural cotton fiber is that air can pass freely through the fabric and at the same time be totally absorbent and cooling. The most famous of all cellular fabrics is Aertex which is the registered proprietary brand name for a leno woven cotton cellular fabric. The name Aertex has become synonymous with other cellular fabrics. Today the name Aertex is used only as the registered brand name for shirts, blouses and underwear made not only from the original leno woven cloth but also knitted fabrics. Cloths constructed with a honeycomb weave are sometimes referred to as cellular, although these types of fabric are much more solid in structure.

Chambray

The name chambray comes from Cambrai, a town in the northern part of France near the Belgian border where the fabric originated. (*See also* Calico, p52.) Chambray is a light, good quality cotton cloth commonly made in stripes and checks, known sometimes as chambray gingham. It is usually constructed with a slightly coarser corded or combed cotton yarn in the weft than warp, woven in plain weave and given a hard but not stiff, smooth finish. Some chambrays are woven with a slight corded effect in the stripe or small dobby motif. A heavier type is also made with thicker yarns making it softer and spongier. This fabric is popular as a cloth for children's and women's dresses, blouses, smocks, aprons, men's dress and working shirts, linings and covering mattresses.

Cheesecloth

Cheesecloth was originally made for the sole purpose of cheese making. The cheese curds were pressed into the cloth, shaped and the cloth retained during the maturing process. Later this fabric was commonly used for covering bacon and packing tobacco leaf (referred to as tobacco cloth). In recent years this soft, unstarched, plain open-weave cotton cloth has been popular for the production of inexpensive shirts made in India. It is usually bleached and can be dyed. This fabric is also referred to as gauze or flag bunting (*See also* Bunting, p20) and when starched is sometimes referred to as scrim. It has many modern uses which include shirts, dresses, curtains, fancy dress costumes, exhibition displays, and lower grades for cleaning cloths. It is still used to cover cheese and meat.

(top and centre) Cellular cloth
(above) Cheesemaking

Chintz

Chino

This fabric was originally made in China although it was soon to be manufactured in Manchester, England and exported to China, where it was purchased by the United States Army stationed in the Phillipines before World War I. It then became a standard summer weight cloth worn by the US Army and was also used by the British Army. It is a rugged cloth able to stand up to hard wear and tear. Chino is twill woven in cotton yarns, with a slight sheen, although today it is often made with a blend of cotton and polyester fibers. It is usually vat-dyed khaki although it is available now in other colors. Used for making sportswear and working clothes, the term chinos or chino pants is often used in America.

Chintz

Chintz comes from the Sanskrit word *citra* meaning spotted or variegated. Cheetah is also from the same Sanskrit word. *Chintes* is the plural of the Hindi word *chit* meaning spotted or variegated. Chintes or chintz is a plain woven cotton fabric decorated with birds, plants and flowers which were originally hand painted onto the cloth in India. These cloths were imported into Britain by the East India Company in the seventeenth century. They became very popular and British manufacturers simulated them by block printing onto British-made cotton cloth and then glazing them with waxes and starch which made the colors much brighter. The importation of chintz threatened the silk industry in Britain and in 1700 a law was passed prohibiting their import. The glazed chintz has been popular ever since as a furnishing fabric used for curtains and loose covers. The original glazes washed out but modern resin finishes are more permanent.

Cleaning Cloths

There are many types of cotton cleaning cloths specially manufactured for various end uses. The most common ones made for domestic use are:

Dish cloths manufactured with an open leno weave or raschel knitting (*See* knitting, p138). Colored yarns are combined with white for decorative purposes.

Floor cloths these are woven like bump cloth with a fine cotton warp and very thick waste cotton weft. Some are knitted using similar yarns. The result in each case is a heavy highly absorbent cloth.

Dusters Traditionally these are woven, napped on both sides to give soft surfaces and dyed yellow.

Stockinette polishers These cloths are weft knitted with finer cotton yarns and used in several thicknesses as a pad for polishing.

(left) A selection of cleaning cloths

Clydella

This fabric name is the registered proprietary brand name for a shrinkproof shirting lighter in weight than Viyella, made from 81 per cent cotton and 19 per cent wool. Other companies produce similar fabrics to this but the name Clydella has become synonymous with this type of blended union fabric. It was originally developed as a lightweight shirting for military wear in the First World War. Since then it is still manufactured in the mill by the banks of the Clyde river near Glasgow in Scotland where it got its name. Clydella is available in solid colors, stripes, checks and is printed. Clydella is sometimes confused with Viyella, made by the same company, but with a different blend of cotton and wool. (*See also* Viyella, p39.)

Corduroy (left to right) thickset, needle and constitution cords

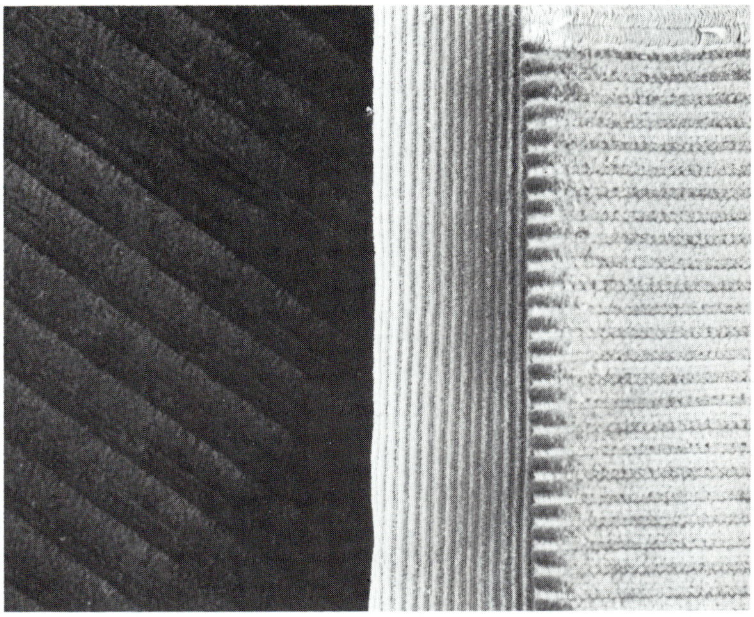

Corduroy

Corduroy is a fabric which was used extensively in the royal households of seventeenth and eighteenth-century France to make rugged, hardwearing male servants' clothing. It became known as the cord du roi.

Corduroy is similar to needlecord, partridge cord, constitution cord and thickset cord. There is also a fancy cord called algoa cord. Woven with a special corduroy weave the floats of soft weft yarn are then cut into pile cords or wales running the length of the fabric. The back of the fabric is more commonly in plain weave although twill is sometimes used. Traditionally corduroy is made in cotton but today many corduroy cloths are manufactured with cotton and man-made fiber blends.

Constitution cord has 5 to 7 cords per inch, thickset cord from 8 to 11 per inch and fine needlecords have between 16 to 21 cords per inch. There are also knitted corduroys. This cloth is used for dresses, jackets, trousers and upholstery.

Cretonne

Creton is a village in France from where cretonne gets its name. This fabric is a strong, white cotton cloth which is sometimes plain but is usually printed with large scale patterns and is similar to unglazed chintz. Made usually in plain weave it is often woven with a random oatmeal weave. Osnaburg cloth (*See* p65) is often used as the base fabric onto which cretonne designs are printed. Warp printed cretonne, also known as shadow cretonne, is woven with a heavy cotton weft producing a chiné effect. Often the printed pattern shows on both sides of the fabric. This cloth is used extensively for upholstery, loose covers and curtains.

Denim

Denim was originally woven in Nîmes in Southern France, known as *serge de Nîmes* and was used as 'sail' cloth for ships crossing the Atlantic Ocean. The warp is usually a hard twist cotton yarn, dyed indigo blue, with a softer undyed cotton yarn in the weft, woven in a compact 2-and-1 or 3-and-1 twill weaves. The smooth surface and structure of denim makes it a very hardwearing fabric. Used in recent years in the manufacture of jeans, it will always be considered the ideal cloth for making work clothes and uniforms. It is sometimes known as engineers' cloth. There are some lightweight striped fabrics similar to denim called galatea (multi-colored) and fodens (blue and white) traditionally used for butchers', fishmongers' and milkmans' aprons. A double jersey fabric using blue and white yarns is made as a substitute for denim.

Dimity

Dimity is a fabric name which comes from the Greek word *dismitos* (*dis*, 'twice' and *mitos* 'warp threads'). Originally a coarse cotton cloth dimity is now a lightweight, sheer, plain-weave cloth usually with raised warp, self-colored stripes of thicker yarn or double threads giving a raised stripe effect. Crossbar dimity is made using double or triple weft threads. This cloth is often sold printed with small patterns or dyed and is popular for women's or children's dresses.

Dimity binding is a twill-woven trimming with smooth edges and a raised diamond weave center. It is also known as bed lace. Dimity ruffling is a narrow, closely plaited braid.

Dotted Swiss

This fabric was originally made in Switzerland and is a soft, sheet cotton muslin with a dot pattern. It is a plain-woven cotton cloth made with dots of heavier self- or contrasting-colored cotton yarns on swivel looms or lappet looms. The base cloth is like a crisp lawn or voile. Imitation dotted Swiss cloths are made by flock printing. Dotted Swiss is most often used for wedding dresses.

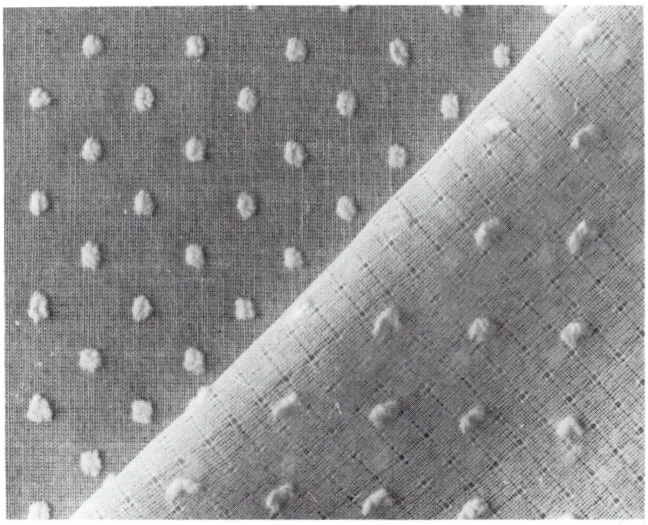

Drill

Drill derives from the Greek word *drillich* which broadly means three warp threads. Drill fabric is made with a 3-and-1 twill weave from good quality, hard twist, coarse cotton yarns. Drills can be undyed, dyed, warp striped or printed. Lightweight drill can be used for shirts. Heavier weight drill is used for uniforms and work clothes. Khaki cloth is a drill and used for army uniforms (*See also* khaki, p62). Middy twill and jean are similar fabrics to drill and satin drill is used for suitings. Florentine drill or French twill is also dyed khaki and used for uniforms.

The French term for drill is *contil* and this fabric is commonly used for mattress covers whereas lighter weights are used for brassieres. This cloth is sometimes called coutille.

(left) Traffic policeman in Dacca, Pakistan, wearing drill uniform

(below) Girl in dungarees

Duck

Duck comes from the Dutch word *doek* meaning a linen canvas which was used for sailors' clothing. There are now many types of duck or fabrics referred to as duck. The basic structure is usually a very tightly woven cotton cloth made with double warp threads and double weft threads in plain weave. It is a strong, durable fabric which can be used undyed, dyed or printed. The most important fabrics in the duck fabric group are number duck, army duck, flat duck, ounce duck, sail duck, belting duck (for driving belts), hosepipe duck, boat or bootleg duck, linen duck, shoe duck, plimsoll duck (used for sneakers, tennis and track shoes), wagon cover duck, tent duck, naught duck. A heavy duck cloth made for tents in India is called dhoosootie.

Dungaree

From the Hindi word *dungri*, dungaree is a cotton cloth which was woven in the Rajapur and Karwar areas of Goa in India. This fabric was originally exported in the seventeenth century to the Malaysian islands including those owned by the Dutch, eventually becoming an important export from India to Britain. The Dutch called it *dangerijs*. Usually this cloth, similar to denim, is constructed in twill weave with the warp and weft both dyed blue. Sometimes known as blue dungaree or bluettes. The term dungaree has become synonymous with hard-wearing working trousers or bib and brace overalls.

(above) Tent made of duck cloth

Duvetine

Also known as duvetyn, the word duvetine is derived from the French word *duvet* meaning down and thus a downy fabric. Made with a cotton warp and weft in 3-and-1 weave the fabric is finished with a heavy nap making a thick smooth fabric sometimes known as suede flannel or suede duvetyne. Dyed grey or brown it looks like doeskin. It is also known as mouseskin or *peau de souris* and used for handbags, trimmings, collars, dresses and jackets. There is an all wool duvetine which resembles velvet. The surface fibers of the fabric are napped by raising with emery rollers, cropped then pressed making a smooth lustrous finished fabric.

Flannelette

A cotton fabric originally made as a cheap imitation for wool flannel. Woven in plain or twill weave in soft cotton yarns the surface of the cloth is raised on both sides. It can be undyed, dyed, woven in stripes or checks. It launders well and is used for sheets, shirts and nightwear, and is usually 'flame-proofed'. It is sometimes known as canton flannel or franella in South America. Boomazey is a twill flannelette printed on the front and napped on the back and is used in Russia for winter shirts and children's clothes.

Fustian

The name fustian comes from the old English *fustane* or *fustyan* derived from the Latin *fustis* meaning a stick or club. Fustian is a very strong, hardwearing pile cloth usually made of cotton but originally constructed with linen warps and cotton wefts. It is assumed that fustian got its name by the fact that the cloth was beetled (beaten) with a wooden stick. Fustian cloths are made on the corduroy principle—i.e. extra weft floats are introduced into a firm backing and are cut to form the pile. The cloth is then beaten to fill out the pile.

There are many types of fustian fabrics: corduroy, moleskin, constitutional cord, beaverteen, imperial cord, swansdown, reformer cord, bullhide, camelot, round top and fustian cord. Fustian was used by the Normans, particularly by the clergy, for chasubles and at one time the Cistercian monks were not allowed to weave any other type of cloth.

(left) Advertisement for flannelette pyjamas

Gauze

A very fine sheer fabric called gazzatum was made originally in Gaza, in Palestine. Woven in silk or linen as well as cotton it was used for veiling and netting. This type of cloth was woven in plain weave but now the term gauze which is derived from Gazzatum or Gaza should be applied to fabrics woven with a leno or gauze construction. This 'weave' structure stabilizes the fabric so that the threads do not slip. Although surgical bandage is often referred to as gauze it is in fact a plain woven cotton similar to cheesecloth, hospital gauze or tobacco cloth. There are many gauze fabrics, some of which have adopted French names (the French word for gauze is *gaze*). In most cases these fabrics are made with silk: *gaze brilliantine*, *gaze damasseé*, *gaze faconnée broche*, *gaze de fil* (linen): *gaze de paris*, *gaze de voilette*, *gaze fond filoche* and *gaze milanaise*. The French term for leno or gauze weave is *gaze tour anglais*.

Gingham

Gingham (*Guingan*, Hindi; *Gingan*, Malay) was originally woven in North East India from cotton and tussah silk. The term means a striped or checked cloth. The original cloth was known as herba in the seventeenth century as there was apparently some confusion over the origin of tussah silk which was thought by Europeans to be spun from a herb. The term gingham is now used to describe an all cotton checked cloth usually woven with equal numbers of dyed and undyed threads in the warp and the same in the weft. Sometimes these checks are edged with double threads in the warp and weft creating the same effect as in dimity. A type of gingham is woven in Peru called cerifos check. Ginghams are used for dresses, shirts, curtains and tablecloths. Another name for gingham is zephyrs.

Gingham

Jaconet

The French word jaconet comes from the Hindi word *jagannath* meaning a thin cotton fabric originally woven in East India. It is a soft closely woven fabric slightly heavier than cambric. It is generally highly glazed on the face of the cloth and used for dresses and children's clothes.

Jasper Cloth

The term jasper comes from the word *iaspis*, which is the same in Latin and Greek, meaning a variegated green quartz. Jasper cloth or jaspé cloth is usually a plain woven cotton fabric where the warp yarn has been dyed or printed in two tones. This gives the woven cloth an uneven effect. The same effect can be achieved by a random arrangement of close toned or contrasting colored warp threads. This type of cloth varies in weight and quality and can be used for furnishings and apparel.

Prospectors panning gold north-west of Sacramento, California in 1849

Jean

Jean fabric gets its name from the northern Italian town of Genoa where it was first made. Originally this cloth was used as lining material and made with a 3-and-1 twill weave producing a smooth faced closely woven cloth. It differs from denim because it is dyed in solid colors or bleached. The plural of jean has become synonymous with hard wearing working trousers. At the time of the gold rush in the mid-nineteenth century in the United States, jean, denim and other heavy weight canvas cloths were used for tents and it was found that these cloths made better working trousers for the gold miners than traditional fabrics. Jean is used extensively for working and sports cloths. Other cloths similar to jean include Argentina and Austrian twill both of which are usually dyed black.

Kain

Kain is the Javanese term used for a length of cotton batik fabric about seven and a half feet long and three and a half feet wide. Also referred to as kain pandjang, bebed, tapih or djarit it is worn as a wrap-around garment in a similar manner to the sarong or kanga and kitengi in Africa. Kitengi is related to kain. Merchants brought kain from the Dutch East Indies to Holland, copied and sold them to the West African countries particularly Nigeria and were subsequently copied and sold to East African countries, where they are now copied by the emerging East African textile printing industry. The pattern of the kain is traditional and is divided into four parts: kepela or central panel, head or end and two bands on either side of the central panel running lengthwise.

Kanga (Khanga), Kitenge (Kitangi)

These shawls and sarongs made in West and East Africa are given a variety of local names and are very precise in their meaning. Made from local cotton usually in plain weave these cloths have very specific dimensions. Sold in pairs, one for the sarong, one for the shawl they are printed with very precise specifications. A kanga is 45 inches wide and 66 inches long. It must have a border all the way round and a central motif no more than 19 inches in diameter. It is often decorated with a commemorative design. A kitenge is 45 inches wide and 72 inches long and has borders along the length of the fabric. It is usually printed with an imitation batik design much influenced by Javanese batik work. Other types of African cotton cloth used for shawls and sarongs include the kidunga, kissuto and kanikas.

(left) Tanzanian women wearing Kangas and Kitenges, dancing in their village

(right) Khadi

Khadi and Khaddar

Khaddar and *khadi* are both Hindi words meaning cloth woven from handspun cotton yarns. This is one of the most commonly used fabrics in India because it is very inexpensive to produce and is exported for shirts and dresses. Other types of khadi made in a similar way are called guzee, garrha and chotari. Apart from the obvious use of making inexpensive clothing this cloth is often used for packing rolls of more expensive materials and for binding corpses in before cremation.

Khaki

Although khaki is known to be a color it is often used loosely to describe cloth of this color. The word khaki is Hindi for dust colored and it was first used to describe the color of the uniforms of Indian Army soldiers during the time of the British Raj of the mid-nineteenth century. Khaki is applied to all types of cloths used by the armies of the world and has become synonymous with rugged hardwearing cloth. Khaki cloths of varying types are now used for sports and leisure wear.

English Army records show that in 1848 Harry Burnett Lumsden equipped his army against the Afghans with uniforms dyed an earthy shade he called khaki, which was a yellowy color.

Lawn

Lawn gets its name from the town of Laon in northern France. A fine linen cloth was made in this town and used for garments worn by the clergy. Lawn is now described as a fine, sheer, plain-weave cotton cloth using high quality yarns. It has a crisper feel than voile but not as crisp as organdie. There are many types of lawn including Indian lawn, Victoria lawn, Persian lawn and bishop's lawn. Liberty of London, England, have made famous their Tana Lawn which began manufacture in the 1920s. It is named after Lake Tana in the Sudan where the raw cotton is grown. It is usually printed with small scale floral designs. This lawn is similar to Egyptian lawn and widely used for dresses and shirts.

Longcloth

Longcloth was originally woven in south India in the Madras area. It is now usually described as a fine, soft closely-woven cotton fabric made from slightly twisted high quality yarns in plain weave. The cloth is normally sized and calendered which gives it a slight lustre. It is heavier than lawn and the weave is more dense than percale. Madapollam is similar to longcloth and both are often sold bleached white. They are most suitable for children's and women's dresses, and also used as sheeting.

(centre above) Khaki worn by the 1st Battalion (25th) King's Own Scottish Borderers, about 1880
(right) Tana lawn by Liberty of London

(left) Madras cotton

Madras

Madras is an area in south eastern India where there is a highly developed handloom cotton weaving industry. There are many types of cloth woven in Madras—Madras Shirting, Madras Gauze, Madras Muslin, Madras Gingham and Madras Handkerchiefs. The term Madras has however become synonymous with a plain woven striped or checked cotton fabric. It is usually made in random checks or stripes in varying proportions using dyed yarns throughout. The dyes are not always permanent and one of the characteristics of this fabric is that the dyes bleed. It is a popular cloth for shirts and dresses and is imitated now in many countries.

Matelassé

The word matelassé comes from the French verb *matelasser* meaning to pad, to stuff or to cushion. Matelassé fabric is basically a double cloth which has been constructed to form a three-dimentional quilted effect. It is usually woven on Jacquard looms from cotton but man-made fibers are frequently used. The padded effect is achieved by introducing soft, heavy cotton yarns into the weft sandwiched between two fine closely woven cloths. *Fourré* is another French term for matelassé. Marseilles is a similar although finer fabric and Marseilles quilts are made in the same way imitating a particular fabric made in the East and used for quilts. Matelassé is commonly used for upholstery, curtains, bedspreads and also for dresses.

Moleskin: A scene at a pottery in Staffordshire, England in the 19th century

Moleskin

As the name suggests moleskin is a fabric which is made to simulate the short, soft, fine fur of the small tunneling rodent. It is a cotton pile fabric which is woven with a special weave based on a satin construction with closely woven floats on the face of the fabric. The floats are cut, steamed to open the fiber to give an even dense nap which looks like a heavy suede. Moleskin is a fabric which is very hardwearing. The lighter weight qualities are used for trousers and working clothes. The heavier weight, with a longer pile, is used for winter coat lining. The term bannigan was given to a moleskin fabric which used to be made for working suits worn by the potters of Staffordshire in England.

Monk's Cloth

It is possible that monk's cloth gets its name from the penitent sackcloth worn by monks and other repentant cloistered people. It is a cloth which is rough, coarse and heavy-woven with a 4-and-4 basket weave usually from cotton although flax, jute or hemp are sometimes used in the weft either natural colored or dyed brown, blue or green. It is not a very stable fabric, because of the loose weave, and tends to sag. It can be used for furnishings but requires careful lining if used for curtains. Sometimes printed it is also known as abbot-cloister, druid or friar cloth.

Mull

Mull is of the muslin family and gets its name from the Hindi word *mulmull* which means muslin. This soft, pliable fabric is made in plain weave from the fine cotton yarns and was originally handwoven in Bengal in India. Often embroidered with flowers it was exported to England in the seventeenth century and used for petticoats. Sometimes it was embroidered in silver and gold. Bishop's Lawn is a type of mull which is often used for ecclesiastical vestments. (*See also* muslin below.) Plain mull fabric is also used in book binding.

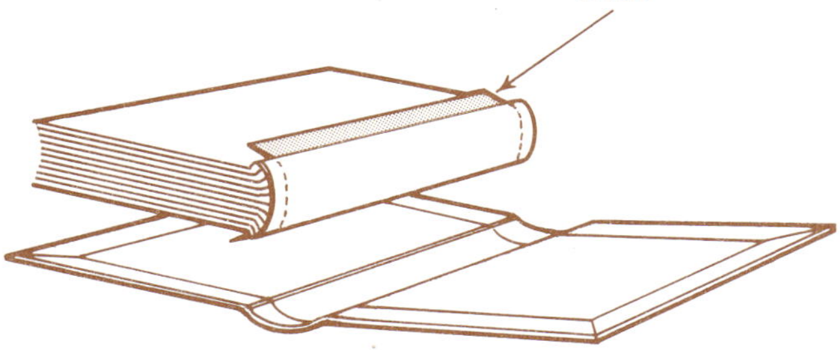

Muslin

Muslin was first woven in Mosul, a city in the northern tip of Iraq near the border of Turkey. It was the name given to a variety of plain woven cotton fabrics but it is a term which has been used in India for the past three hundred years to describe a thin, fine, soft cotton cloth. In the United States many more closely woven cotton fabrics, even some types of sheeting, batiste, lawn, cretonne, longcloth or percaline, are referred to as muslin. The term raw muslin is used in America for unbleached muslin. Mutton cloth, butter muslin, cheesecloth, mull, paper muslin are all cloths of the muslin family. Book muslin and binding muslin have hard stiff finishes but are not true muslins. There are several Hindi words for muslin: *malmal*, *mollmol* or *mulmull* (*See also* mull above). There are also several other local Indian names used to describe different muslins which include alabalee, ajiji, alliabably, jhuna, shabnam and sullah.

Nainsook

The word nainsook comes from two Hindi words—*nain* meaning eye and *sukh* meaning delight. In the seventeenth century this Indian fabric, sometimes called nansook, nyansook or nainsook, was thought to give 'pleasure to the eye'. It is a lightweight, plain-woven, cotton cloth similar to jaconnet. English nainsook has a soft finish and French nainsook has a hard, crisp finish. Sometimes this fabric is made with a closely woven satin or twill stripe forming a corded effect at intervals across the fabric. Nainsook checks in the United States are made from a combination of small random checks plain woven in colored yarns and bordered by warp and weft satin or twill stripes. Nainsook is heavier than lacon and is usually sold undyed, in plain pastel colors or printed. It is usually used for lingerie or dresses.

The Emperor Akbar enthroned, about 1600. The figure on the left is wearing a muslin skirt

A 1940s bride in an organdie dress

A British lifeboat crew in 1942 wearing oilskins

Oil Cloth

Oil cloth, known as American cloth in the UK, is a plain woven cotton fabric, coated on one side with a mixture of linseed oil and pigment. The pigment is often white but can also be tinted. The fabric is then given a glazed finish making it waterproof and is easily sponged down. One of the problems with oil cloth is that it cracks. At one time this fabric was known as imitation leather. It has now been superseded by cloths with various plastic finishes which are more pliable and durable. American cloth, and oil cloth were used extensively for inexpensive upholstery, kitchen tablecloths, shopping bags and sometimes rainwear. Enameled cloth and leather cloth are similar to oil cloth. Lancaster cloth is a similar fabric printed with an imitation marble design.

Oilskin

Oilskin is usually made from a closely woven cotton cloth although it can also be silk. The plain woven fabric is impregnated with linseed oil, dried and oxidized to a hard, smooth, translucent finish making it completely waterproof. The cloth becomes stiff and retains the smell of the oil which also gives it a distinctive golden yellow color. Before the invention of plastics and man-made fibers this fabric was the only type available for seamen's waterproof clothing and was used in the manufacture of slickers and sou'westers. A fine silk fabric treated with boiled linseed oil was used for surgical purposes.

Organdie

Organdie (organdy) is a very thin light fabric woven from fine, tightly-twisted, cotton yarns. It is transparent and usually has a permanent, crisp, starched finish. Although some stiffening treatments can be washed out organdie can withstand repeated laundering and only needs to be ironed to bring it back to its original condition. Organza is a pure silk fabric which resembles organdie. Organzine is a two-fold, fine filament, silk thread commonly used as warp yarn.

Osnaburg

Osnaburg is the name of a fabric originally woven in the city of Osnabruck in north west Germany. At one time it was made of linen but now it is a rough, strong, plain-woven, cotton cloth made with coarse yarns sometimes spun from cotton waste. Quite often this fabric which is similar to cretonne is used as a finishing fabric either undyed, dyed or printed although it is more commonly used in its unbleached state for bags for sugar, grain or cement.

(left) Osnaburg printed sack

Oxford cloth

Oxford cloth was never woven in the city of Oxford but gets its name through its popularity as a shirt fabric worn by the undergraduates of Oxford University in England. It is a soft, absorbent, sturdy, cotton shirting with a silky lustre finish and is very popular for shirts or dresses in the United States. This fabric is made in plain weave with two fine warp threads woven as one giving the effect of a 2-and-1 matt weave. Sometimes stripes are added in fancy weaves. Oxford cloth is now made in various blends of cotton and man-made fibers. It wears well and can be laundered easily.

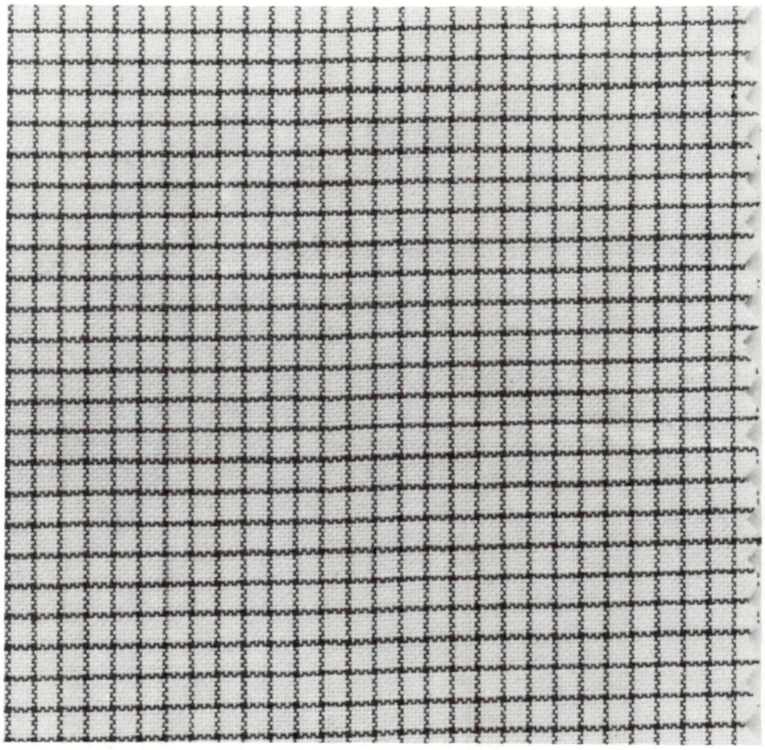

Oxford cloth

Percale

Percale comes from a Persian word *pargalah* which describes a type of cotton fabric originating from Iran. Percale is now the name given to a fine, smooth, cotton fabric without any luster. Finer than muslin it is made in plain weave from good quality yarns. Percale is sometimes printed and normally starched and heavily pressed. Percale is used for dresses, shirts and particularly for sheets. Percaline is the name given to a lighter-weight, cotton cloth which is usually bleached or dyed, glazed and sometimes given a moiré finish. This is used for summer weight clothing and linings.

Piqué

The term piqué comes from the French verb *piquer* meaning to quilt. The 'quilting' of this fabric is part of the weave structure resulting in a fine, three-dimentional, embossed effect similar to a Bedford cord. In the United States the wales of this cotton cord run the length of the cloth whereas the English piqué rib is across the fabric. A pin wale piqué is a very fine, corded cloth and a waffle piqué is made in a small honeycomb pattern which retains the characteristic embossed look. There are also bird's eye piqués and embroidered piqués. Sometimes many of the wide variety of piqué cloths are printed but most are bleached or dyed. The versatility of this cloth stretches from children's and women's dresses, blouses, men's dress shirts and sportswear to draperies.

Waffle piqué

Plissé

Plissé

Plissé is a French word which means wrinkling, crinkling or pleating and is used in a variety of ways to describe different fabrics. In France a plissé fabric has small folds, pleats or tucks made by a special weave structure. In the United States the term plissé or plissé crêpe is used to describe a plain-weave cotton fabric which has been treated in certain areas with caustic soda to shrink the cloth. The caustic soda solution is printed onto the cloth in stripes or patterns and produces a permanent crinkled effect in those particular areas. The effect is permanent and the crinkles cannot be ironed out. The term Seersucker is often used also to describe this type of fabric although the crinkled effect in Seersucker is obtained by the construction and use of special yarns in the warp. All of these types of fabric can be used for dresses, jackets, curtains, bedspreads or lingerie.

Poplin

Poplin comes from the French word *popeline* which is a cloth originally made in the papal city of Avignon in Southern France for church vestments. Poplin is a lightweight, closely-woven, cotton fabric with a fine rib across the width of the cloth. This rib is created by using a fine mercerized yarn in the warp and a thicker one in the weft. There are many weights and types of poplin the most common of which are used for shirts and pyjamas. The original poplin was woven with a silk warp and worsted weft. This fabric is known also as popeline or Irish poplin.

Sateen

Sateen is a weave which is usually associated with cotton cloths although man-made fibers are sometimes used either by themselves or blended with cotton. A cotton sateen fabric is made with either a five- or eight-end satin weave where the weft thread, which is usually coarser than the warp, is on the face of the fabric. Unlike satin, the warp need not be so closely set. The yarns used are mercerized giving a smooth lustrous surface to the cloth. Sateens can be plain, dyed or printed and used for a variety of purposes including draperies, upholstery, mattress covers, linings and sportswear. (*See also* satin, p89.)

Seersucker

Seersucker comes from the Persian for milk and sugar: *shīr o shakkar*. The contrast between sugar and milk is a good description of this fabric. It is a cloth which has smooth, plain stripes alternating with puckered or crinkled stripes. The stripes are in the length of the fabric and can be any proportion. The fabric can be produced in three different ways: by stripes in the warp being under varying tensions, by using two yarns of varying twist in the warp or by printing the stripes with a resist and treating the cloth with caustic soda which crinkles the part of the fabric not been printed. Seersucker is usually dyed in solid colors or it can be printed. Seersucker gingham is made in a similar way. Usually seersucker requires no ironing and is an ideal fabric for dresses, men's summer jackets, children's playclothes, housecoats, bedspreads and curtains.

Sponge Cloth

As the name describes most sponge cloths are made to absorb moisture such as a floor or cleaning cloth. These coarse-weave cloths are usually made with heavy, low-grade cotton yarns in plain weave and sometimes leno. There is a specific weave called a sponge weave which produces a spongy cloth with a cellular construction. This fabric, made of soft cotton yarns, is more commonly used for bedcovers. (*See* cleaning cloths p55.)

Stockinette

Stockinette is a knitted fabric which derives its name from a stocking stitch used originally to make socks and stockings. It is a fabric which is now associated with cleaning cloths although it is a useful cloth for making dresses, shirts and nightwear.

Surgical Cloths

Surgical cloths which include bandages for humans and animals, come under various categories including plain-woven cotton muslin, woven cotton gauze, woven stretch bandage containing elastic material, woven crêpe bandage and knitted bandage containing no elastic material, non-woven fabric and woven cotton napped lint.

Tarlatan

The origin of the word tarlatan is uncertain and there are variations of the word which refer to slightly different types of fabric. Tarlatan is a lightweight, very open, plain-weave cotton cloth which is stiffened or glazed on one side. It resembles scrim only it is woven in much finer cotton yarns and is very transparent. It is often called Argentine cloth and can be used for Christmas stockings, fancy dress costumes, fruit packing, coat lining, display and millinery. Tarlatane is a very similar cloth but slightly more open and thinner yarns are used. Tarlaton or tarlton are alternative spellings of tarlatan.

Seersucker

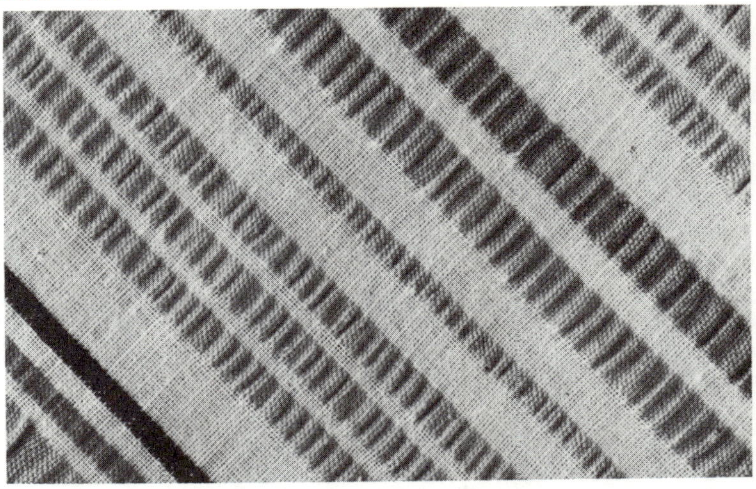

(above) Stretch bandage

(opposite) T-shirt made from stockinette
(right) Traditional Christmas stocking made of tarlatan

I'd be lost without it.

Toweling

The origin of the word towel goes back to the old High German word *dwahan*, meaning to wash, from which the modern German word *zwehle* comes. A towel is a piece of cloth used specifically for drying anything wet and therefore must be made from highly absorbent materials. The best fiber to use is cotton. There are several types of toweling including terry, turkish, huckaback, honeycomb, damask, crash or knitted.

Terry cloth (or Turkish toweling), from the French *tiré* meaning drawn, is a rough-faced cloth covered both sides with small uncut loops of cotton. This toweling can be woven plain, in stripes or with Jacquard patterns, and is used extensively for bath, hand and face towels, British nappies, and bar counter mats. A terry toweling made with linen is used for saunas and animals. A machine-knitted toweling is made with loops on one side and used for stretch sheets and clothing.

Ticking

Tick comes from the Latin *theca* meaning a cover or case usually made of cotton or sometimes linen. Ticking is a very closely-woven stout fabric made of tightly-spun cotton yarns. It is available in several forms including damask or plain, solid shade fabrics. Traditionally ticking is woven from dyed yarns in a combination of thick and thin stripes on a white background using a 2-and-2 twill or herringbone weave. The cloth has a smooth, lustrous surface and can also be given a water repellent finish. Ticking was at one time referred to as bedstout, inlet and bed tick. Limoges are brightly colored tickings with a hard glazed surface. Limoges also refers to coarse hemp cloths used for bags in France. It is commonly used for pillow cases, mattress covers and bolster covers.

Velour

Velour is the French word for velvet and gets its origin from the Latin *villosus* meaning hairy. Velour is a pile fabric which is usually made of cotton and piece-dyed in solid colors. The pile can be on both sides of the fabric, is made of coarser yarns and more dense pile than velvet or velveteen, and is sometimes referred to as plush. The term velour is often used to describe a napped finish cloth similar to duvetyn. A knitted velour is made with a fine pile surface and is used for sweaters and sportswear. Woven pile velour is more suitable for draperies and upholstery and napped velour finished cloth for suits and coats. A felt-like fabric called velour is also made with the hair of the rabbit, hare or nutria and is identified by its lustrous, heavy, hairy nap and is commonly used for hats.

Huckaback toweling

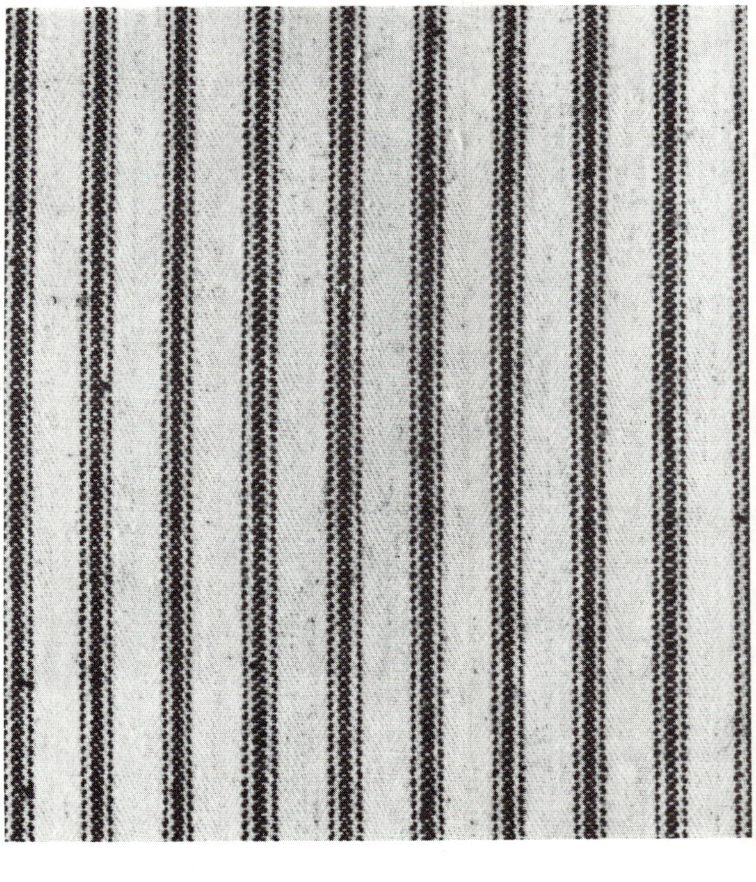

(centre) Jacquard terry toweling used for bar mats
(right) Ticking

Velveteen (left) with woven stripes and (right) printed

Velveteen

Velveteen is often referred to as cotton velvet and was first produced in Manchester, England, in the early part of the eighteenth century. It is a fabric with an even, all-over, short, closely set pile. Mercerized cotton yarns are usually used to make this cloth although rayon is also often used. The pile of the fabric slopes slightly to create a slight sheen to the surface of the fabric. Velveteen is made with a weft float construction. After weaving the weft is cut and it is then brushed and steamed to produce the finished even pile. Velveteen plush has a slightly longer pile and hollow-cut velveteen has grooves cut or constructed into the pile. Velveteen can be used for dresses, coats, suits, draperies or upholsteries.

Venetian Cloth

Venetian cloth is a strong, smooth faced, lustrous fabric resembling silk Venetian originally woven in Venice. Although this fabric is more commonly woven with cotton yarns in satin weave it can also be made of worsted wool or silk. Sometimes the surface of the cloth can be napped and is usually either dyed in plain colors or bleached white. Venetian cloths can be used for linings, dresses, jackets, draperies and cushion covers. Wool Venetian cloth is used more for suits, coats and upholstery.

Voile with satin stripes

Voile

The French word for veil is *voile* and it is for this end use that this fabric was originally made. Voile is a sheer, open weave, light weight cotton cloth which drapes well into soft folds. Although there are also silk voiles and wool voiles, cotton voile is the most common now. Made with high twist smooth cotton yarns the cloth is woven with an even clear surface. Cotton voile is often woven with clipped spots known as clip dot voile. There are other variations of voile including drawn thread and embroidered voile. It is used for lingerie, blouses and curtains.

Winceyette

Wincey and winceyette are two similar types of fabric the names of which come from Linsey-Woolsey which is a play on words of Wool, linen, and kersey. Linsey-woolsey was a fabric which was produced in Lindsey, Suffolk, England made of either cotton or linen in the warp and wool in the weft. It is a plain woven cloth, using soft cotton yarns, which is raised on one side making it a warm washable fabric suitable for nightclothes or bedsheets.

Silk
The History of Silk

The origin of the word silk comes from China where the first silk was reeled from the cocoon of a silkworn:

Chinese—sse	French—soie
Greek—serikon	German—Seide
Latin—sericum	Korean—sir
Italian—seta	Russian—sheolk
Spanish—seda	

The word sericulture comes from the Latin *sericum*, meaning the cultivation of silk. When written in Chinese the characters for silkworm literally mean heavenly insect.

The history of cultivated silk production or sericulture dates back to about the year 2640 BC when the Chinese Empress Hsi Ling Shi gave the silk industry her royal patronage. This may be so, but according to 'An Essay upon the Silkworm', published by Henry Barham in London in 1719, silkworms survived the Great Flood in the Ark when it came to rest on Mount Ararat, and were subsequently taken by Noah to China. It is known that the Chinese were the first to develop silk and reel it from the cocoon and that they kept up a monopoly for over 3000 years. Eventually, after several hundred years, knowledge about the silkworm reached Japan and then Korea.

Chinese legend says that in 400 AD a silk moth and a seed of the mulberry tree were taken to India by a Chinese princess who concealed them in the lining of her head-dress. However, Sanskrit writings claim that silk manufacture was introduced into the West by two Persian monks who succeeded in bringing a small supply of silkworms to Constantinople in 552 AD. It was not long after this that sericulture spread throughout the whole Byzantine Empire and eventually the Arabs, Spanish and Italians developed a silk industry. It was during the Renaissance that the cultivation, manufacture and use of silk expanded throughout Europe. Twelve years before Christopher Columbus discovered the New World, Louis XI of France established the first silk mill at Tours in France.

Having been unsuccessful in establishing sericulture in Britain, James I in 1622 issued instructions to his colonists in Virginia to breed silkworms in preference to 'that pernicious and offensive weed, tobacco'. A slogan was used by the Government to promote its policy:

> Where worms and food do naturally abound,
> A gallant silken thread must there be found.
> Virginia excels the World in both,
> Envy nor malice can gainsay this troth.

Weaving was a well established craft in Britain and had been since Edward III brought Flemish weavers to England in the early fourteenth century. Another influx of immigrant workers, this time French Huguenots, came to England after Henry of Navarre's Edict of Nantes was revoked in 1685 and 50,000 families of French Protestants escaped from France. Despite efforts to stop them, many of them came to England and among them were a considerable number of silk weavers. The principal settlement for them was at Spitalfields in East London. The Huguenots brought with them the expert knowledge of weaving velvets, brocades and satins.

Meanwhile every effort was being made to develop a silk industry in America. By 1838 it seemed there was a great future in silk production. After considerable investment and speculation in planting the South Sea Island mulberry tree, the *Moris multicanlis*, it was found unfit for silkworm rearing and the potential silk industry collapsed in 1839. Today the main silk-producing countries are China, Japan, Italy and India.

(above) The White Mulberry (*Morus alba*), from *Gerard's Herball*, 1636

(opposite) King James I, about 1620, by John de Critz

Silk Production

Silk is a continuous filament of protein substances produced by the silkworm. The silkworm produces two protein substances within its body—fibroin which forms the main core of the silk filament and sericin which is the so-called 'silk gum' which covers the fibroin. The sericin is a most important component of the silk when it is processed, but it is finally removed before dyeing and finishing leaving the fibroin which is the actual silk fiber. In order to produce this protein material the silkworm, which is the caterpillar of the silk moth, feeds on the leaves of plants, much in the same way as a cow feeds on grass and converts the grass in its body into the protein found in dairy products.

There are several species of silkworm but the one which is the most important and produces the majority of silk for the textile industry is the *Bombyx mori*, so-called because the mulberry leaf provides it with its diet (the Latin for mulberry is *Morus*). The most suitable variety of mulberry leaf is from the white mulberry (*Morus alba*) bush. It was the black mulberry (*Morus nigra*) which was grown in England in the seventeenth century in an attempt to develop a sericulture industry. In contrast to the *Bombyx mori* silkworm (the moth has a wingspan of 2 in/5 cm) there are other species of silkworms which produce what is known as tussah or wild silk. The antherea and attacus silkworm (the moth has a wing span of 6 in/15 cm) are the best known producers of wild silk. Antherea is a term which comes from the Greek *antheros* meaning flowery. Unlike the *Bombyx mori* both the antherea and attacus silkworms feed on the leaves of the oak, castor oil, and cherry trees. The silk produced is much coarser and varies in color from yellow ochre to grey to brown. The antherea is known more commonly as muga, mooga, moonga or mounga and is found in north east India especially in Assam. Some antherea silk is also grown in China and Japan. Attacus is a similar silk worm and produces a wild silk known as atlas silk or eri silk.

(below) A plantation of *Morus alba* in Japan, not to be confused with the Black Mulberry (*Morus nigra*), found in England and the U.S.A.

(below) The cocoon cut open to reveal the fully formed chrysalis

(below) Silk moth emerging from its cocoon

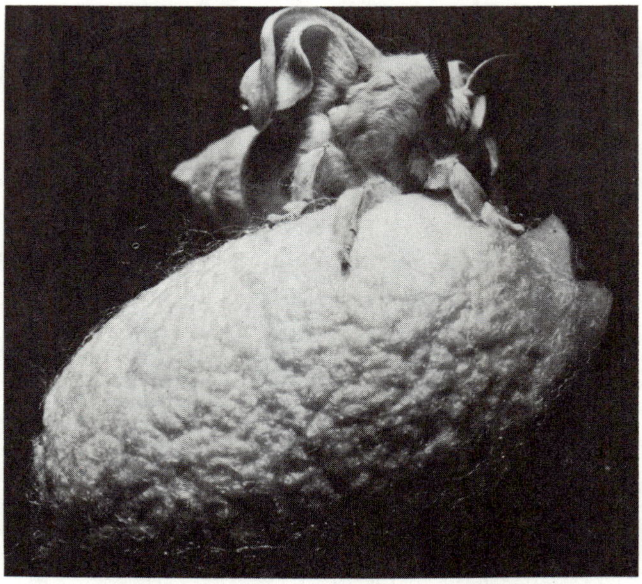

(opposite) Silkworms feeding on mulberry leaves

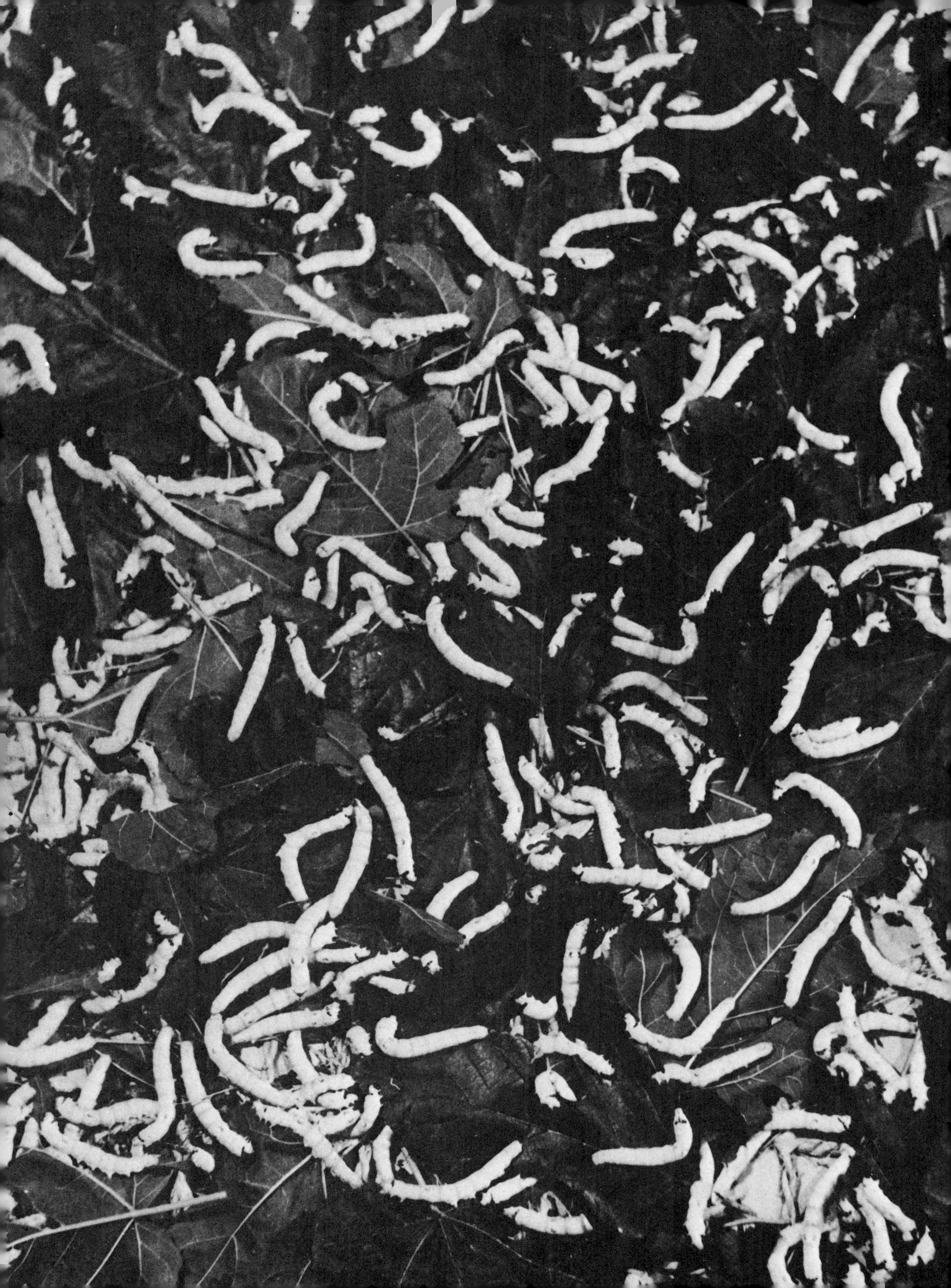

Sericulture, the cultivation of silkworms to produce silk, is a delicate process requiring care and patience from moth to cloth. When the leaves of the white mulberry bush begin to bud in the spring the eggs of last year's *Bombyx mori* moths which have been hibernating, often in the cold dry atmosphere of the mountains, are brought down to the mulberry district to hatch. Over a period of ten to fourteen days and in a temperature which increases from 55°F (12.8°C) to 75°F (23.9°C) the eggs, which are no larger than pin-heads, hatch into baby caterpillars. The ravenous caterpillars start eating and growing immediately. On a diet of mulberry leaves the caterpillar or silkworm grows and discards its skin four times, becoming a hairless creature measuring 3–4 in (7.5–10 cm) long. It is estimated that over 36,000 caterpillars are hatched from 1 ounce (25 grams) of eggs and one ton of foliage is consumed by this number of caterpillars to produce eventually 12 lbs (5.5 kg) of raw silk.

A viscose solution is emitted through two holes in the head of the silkworm, coming from a pair of glands running the length of its body. It solidifies under tension to form an endless pair of filaments stuck together by the gummy sericin (the two filaments look like one at this stage). By moving its head from side to side in a figure of eight movement, the wall of the cocoon is gradually built up from the inside where the process continues even after the silkworm is lost from sight. The finished cocoon is about 1½ inches (4 cm) long and ¾ inch (2 cm) wide, and once the sericin dries it becomes very hard.

It is estimated that the cocoon of silk from one *Bombyx mori* silkworm can produce a mile of filament silk. After a period of ten days, once the cocoon has been completed, a chrysalis is formed and it is then that the silk must be unwound or reeled from the cocoon. At this stage selected cocoons are put on one side from which moths will emerge to produce eggs for the next season's production. The life cycle of the *Bombyx mori* is completed only once a year and is therefore referred to as monovoltine. Other types of silkworm, some of which can complete seven life cycles in one year are called polyvoltine species.

A fully grown silkworm ready to spin its cocoon

(below) Female silkworm (*Bombyx mori*), laying eggs

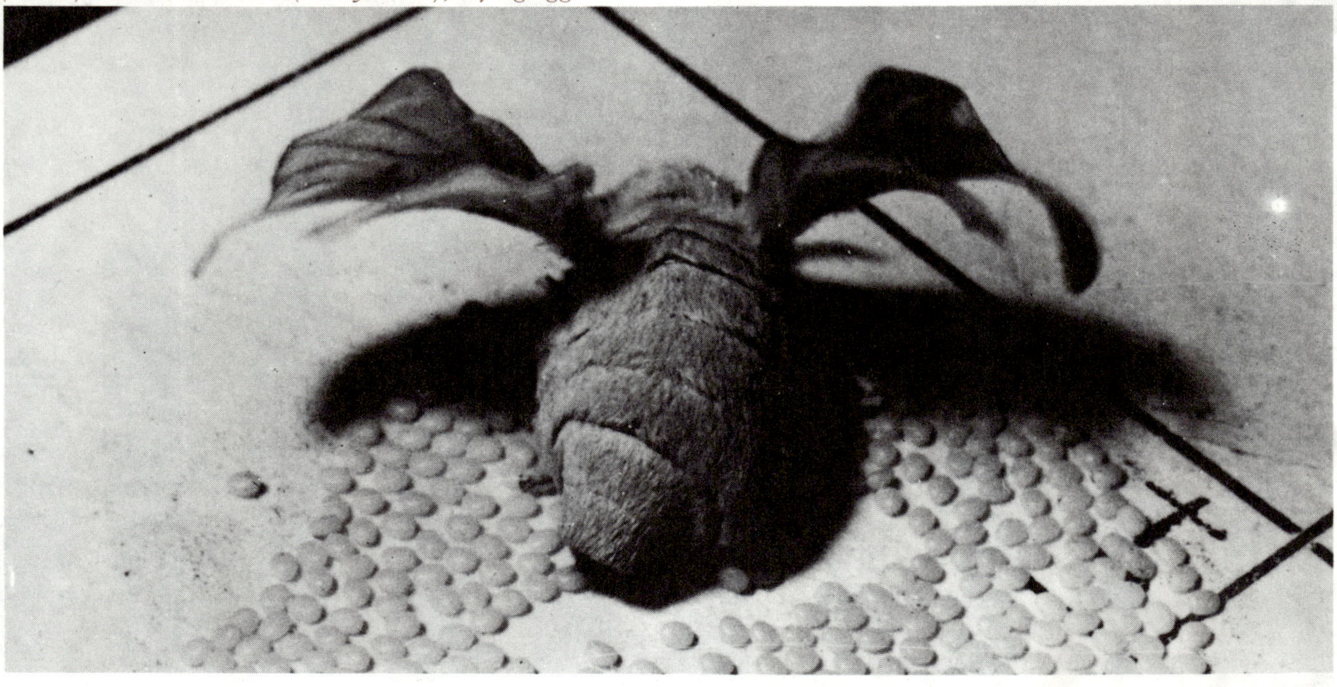

(opposite) Silkworms on their feeding trays

The double filament (two brins) of silk from which the cocoon has been built is known as a bave. The process of reeling starts by softening the cooon by immersion in hot water. The surface of each cocoon is then lightly brushed to find the end of the bave and between five and ten baves are collected together and the reeling begins. This produces the raw silk which is almost ready for use. The final stage is known as throwing. The term throwing comes from the Anglo-Saxon *thraw* meaning to twist or spin. A throwster sorts the skeins of raw silk for quality and through a series of processes of soaking, drying and winding will put a twist into groups of filaments to form yarn which can be used for weaving or knitting. Not all silk is thrown. Some is spun into thread or yarn like cotton. This type of silk yarn is usually produced from waste silk or cocoons which have been pierced by an emerging moth.

During the process of boiling off the sericin, either in the yarn state or in the cloth, the weight of the silk is reduced by as much as 25 per cent. The more sericin boiled off, the better quality the silk. To restore the weight into the silk (hence the term 'weighted silk') the yarn or cloth is processed with tin and iron salts. Having boiled off the natural gum, sericin, from silk, and rinsed thoroughly, the yarn or cloth can be dyed. At this stage silk takes on a characteristic handle which is known as scroop. Scroop is the crunchy, rustling feel which is one of the attractive features of silk. Sometimes silkworms build their cocoons too close to each other, often merging one cocoon with another. When these cocoons are reeled there is more likelihood of producing threads with slubs or bumps at intervals. This type of yarn is known as Douppion.

Silk fabrics need particular care. Some can be washed but when in doubt, dry clean. Fabrics such as taffetas and brocades should always be dry cleaned but the main rule to observe is never to allow silk fabrics to become too soiled before cleaning. Perspiration stains on silk are often difficult to remove and also weaken the fabric. If a piece of silk fabric or garment is washed make sure that the dye is fast. Dip a corner of the cloth into tepid water, squeeze dry, place on a piece of cotton and cover with a warm iron. If there is no color on the cotton, the garment may be washed. Never soak, boil or bleach silk. Wash in warm suds (100°F/40°C) only. Rinse well. Remove surplus water by rolling the fabric or garment in a clean towel, but never leave it to dry out completely in the towel. Press silk on the wrong side with the iron at a warm setting, but do not use a steam iron. If the fabric is excessively or unevenly damp, water staining may occur when ironing. These stains can be removed by immersing the fabric or garment for 2 or 3 minutes in warm water, allowing to dry and re-ironing.

Hanks of Indian tussah silk yarn

(below) Cocoons being examined and sorted prior to silk reeling

(opposite) Wooden racks sectioned with cardboard in which silkworms spin their cocoons

Aerophane
The term aerophane comes from a combination of the word aero meaning air and the Greek word *phainesthar* meaning to appear. Broadly it means a silk gauze fabric 'lighter than air'. Usually woven in an imitation crêpe weave, it is dyed in solid color and is used for trimming dresses and hats when cut on the bias.

Atlas
The term atlas is used in Europe to describe a silk-faced fabric with a cotton back made with an 8-end satin weave. It is very shiny on the face and matt on the reverse side. This fabric is used for dresses and linings. Originally the word came from India. The silk produced from the cocoon of the attacus attissima, known also as attacus atlas, ailanthus or atlas silk is similar to tussah only darker. It was used in India to weave richly-colored, striped silk cloths and was exported to Europe in the early eighteenth century. Another name for atlas is fagara silk. (*See also* atlas, p48.)

Bengaline de Soie
Bengaline de soie is an all-silk fabric although the term bengaline is used to describe a variety of cloths made from different fibers. The word bengaline originates from Bengal in India. It is a lustrous warp-faced cloth with a corded effect across the width of the cloth. The warp threads are set close together and a thicker soft weft or filling is woven across to produce a rib similar to poplin. Bengaline is a strong durable fabric in all its forms and drapes well. At one time it was used widely as a mourning cloth but now any bengaline fabrics can be used for women's dresses, ribbons (like grosgrain) and hats. Other types of bengaline include *bengaline maquise*, *bengaline radrant*, *bengaline russe* and *bengaline velour*.

Bolting Cloth
The term bolting comes from the French word *blutage* meaning to sift. Originally bolting cloth was made specifically to sift flour from bran. It is a plain-woven, sheer silk fabric and is still used in flour mills but has become a popular fabric to use in making silk screens for printing. It is also sometimes used as a foundation for wigs. This fabric is now frequently made from filament nylon or polyester and stiffened to resemble the original silk cloth. It is also known as miller's gauze.

Bengaline de soie (left), and grosgrain (right)

(right) Screen printing using bolting cloth

Bourette

Bourette is from the French word *bourre* meaning hair or floss. Bourette fabric, woven from bourette silk yarns, is a light-weight, rough-faced cloth made in either plain or twill weave. The yarn, called bourette silk which gives the cloth its distinctive character, is spun from silk waste produced in the manufacture of schappe silk. It is bumpy and irregular. Although this cloth can be used for apparel it is more commonly used as curtain fabric. The small hairy lumps, nubs or noils produce a fancy effect of brightly colored spots of color in the cloth.

Brocade

The Latin word *brocare* means to figure. A brocade is a richly figured cloth. Originally a heavy silk fabric with floral and scroll patterns woven in gold or silver thread, it was first produced in China and Japan. Now brocades are Jacquard woven with richly figured patterns emphasized sometimes by contrasting colors or more usually by contrasting satin weave figures with a plain weave or twill background. Brocades are often made with man-made fibers. Lighter weights are used for apparel and heavier weights for furnishings. A brocantine is a brocade with a raised pattern imitating embroidery.

Brocatelle

Brocatelle is similar to brocade but the figures are puffed out giving it a very distinctive three-dimensional quilted or blister effect. This fabric was originally woven in silk with lustrous warp satin figures on a less glossy taffeta background, the figured areas being padded either with a soft heavier wool or cotton in the weft. Brocatelles are now made in wool, cotton, silk or man-made fibers, are very firm in construction and used for upholstery or drapery. Lightweight cloths are used for dresses. *Brocatelle de passementerie* is made with a cotton warp and wool filling.

Broché

The French word *broché* means 'figured' and the name is given to a variety of fabrics including: an all-silk cloth where the pattern is produced by swivel or lappet weaving; a silk fabric decorated with an imitation embroidered effect made by introducing extra weft or extra warp threads into the basic cloth without becoming part of the structure; *broché coutils*, a Jacquard woven cloth made for corsets; and *broché quilt*, a cloth made specifically for a bed cover. The warp is woven in two alternating colors to form alternately the figure and background. The weft is completely hidden.

Chiffon

Chiffon is a French word which literally means rag but it is used generally to describe a light, flimsy silk fabric. The finest of all silk cloths it is woven in plain weave from single, hard twist filaments of silk. It is strong yet delicate. Chiffon is sometimes called *mousseline de soie*. The term chiffon is often used in conjunction with other fabric names to indicate the lightness of a cloth. Chiffon batiste is a term used in Britain for a lightweight, sheer, worsted fabric. Chiffon crêpe is a lightweight crêpe fabric, similar to georgette. Chiffon net is a fine black net. Chiffon taffeta is a soft, lustrous, lightweight taffeta. Chiffon velour is a lightweight soft velour. Chiffon velvet is sometimes known as transparent velvet or wedding ring velvet.

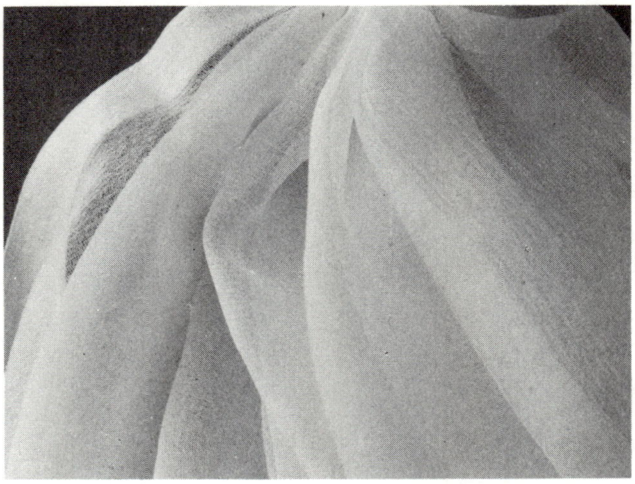

Chiffon

Corah Silk

The Hindi word *kora* means virgin and it is from this derivation that corah or cora as it is sometimes spelt gets its name. Corah silk is a lightweight silk fabric made in India from natural, raw, unwashed silk. After weaving the cloth is washed to remove the gum leaving it a creamy white color. Although this fabric was originally made from wild silk it is now produced from cultivated silk and is either dyed or printed. The term *corah* also refers to an Indian silk handkerchief.

Crêpe de Chine

Originally woven in China, *crêpe de chine* is an all silk fabric. It is light in weight and usually constructed with a plain, slightly twisted warp and crêpe wefts, unlike georgette where both the warp and weft are crêpe yarns. There are more threads in the warp than weft and it is woven in plain weave. *Crêpe de chine façonné* is a Jacquard woven brocade fabric. *Crêpe de chine travers* is constructed with a heavier weft thread every $\frac{3}{16}$ of an inch, producing a rib across the fabric. Moss crêpe or mourning crêpe are similar fabrics to *crêpe de chine*. Nagoya silk is a Japanese-made *crêpe de chine*. A slightly stiffer *crêpe de chine* made in Japan is called kabe crêpe.

(right) A Victorian funeral where mourners wore black crêpe de chine round their hats and also in the form of a sash around the body

An 18th-century gilt chair upholstered in silk damask

Damask

Damask was originally known in England as early as the thirteenth century. The name was applied to a richly decorated silk fabric from Damascus in Syria although many damask fabrics are now woven in cotton, linen, rayon and wool. The cloth has the characteristic of being Jacquard woven in satin and reverse sateen weaves. This produces areas of lustrous satin background with contrasting matt areas. The cloth is reversible. Damask differs from brocade which is not reversible. The French word for damask is *damas* or *damassé*. Damassé brocat has silver and gold in the weft, damassé Chine has printed silk warps. Lightweight cotton damask is used for tablecloths and table napkins. Heavyweight damasks are more suitable as upholstery and curtains.

Duchesse Satin

Duchesse or duchesse satin is a highly lustrous smooth all-silk fabric. It is a warp-faced cloth made with either an 8- or 12- end satin weave. As the name indicates it is a luxurious and expensive fabric used chiefly for wedding and evening dresses. Duchesse mousseline is a variation of duchesse satin but woven in a fancy twill weave. A similar fabric is shoe satin chiefly used for ballet shoes. Duchesse lace is a pillow lace similar to guipure lace, *guipure de bruges* or *point duchesse*.

Epingle

Épingle is a French word meaning pin which describes the lustrous, fine corded effect of this fabric. Originally made of all silk there are now a variety of different types made from man-made fibers, worsted or cotton yarns. The cloth is normally woven in a plain weave with small ribs running either in the warp or weft. The small pin-like ribs alternate with heavier ribs and also in contrasting colors. This fabric is used for dresses or men's ties. Epingle brocade is a Jacquard-woven, figured fabric with an épingle-ribbed background across the width of the fabric.

Epingle crepon is similar to *épingle brocade* but with a silk and worsted weft alternating. *Epingle façonné* is similar to *épingle brocade* but with a silk warp and a worsted weft. Epingline has a silk warp and worsted weft which produces a rib the length of the fabric.

Rita Hayworth wearing a duchesse satin dress

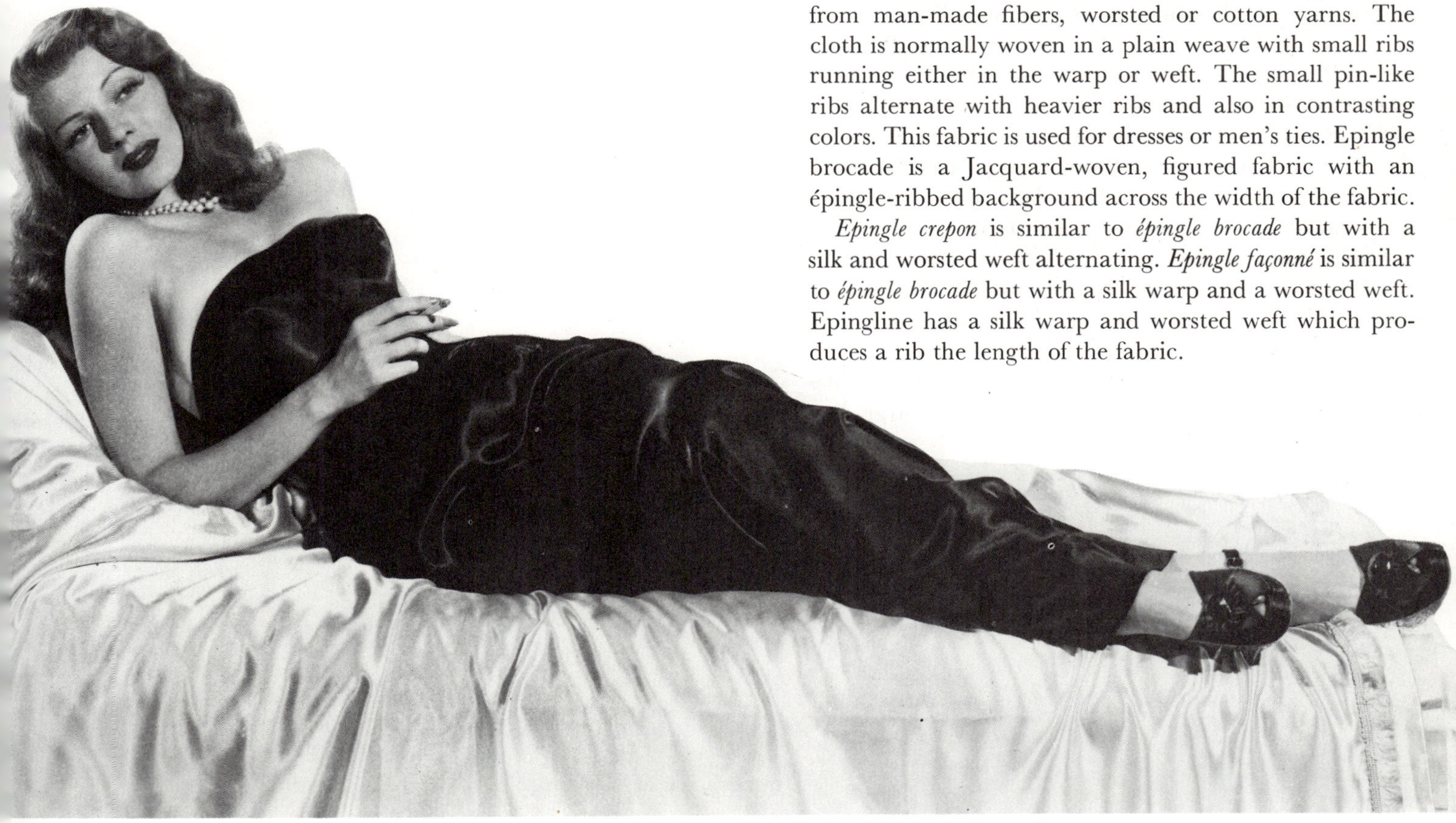

Faille

The word *faille* is a French term for a scarf-like women's headdress and it is from this usage that the fabric gets its name. *Faille* is a fine, slightly stiff silk fabric, woven in plain weave. It is slightly lustrous with flat ribs across the width of the fabric created by heavier yarns in the weft. The fabric has body and drapes well. It can also be made in cotton, man-made fibers and sometimes wool. *Faille* cotton is a British term for a cloth made with a silk warp and cotton weft. Other faille fabrics include: *faille de chine*, *faille crêpe*, *faille française* and *faille* taffeta. Most faille fabrics lend themselves to being given a moiré treatment and are used for women's evening dresses and underskirts for sheer fabrics.

Foulard

Foulard was originally woven in India. It is made with a 2-and-2 common twill weave in all silk, although now it is sometimes made with cotton or man-made fibers. Foulard is a particularly soft lustrous fabric, prints well and is used often for scarves, linings and men's ties. A 29-in (73 cm) wide, piece dyed, silk foulard cloth woven in China is called hongchow. A fabric called *foulard poile de chevre* was woven of goat's hair in Britain in the late nineteenth century. Foulardin, a lightweight cotton fabric made in Austria, was made to look like silk foulard.

Grosgrain

Grosgrain, also known as grogram, is a fabric which derives its name from the French *gros* meaning large and *grain* meaning cord. Therefore the term largecord would aptly describe this fabric which is a strong, all-silk cloth with pronounced ribs across the cloth heavier, more rounded than faille. Like faille, grosgrain is a suitable cloth for moiré treatment, having a fine warp compactly woven with a coarse weft in plain weave. It is commonly used for dresses, and neckties and in ribbon form is used for binding and trimming. There are other fabrics using the prefix gros and which are similar cloths to grosgrain. *Gros de Londres* has one or more fine ribs between each large rib. *Gros d'été* has two different warps giving an accentuated ribbed striped effect. *Gros des Indes* is even more accentuated than *Gros d'été* and *Gros de Lyon* is similar to *Gros d'été*. *Gros de Tours* has the same ribbed effect but resembles taffeta. *Gros de Tours* is also the name used in Argentina for Jacquard-woven cotton bedspreads.

Georgette

The name georgette, sometimes referred to as a crêpe georgette or georgette crêpe, was originally a trademark for a silk crêpe fabric named after a French milliner Madame Georgette de la Plante. It is lightweight sheer fabric with a fine textured surface with less luster than *crêpe de Chine*. The crêpe effect is achieved by using hard-twist, crêpe silk yarns in the warp as well as the weft. The cloth is made with plain weave and is soft to handle and is usually hard wearing. It is used for dresses, lingerie, millinery and curtains. Another fabric in the same family is crêpe Elizabeth. Similar to georgette in weight and construction it has a pebbly, mottled appearance.

Habutai

Habutai is the most popular spelling of the name for this fabric but habutaye and habutae are also used. The word is translated from the Japanese meaning a lightweight, soft, handwoven silk cloth still with the natural gum in it. A more common term for this cloth is Jap silk. It is woven from yarns comprised of 12 to 16 filaments of raw silk and slightly twisted. The fabric is made in plain weave and used for dresses, linings and curtains. It is also commonly used by conjurers requiring lightweight handkerchiefs which can be dyed in brilliant colors. Other names for this cloth are karamata and kaga. A lower grade habutai cloth is called khaiki.

(opposite left) A conjuror performing a trick with habutai silk handkerchiefs
(opposite right) Mosquito net in India in the days of the Raj
(opposite below right) Marquisette

Morocain
Morocain gets its name from a fabric which was originally woven in French Morocco. The term is now used to describe a heavy crêpe fabric which has slightly wavy ribs across the width of the cloth. It is heavier than, but resembles Canton crêpe. This cloth is now produced in man-made fibers as well as silk and the crinkled appearance is achieved by the use of highly twisted crêpe yarns in the warp with softer yarns in the weft. This cloth is used for dresses.

Marquisette
The term marquisette comes from the French meaning the entrance, canopy or awning to a tent or marquee. The fabric was originally made to use as mosquito netting, acting as a strong transparent screen. Made originally in silk this fabric is now also made in cotton and man-made fibers, It is a lightweight, fine, crisp, open mesh fabric made in leno or gauze weave sometimes including a simple dobby or Jacquard pattern. This cloth is used for curtains, dresses, and children's wear.

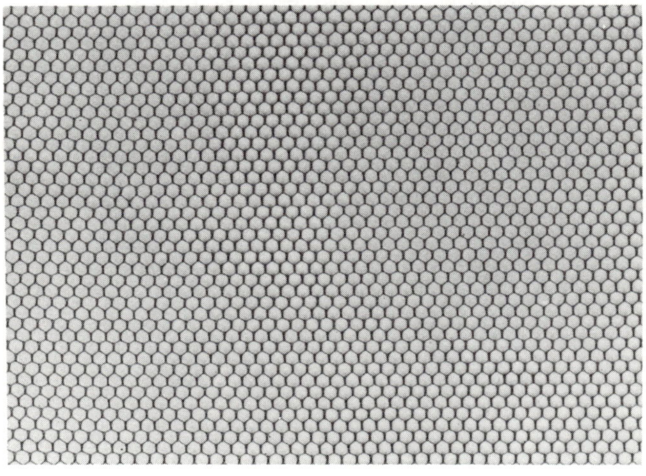

Mashru
The Arabic word mashru means lawful or permitted. For religious reasons Muslims, the followers of Mohammed, may not pray in pure silk cloth or any cloth made from animal fibers. A cotton-back, silk-faced fabric was woven so that the cotton could be worn close to the skin by orthodox Muslims. Originally woven by handweavers in Punjab and Sind in India a much finer quality satin striped cloth of the same type is woven in Ranjore, Hyderabad and Trichinopoly.

Mienchow
The term Mienchow is given to a variety of silk fabrics woven in different parts of China—some in the Red Basin or Szechwan province of central China, some in the eastern province Kiangsi and in the northern province of Shangtung. Although all these handwoven narrow cloths are made with plain weave the quality of the yarn varies but is generally made from mulberry silk, a waste silk. After weaving, the fabric is boiled-out to remove the natural gum. The rough cloth is then dyed blue, violet or scarlet and used by the locals for underclothing.

Milanese
Milanese is a type of warp-knitted silk fabric made originally on machines in Milan, Italy. This cloth is sheer and very lightweight. During the knitting process two sets of threads cross over making the characteristic diamond effect on the back of the fabric, leaving a surface of fine ribs on the face. It is a run-resistant or ladder-proof construction making it an altogether strong fabric. It is made in several weights and is used for underwear, lingerie and gloves.

Moiré
The term *moiré* is a French word which describes a finishing process which produces a watery appearance on the surface of a fabric. The best results are obtained on silk fabrics although the effect can be achieved on cotton or man-made fiber cloths. The base cloth should be of a type which has been woven with a fine rib or cord effect running across the fabric. This is done by weaving a cloth with a fine close warp and a heavier weft or filling. This produces cloths like faille, grosgrain, poult or taffeta. Two folds of cloth are put through heavy rollers under heat, the ribs are squashed against each other, but not in perfect registration therefore producing a rippled effect. There are various moiré effects: *moiré française*, *moiré antique*, *moiré renaissance*. These fabrics can be used for dresses, coats, linings and trimmings.

(above)
Suliman the Magnificent, who ruled the Ottoman Empire in the 17th century, probably wearing mashru
(below) Moiré taffeta

Early 19th-century dinner dresses, (left) with muslin sleeves

Mousseline de soie

Mousseline de soie is French for silk muslin (*see also* Muslin, p64). It is a crisp lightweight fabric similar to chiffon but more closely woven and not as soft as voile. It is woven in plain weave from good quality yarns. The amount of stiffening size varies in the fabric but this can be washed out. Usually obtainable in plain colors it is used as dress fabric.

Ninon

Ninon is a French derivation from the name Anne although it is not known how this fabric got its name. It is a smooth, crisp, thin, lightweight fabric originally made from very fine, highly twisted silk yarns with two or three threads weaving as one in the warp and the weft. These were known as double or single ninons. The finest single ninon is now more common. In general ninon is heavier and not as soft as chiffon and is used for scarves, dresses and curtains. Ninon is now also made from man-made fibers and a ninon voile is a term used in the United Kingdom for a cotton voile made to imitate ninon.

Ottoman

The Ottoman Empire emerged under the Sultan Othman or Osman who assumed government in Turkey during the thirteenth century. At the time a pure silk, luxurious fabric called Ottoman was woven in Turkey. Ottoman is a firm, lustrous, plain-weave fabric with a cord effect across the width of the cloth. The ribs, which are larger and rounder than *faille* or other silk-ribbed fabrics, are often woven with worsted yarn in the weft to give bulk to the ribs. Ottoman soleil is the smallest rib across the fabric. Ottoman cord is woven with the ribs down the length of the fabric and are in different sizes arranged alternately. Ottoman plush is a dense silk plush woven on a heavy ribbed background. These fabrics can be used for dresses, coats, trimmings and curtains.

Panne Velvet

The term *panne* in French means shag. Panne velvet is a cloth with a longer pile than velvet but shorter than plush. The pile of panne velvet, which is normally pure silk, is pressed down and flattened under the pressure of heavy rollers, the pile is laid in one direction giving the fabric a heavy lustre. Although panne velvet is now made in man-made fibers and wool it is a fabric which was always made of pure silk and has been popular since the Middle Ages. Lighter weight types are made called pannette or chiffon velvet. Other names for panne velvet are paon velvet or mirror velvet.

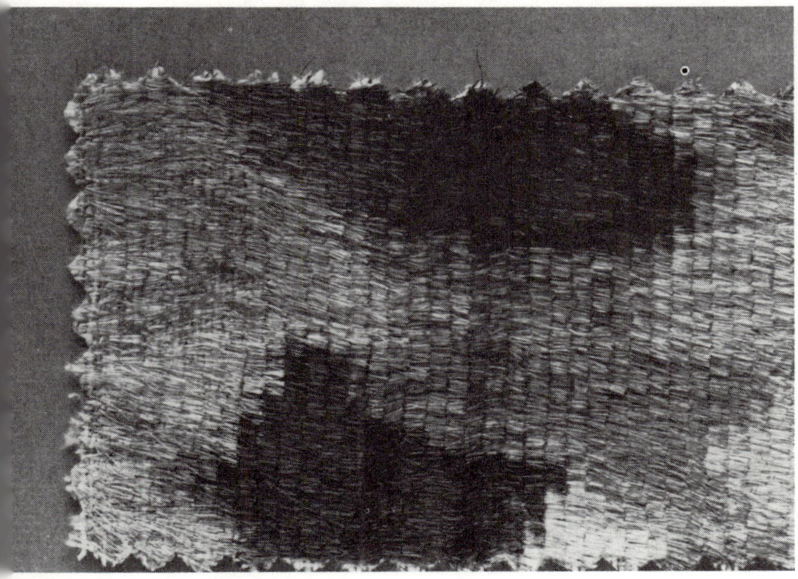

Printed panne velvet

Parachute Silk

As the name suggests parachute silk is a pure silk fabric made specifically for parachutes and was in great demand during World War II for man-carrying parachutes. This fabric was also used for cartridge bags for naval guns. The cloth is closely woven in plain weave from the best quality silk yarns. Since World War II man-carrying parachutes have been made from nylon and cargo parachutes from rayon. Parachute silk is used for dresses, blouses, lingerie and parachutes.

Pongee

Pongee is a term which comes from the Chinese *pen-chi* meaning home loom or woven at home. It is used to describe a whole variety of hand-woven fabrics originally from northern China made from the silk of the silkworm which feeds on oak leaves. Shangtung, hohan, antung and ninghai are all types of pongee silk. The warp is usually finer than the weft, and the characteristic slubs of wild silk create a nubbed effect in the cloth giving it a coarse, irregular appearance. Although pongee is naturally honey colored, all pongee clothes dye evenly and can be used for dresses, blouses and lightweight suits.

Poult

The phrase *poult de soie* comes from the word *paduasoy* meaning a silk cloth from Padua (or Padova) in Northern Italy where it was first made and presumably worn by the Venetians. Poult, as it is now known, is a fabric similar to faille or grosgrain, but finer. It is woven in plain weave with a closely set warp and slightly heavier weft making fine ribs or cords across the width of the fabric and it can be moiréed. This cloth is used for dresses and linings.

Radium

Radium is a firm, closely woven fabric which is smooth and soft. Originally the warp was made of untwisted silk and the weft was made from alternate right and left hand twisted silk yarns. Usually the weft is a different color to the warp and when tightly woven creates a shot effect when light is reflected from its lustrous surface. This cloth is used for dresses, lingerie and linings.

Radzimir

Radzimir, sometimes spelt Rasimir or Rhadzimir, is a condensation of the French *ras de Saint Maur* meaning a smooth flat cloth from Saint Maur which is in St Germain des Près, Paris. This cloth is a fine, lustrous, heavyweight silk dress fabric made in plain weave with a fine warp and heavier weft making a rib across the fabric like faille or grosgrain. This fabric was at one time woven in Britain in considerable quantities. It is generally dyed black and used for mourning.

Hand-painted silk

Radium

Satin lingerie

Satin

Satin is the name of a weave. There are many variations on the weave. The word satin comes from Zaytoun now known as Chuanchow, a seaport in south eastern China. Satin, which is traditionally made of silk, is a smooth fabric usually with a thick, lustrous, unbroken surface texture. The weave structure of a satin fabric allows the densely set warp threads to completely cover the weft. The cheaper qualities of satin, like paillette, show only four out of five threads on the surface (5-end satin). Satin mervilleux shows six threads out of seven on the surface (7-end satin). The most luxurious satin, duchesse satin, is woven with seven out of eight warp threads showing on the surface (8-end satin). There are many types of satin fabrics. Some are still woven in silk but others are now made in cotton or a variety of man-made fibers. Some of the most common satins are:

Charmeuse A fine lustrous surface and dull backed fabric.
Ciré satin Often dyed in metallic colors. Wax applied with heat under pressure to produce a stiff, leatherlike, high lustre fabric.
Crêpe back satin Satin on one side, crêpe on the reverse side.
Satin Canton or Canton crêpe A soft, heavy fabric with a lustrous surface and crêpe back.
Panne satin Stiff and highly lustrous fabric.
Antique satin Heavy, dull lustred fabric usually woven with uneven yarns.
Shoe satin Silk face and cotton back.
Satinette A very thin silk satin.

Shantung

Shantung silk fabric was originally made of wild silk yarns on handlooms in the Shantung province of northern China. It is a rough, plain-weave silk fabric made of uneven yarns producing an uneven textured effect. Sometimes there is evidence of thicker threads being used in the weft. The term shantung is also used to describe a heavyweight pongee. There are now man-made fiber and cotton shantung fabrics characterized by the irregular rib effect in the weft alternating with a regular yarn. This fabric is used for dresses and curtains.

Shot Silk

The term shot silk often refers to a silk or man-made fiber and is identical to changeable taffeta. It is a closely woven fabric made in plain weave using lustrous yarns. The shot effect is created by using different colored yarns in the weft to the warp making a fine checkerboard of the two colors. The yarns being shiny reflect the contrasting or complementary colors and produce a luminous iridescent effect. Sometimes Thai silk is made in this manner. It is used for dresses and furnishings.

(left) Samples of Thai silk

Surah

Surat is in north-western India where a fine silky cotton is cultivated, and it is from this town that the term surah or surah silk was taken and used in France to describe a soft silk fabric made in twill weave from rough-spun silk yarns. The cloth is usually made from dyed yarns. Surah chevron is a similar fabric only woven with a fine herringbone pattern. Other types of surah include *surah ecossais quadrille*, being woven in tartan effects; *surah gros cole*, a heavy, closely-woven, thick silk fabric with a lustrous finish on both sides. These cloths can be used either for dresses or furnishings.

Taffeta

The term taffeta comes from the Persian word *tafta* meaning a glossy twist. Hence it is usually found that taffeta fabrics are made from high twist silk or man-made fiber yarns giving the fabric the characteristic crisp paperlike quality for which taffeta is well known. The terms taffatie and taffety were used in Bengal, India where silk fabrics similar to those woven in Persia, were also made and exported to Europe in the seventeenth century. In medieval Europe the term taffeta was used to describe a series of lightweight silk fabrics. Now the term taffeta usually means a plain weave cloth with a fine, smooth, crisp, lustrous or matt finish. The cloth usually has a fine rib across the width making it possible to emboss a moiré effect into it. There are other variations of taffeta which include: antique taffeta, usually stiffer and sometimes having an iridescent effect; faille taffeta with a more pronounced rib across the cloth; paper taffeta, a lightweight cloth with a crisp paperlike handle; tissue taffeta, a transparent very lightweight cloth; and taffeta chameleon or shot silk. Taffetas can be used for dresses, curtains, upholstery and umbrellas.

Tricot

The French term *tricot* meaning knitted fabric, is used to describe a variety of warp knitted fabrics which were originally made only in silk but are now made in man-made fibers and cotton. The main characteristic of this type of fabric is that it is usually light in weight having vertical wales on the face of the cloth and crosswise ribs on the reverse side. This fabric has very little stretch in the structure of it and is run or ladder resistant. Tricot is sometimes called double-warp tricot, two-bar tricot, glove silk or Charmense. This jersey-type cloth can be used for all types of dresses, blouses, underwear and gloves.

Taffeta dress, about 1910

'Come Dancing' contestants. The lady is in tulle

Tulle

Tulle gets its name from the French town of the same name. Tulle is a net fabric which at one time was made only of pure silk and now can be made of man-made fibers or cotton. The distinctive feature of tulle is the hexagonal mesh which was first made on machinery in Nottingham, England, in 1768. The invention of the bobbinet machine in 1809 helped the industry to expand and it was in 1817 that a factory opened in Tulle, France. Tulle crinoline is a pleated fabric made with graduated sized mesh. Tulle grec has a larger mesh and tulle grenadine has rows of alternate black and white mesh. Tulle, which is also known as malines lace, is used for dress making and trimming, millinery and theatrical costumes. It is difficult to launder this fabric and care should be taken in dry cleaning it.

Tussah

The word tussah comes from the Hindi word *tasar* which is derived from the Sanskrit *tasara* meaning shuttle. Other spellings include tussas, tusser, tussore, tussur and tussus although tussah is the most common in the English language. Tussah is wild silk and cloths made from this silk were originally made in Bengal, India. It is a stiff, rough, coarse silk which has a characteristic yellow/brown/ecru colour and is not easy to dye or bleach. Seventeenth-century merchants returning to Europe from India referred to this silk as herba because it was thought it had been spun from a plant or herb. The wild silk worm spins its cocoon onto a plant which then looks to be part of the plant. There are many tussah silk cloths. Tussah silk can be knitted or woven and usually the fabrics are more suitable for coats and furnishings. Tussah silk can also be spun into fine yarns and is used in pongee and shantung. Coarser fabrics are katey and ninghai. Tussah silk is often used together with cotton or wool.

Velvet

The word velvet comes from the Latin word *vellus* meaning a fleece. Velvet is a warp cut, pile fabric originally made with a silk pile and cotton back. It is a fabric with a rich soft texture and is woven face to face in the same way as Wilton carpet. Velveteen (*See* p71) is a weft-pile fabric. The distinguishing feature of velvet is a succession of rows of short cut tufts standing close together presenting a uniform surface which is lustrous in appearance and soft to the touch. The quality of velvet is determined by the closeness of the tufts and the density and construction of of the backing. There are many different types of velvet. Some are almost transparent. Chiffon velvet is a lightweight, soft fabric with short dense pile. Lyons velvet is a heavier weight fabric with a crisp handle. Panne velvet is a cloth with the pile pressed down in one direction. Brocade velvet is a velvet with a pattern which has been chemically burnt out of part of the pile. This is sometimes called façonne velvet. The uses for velvet are wide-ranging and include dresses, coats, shoes, curtains, upholstery and hats. Most velvets should be dry cleaned.

Other Plant Fibers

The following plants produce fibers most of which can be spun into yarn and made into fabric. They are divided into three main groups:

1 STALK OR STEM FIBER (bast)

Flax
Hemp
Hop
Jute
Kenef
Nettle
Ramie
Sunn
Urena

2 LEAF FIBER

Abaca
African Bowstring hemp
Banana
Esparto
Henequen
New Zealand Flax (or New Zealand Hemp)
Papyrus
Pineapple
Raffia
Rice
Sisal
Yucca
Manilla Hemp

3 SEED FIBER

Bombax
Cotton
Kapok
Milkweed
Pulu
Coir

(above) Hops (*Lupus falictarius*)
from *Gerard's Herball*, 1636
(right) Yucca showing the cassava root,
from *Gerard's Herball*, 1636
(opposite) Maoris dressed in pui-pui skirts made from New Zealand flax at a concert in Rotorua, New Zealand

Rubber is also included in this list because it is a processed substance from a plant which can be made into a fabric. Rubber, the milky fluid from tropical rubber trees, is also obtained from temperate climate plants like dandelions. Most plant fibers, other than flax and the seed fibers, are cultivated for the production of cordage, string and coarse fabrics. Most of the harvesting of these plants and also much of the processing from plant to fiber can only be done by hand.

The group of fibers which come from the stalks of certain plants are known as bast fibers and other than cotton form the largest part of the production of natural fibers in the world. For several thousand years bast fibers have been used for making textiles but there is no record of how the first discovery was made that there are strong flexible fibers inside the stems of plants. It can be assumed that the discovery was by accident when, in all probability, a bunch of rotting plants was picked up and twisted into a primitive rope.

Leaf fibers have been used by the islanders of Polynesia for making 'grass' skirts for hundreds of years. The long pointed leaves of the New Zealand flax plant are used for making piu-piu skirts, the traditional patterns being produced by scraping the meat of the leaf away in certain areas, exposing the fibers of the leaf and then dying them black. As the leaf dries out it curls producing a tube. The piu-piu is made up of several leaf tubes the ends of which are woven into a waistband. Cotton is by far the best known of all the seed fibers and constitutes a section of its own in this book. However, other seed fibers are put to good use in a variety of ways. Coir matting, for example, is increasingly popular as a floor covering.

Man-made fibers are gradually taking over the jobs for which the tough natural fibers were once used. But there are advantages and disadvantages on both sides. Fabrics and cordage made from man-made fibers are definitely more durable and in most cases stronger but the inherent tactile and visual qualities of the natural fibers are much more agreeable to live with.

A Japanese gentleman wearing a traditional bast-fiber garment

An Irish linen cottage table cloth

(opposite) New Zealand flax plant

Aida Canvas

Aida canvas is a coarse, open fabric usually made of linen although cotton and wool are sometimes used, blended with the linen. The fabric is stiff and is usually tan or brown in color and woven in plain or hopsack weave. The main use of this is for embroidery. Sometimes known as Java canvas or oatmeal.

Arras

Tapestries have been woven in Arras since the middle ages and the name of this city in northern France has become synonymous with all types of wall hangings. Arras is a term given to an open-weave, coarse linen cloth which is embroidered with simple patterns and used as hanging curtains, table and cushion covers. At one time the term arras also applied to certain worsted fabrics woven in this locality. This area is also famous for bobbin lace.

Bark Cloth

The inner bark of many varieties of tropical and subtropical trees, such as the paper mulberry (*Brousonnetia papyrifera*) and types of *Fiscus* tree are soft enough to be processed into a cloth. The fibrous layer of the inner bark is soaked and beaten out evenly with a wooden mallet or club to a pliable thickness, sometimes as thinly as a fine muslin. The cloth can then be bleached, dyed, painted or printed. Tapa or kapa (Hawaii) or masi (Fiji) cloths are bark cloths which are used as decorative wall hangings or clothing. Bark cloth is strong and cool to wear. A woven fabric called bark crêpe is made with a silk or man-made fiber warp and wool weft simulating bark cloth.

Printed burlap furnishing fabric

Burlap

The origin of the name of this fabric is uncertain but it is used in the United States to describe a plain woven jute fabric. The term hessian is used in Great Britain to describe the same type of fabric. It is a strong fabric and in its unfinished state can be used for bagging and upholstery. It is often used as curtains or upholstery fabric when printed and dyed and is an inexpensive cloth which is sometimes laminated onto wallpaper. Gunny or sacking cloth is a coarse burlap.

Butcher's Linen

This fabric was originally manufactured for butcher's aprons. It is a strong, heavy linen cloth usually woven in plain weave in dark blue and bleached white stripes. It is now more common to see this fabric made from cotton woven in common twill weave. The same quality linen cloth, when all white, can be used as a suiting.

Cambric

Cambric was originally woven in Cambrai in northern France. It is a plain-weave, soft linen fabric, sometimes also woven in cotton, with a slight lustrous finish on the face of the cloth. Cambric is made in many qualities, some as fine as lawn, the coarser types sometimes being backfilled with china clay or given a starched finish to give the cloth more weight. It has many applications—handkerchiefs, aprons, shirts, underwear, linings—and is used also for church embroidery and tablecloths. Cambric muslin is a fine, bleached, glazed cotton fabric and cambric grass is another name for the Ramie plant.

Canvas

Canvas is a broad term used to describe many heavy cloths, woven linen and cotton fabrics. The Latin word *cannabis*, from which the word canvas comes, suggests that it was originally made of hemp. The word canvas is often used interchangeably with duck although duck is generally made of cotton. Canvas made of linen or unbleached flax is stronger than canvas made of cotton.

There are special weights of canvas made for sails, tarpaulins, tents, boxing rings, judo mats, embroidery and for artists to paint on. By itself canvas made of flax will not altogether be waterproof and is therefore treated with various waterproofing materials depending on the end-use. Traditionally tarpaulins were painted with tar. Sails were often painted with tar, red lead, oil or varnish and artists' canvas is painted with white primer. Where canvas was once used for tents, sails and tarpaulins man-made fibers have now replaced flax and cotton. (*See also* canvas p53.)

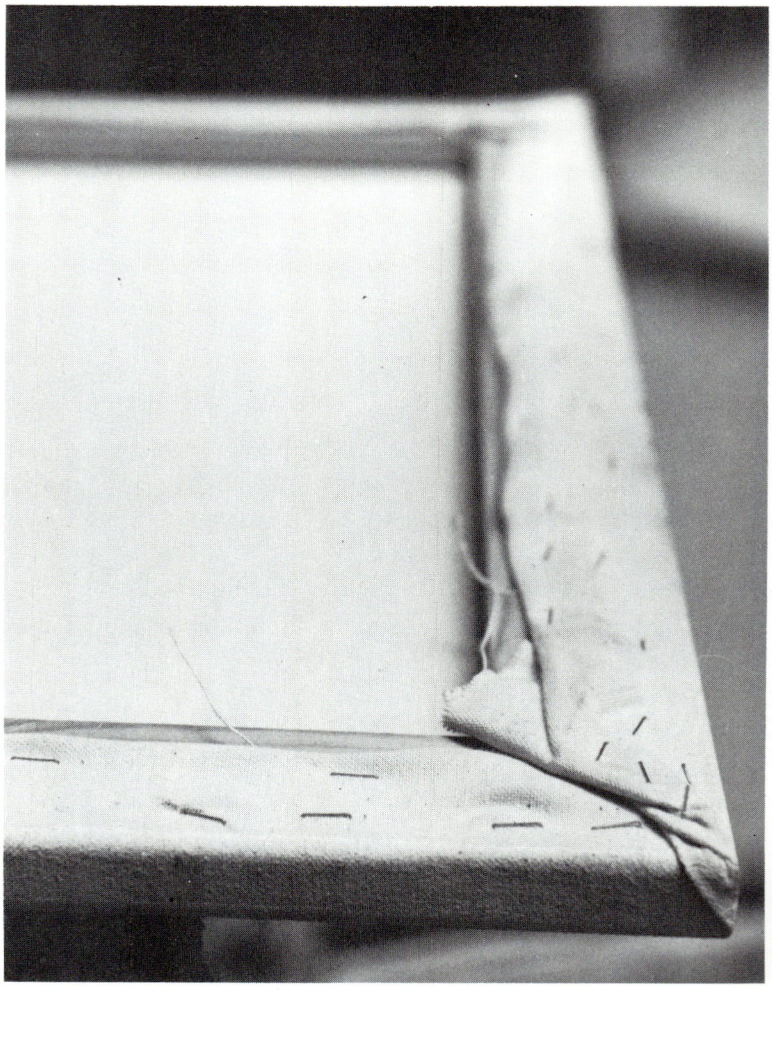

An artist's canvas

The Indian nut tree from *Gerard's Herball*, 1636. It is now known as the coconut plant from which coir is obtained

Coir

The Tamil word *kayira* means rope and it is from this that the word coir comes. Coir is the seed fiber obtained from the outer layer or husk of the coconut. Most coir comes from Ceylon and there are basically two grades: kogalla, the best, and Colombo. It is naturally reddy brown in colour and being already quite fibrous requires the minimum of processing. Once the husk has been hacked from the coconut it is then wetted in water separating the fibers and rotting away the other vegetable matter. The stiff, long, round, smooth fibers are between 4–10 in (10–26 cm) long and similar to horsehair. The long fiber is coarse yarns from which mats, cordage and packing cloths are made.

Crash

The word crash comes from the Russian *krashenina* meaning colored linen. It is a fabric which is made in a variety of weights and types but generally is considered to be a rough textured cloth made with uneven, knotted yarns. It is usually made in plain weave although twill is sometimes used. Crash was originally made from flax but cloths bearing the same name are often made from cotton or a combination of flax and cotton or jute and cotton. It is used for a variety of purposes: toweling, and more particularly hotel toweling made with Jacquard woven names of the hotel or club, table linen, drapery, embroidery and needlework. At one time the term crash also referred to a piece of heavy flax cloth which was put down to cover a carpet to protect it.

Damask

Although originally woven in silk and named after a richly decorated silk fabric first woven in Damascus in Syria, damask is also closely associated with the linen industry. The lustrous quality of the linen fiber, Jacquard-woven, with the characteristic satin and reverse sateen weave produces a firm reversible fabric which can be used for tablecloths and table napkins. Usually linen damasks are woven with fine bleached yarns.

Flax

Flax is a bast or stem fiber. The word flax comes from the Anglo-Saxon word *fleax*. The botanical name for flax is *Linum usitatissimum* from which the word linen comes. Flax is the most ancient of all textile fibers. It is known to have been used for textiles more than 7000 years ago. The early Egyptians gathered wild flax from the banks of the Nile and made it into rope, cord, fishing lines, fishing nets and cloth. The mummies of the pharaohs of Egypt remain wrapped in flax garments which have not decayed. Nine hundred years ago the Bayeux Tapestry was embroidered on a fabric made from flax to commemorate the Battle of Hastings. It was Louis Crommelin, a linen weaver who fled from France to Ireland in the eighteenth century who improved the processing of flax fiber and thus contributed to the importance of the Irish linen industry.

Russia is the largest producer of flax. Most iron-curtain and mid-European countries grow flax. Belgium also cultivates a large amount of flax. The main flax growing area in the United States is in Oregon.

Flax is one of the strongest of all vegetable fibers. Unprocessed it contains 70 per cent cellulose. Once boiled, bleached and dried the resulting fiber, which is called linen, is almost 100 per cent cellulose. There are basically two types of flax grown. Fiber flax is grown mainly to produce fiber; seed flax is grown for its seed and used mainly for the production of linseed oil. It is grown sparsely, is short stemmed and produces a high yield of seeds. Fiber flax grows close together between $3\frac{1}{2}$–4 ft (1–1.2 m) tall allowing the fibers in the plant to grow long and straight. When harvested seed flax is cut, but all fiber flax is pulled. This maintains the full, undamaged length of the fiber which extends down to the root.

The harvesting of fiber flax is still done by hand, although in recent years most is mechanically pulled. Once harvested it is dried in the field and the seeds for replanting are gathered. The dried plant is then ready for retting (rotting). The process of retting involves the soaking of the flax plants, sometimes referred to as the straw, in order that the woody core and gums will decompose and loosen the fiber from the other vegetable matter. In the more traditional flax growing areas like Belgium and Ireland the retting is done in ponds and rivers but the process is generally carried out in large tanks.

After a period of between four days and three weeks the retted flax is dried. To separate the fiber from the

Section from the Bayeux tapestry, embroidered on flax cloth, depicting the Battle of Hastings in 1066

waste it is passed through scutching rollers and hackled (combed) on strong steel pins passing through the hackling machine several times until the fiber is clean. The term line applies to the longest, smoothest fibers which are separated in the hackling process from the tow fiber. The flax is now ready for carding, drawing and spinning into yarn.

The natural color of flax is a grey brown and it is at this stage, after spinning that flax is bleached. A process has been developed in Northern Ireland to bleach flax at an earlier stage immediately after hackling. This makes it possible to blend pure white linen with other fibers. Fabrics woven from flax or linen require little care. They are washed or boiled using a mild soap or detergent. It is best to remove stains of any type before laundering. Fruit juice, tea or coffee stains can be removed from line cloths by pouring boiling water through the cloth. Rust stains can be removed with vinegar, lemon juice, acetic acid or salt. Grass staining can be removed with hydrogen peroxide and grease spots removed with benzine, gasoline, kerosene, carbon tetrachloride or any proprietary brand cleaning fluid. Avoid excessive starching and creasing which causes the fibers to crack. When folding linen do so with the least number of soft folds and avoid sharp creases. Linens can now be treated with resins to make them crease resistant. Linen should be ironed damp or with a steam iron and to retain the lustre of some fabrics should be ironed on both sides. Flax is highly absorbent and being a good conductor of heat is cool to wear.

New Zealand flax (*Phormium tenax*), known to the native Maori as harakeke, unlike the bast fiber flax described above, is a large plant with long spear-shaped leaves, yielding a fiber used for making mats, belts, nets, ropes, cords, cloaks, traditional taaniko weaving and piupiu (skirt) making.

(below) Egyptian painted papyrus scroll showing a flax canvas sail

(below) A vignette from the Egyptian painted papyrus of Nakht showing flax gathering

Flax plant (*Linum usitatissimum*) from *Gerard's Herball*, 1636

Glass Cloth

The term glass cloth is often confused with cloth made of glass fiber or cloth coated with powdered glass although both of these descriptions would be true. Glass cloth, in this context, is however a fabric made of flax woven with the specific purpose of producing a cloth for drying up glasses. It is usually woven in plain or twill weave with bleached linen yarns. Often a Jacquard woven stripe is woven down the center. This cloth is sometimes referred to as a tea cloth or tea towel.

(above and below) A linen glass cloth

Hemp

Hemp is a bast or stem fiber fabric. The word hemp comes from the Anglo-Saxon word *henep*. The botanical name for hemp is *Cannabis sativa* from which the word canvas comes. African bowstring hemp, sisal hemp, sunn hemp, Bahama hemp, New Zealand hemp, Chinese hemp and Manilla hemp are not true hemps and are not related to the *Cannabis sativa* plant.

Hemp is known to have been used as a textile fiber in China, Persia and Japan 5000 years ago. It came to Europe in about AD 500 and the United States in 1645. Russia is the largest producer of hemp fiber followed by Italy and Yugoslavia. Many other countries including the United States produce small quantities but most commercial quantities are imported. The hemp plant grows from 7–10 feet (2–3 m) high and the stalk is about half an inch thick. Unprocessed it contains about 77 per cent cellulose. Unlike flax, hemp is usually cut in the field and not often pulled. It is spread out in the fields to be retted (rotted) by the dew and processed into fiber in a similar way to flax. The fiber produced is creamy white to yellow-brown in color. It is lustrous and as strong as flax. Hemp fiber can be spun into yarns resembling flax although most cloth made from hemp is usually more coarse. Hemp is used for making string, cord and rope.

Hemp plant (*Cannabis sativa*), from *Gerard's Herball*, 1636

Holland

This cloth was first produced in Holland. Sometimes referred to as brown holland it was made of unbleached flax. Holland is a fine, plain-woven fabric now made in bleached and dyed linen yarns. The cloth is heavily sized and sometimes glazed. This produces a crisp, hard, flat, semi-opaque fabric which should be rolled not folded. Holland is used for roller blinds, and blackout cloth. It is sometimes called shade cloth. Cotton is now used to produce similar cloths which are called holland.

Hop Pocketing

Hop pocketing is a special fabric woven from jute yarns and ultimately made into a large bag into which dried hops are packed for despatch to breweries. At one time these sacks or bags were made from jute or hemp cloth made with a weave which was to be known as hopsack weave (*See* p148). The term hopsack now usually refers to a woolen cloth woven in hopsack or basket weave. Now hop pocketing is woven with a 2-and-1 twill.

Moving the hop pockets at one of the Guinness breweries

Jute

Jute is a bast or stem fiber. The word jute comes from the Sanskrit word *juta* meaning matted hair. Jute comes from two similar plants botanically known as *Corchorus capsularis* and *Corchorus olitorius*. It is not known when jute was first used as a textile fiber but trading in jute cloth from Bengal started in the sixteenth century. Today most jute still comes from the river delta area of East Pakistan.

The jute plant grows between 5–16 feet (1.5–5 m) high and the stalk is about $\frac{1}{2}$–$\frac{3}{4}$ inches (1–2 cm) thick. Unprocessed it contains about 64 per cent cellulose. The fibers are about 4–7 feet (1.2–2 m) long. The stalks of jute are first retted (rotted) in water then the bark is pulled off the jute fiber which is then ready for softening. The softening is done by passing the woody fibers through heavy, fluted rollers at the same time as oil and water are poured over the fibers and allowed to soak for 12 to 24 hours to soften the fibers. The remaining processes of carding and drawing are similar to those of flax. Yellow-brown in colour, and unlike hemp and flax, jute tends to disintegrate in water and is not very elastic making it unsuitable for rope manufacture. It is a moderately strong and lustrous fiber. Jute can be dyed but does not bleach well and is used in weaving burlap, hessian, pocketing, sacking, carpet backing, bagging, tarpauling, scrim and mixed with other fibers is used for horse blankets.

Jute sack full of cashews
on a co-operative in Senegal, West Africa

Kapok

The Javanese word *kapuk* is given to the silk-cotton tree or kapok tree (*Ceiba pentandra*) which is a native plant to Java. The tree is one of a whole family of trees (*malvaceae*) which grow in tropical countries. The bombax tree is one of these and the lightweight fiber produced from the seed pod of both the kapok tree and the bombax tree are similar. The fiber varies in length between $\frac{3}{4}$–1 inch (2–2$\frac{1}{2}$ cm), is lustrous, brittle, resistant to moisture, resilient and it floats. The color ranges from white through grey to brown. Kapok and bombax cotton, as they are known, are two of the four natural vegetable fibers which can never be spun into a yarn by themselves. The fiber lacks strength and elasticity. This fiber is mostly used as a stuffing or padding for pillows, mattresses, pallets, and life preservers. Kapok is also known as Java cotton or silk cotton. The oil from kapok seed is used in soap making.

Kenaf

Kenaf is a soft bast or stem fiber from the stalk of the plant *Hibiscus cannabinus*. It is similar to jute and processed in the same way to produce the fiber although the fiber, which is between 5–8 feet (1.5–2.5 m) long, is more lustrous, harder and stronger than jute. It is lighter in color than jute, varying from pale yellow to grey. The kenaf plant grows in Central Asia, India, Africa and Cuba. It is chiefly used for making ropes and string but can be spun into a yarn fine enough to make a coarse canvas. In India it is known as ambari or deccan hemp and in Africa, lipatam or gombo.

(opposite) Weighing jute bags
containing cocoa in Ghana, West Africa

Linen

Linen fabrics are made from processed flax (*Linus usitatissimum*). Usually the term linen is used once the flax fiber has passed through the preliminary stages and is converted into a spun yarn. Linen yarns possess unique qualities of strength and luster and do not rot. The use of linen has been superseded by man-made fibers but in many instances linen cannot be replaced. With the advent of crease-resistant resin finishes linen fabric is much easier to care for when used for dresses and suits. Press linen while it is still damp; to retain its luster some fabric needs to be ironed on both sides. Linen is highly absorbent and cool to wear.

The following are some of the traditional uses of linen: in thread form, for sewing shoes and cricket balls; in fabric for handkerchiefs, table linen, embroidery cloths, household textiles and apparel.

Mummy Cloth

Mummy cloth was a cambric type fabric which was specially woven by the ancient Egyptians for wrapping and binding the dead bodies of their Pharaohs' queens and in certain cases their animals before burial. Flax grew on the banks of the Nile and it was a general rule that only persons of royal blood could wear linen. Wide fabrics as well as narrow bandages were woven and these were carefully wrapped around to preserve and protect the body. When the tomb of Tutankhamen was opened in 1922 after almost 4000 years, it was found that much of the linen mummy cloth was well preserved. Mummy cloth should not be confused with momie cloth, momie toweling or momie crêpe which are all cloths made of cotton using a granite or crêpe weave.

Spinning flax by hand

Jacquard-woven damask Irish linen hand towels

Common stinging nettle (*Urtica urens*) from *Gerard's Herball*, 1636

Nettle

Nettle fiber is obtained from two varieties of stinging nettle: *Urtica dioica* and *Urtica urena*. It has been used as a textile fiber for making fabric since ancient times and when fully processed resembles linen. The stinging nettle grows chiefly in Europe and was originally cultivated in Germany for the purpose of producing fiber. It is rarely seen in the United States. The stalk of the nettle is processed by retting, scutching, hackling, cording and spinning in the same way as flax. The output of fiber nettle-processing is quite small therefore making it an uneconomic industry. An East Indian term for nettle fiber is *bichu* which is woven into a coarse, plain-weave fabric called bongra or borre.

Papyrus

Papyrus is known as the paper reed, *Cyperus papyrus*, which is grown on the banks of the Nile in Egypt. Before it was ever used as a textile fiber some 4000 years BC, the reeds were used to make the earliest form of paper. The Papyrus reeds were unwound and laid side by side, then a second layer placed at right angles across the first. These two layers were then hammered to form a flat crisp sheet. Not until much later was papyrus reed, which stands from 6–8 feet (2–2.5 m) high, used to make fiber to spin into yarns from which cloth can be made. Papyrus cloth can be used for canvases of various types and sails.

Ramie

Ramie is a bast or stem fiber. The word ramie comes from the Malay word *rami* meaning rhea or China grass. The botanical name for ramie is *Boemeria nivea*. The history of ramie as a textile fiber is not known but it is cultivated in the East Indies, Japan, China, India, the Phillipines, Russia, Latin America and Florida.

The plant, which is dark green in color, is a non-stinging nettle and grows to a height of 5–8 feet (1.5–2.5 m). The diameter of the stalk is about $\frac{1}{2}$–$\frac{3}{4}$ inches (1–2 cm) thick. Unprocessed it contains 83 per cent cellulose. The fibers range from $\frac{1}{2}$–20 inches (1–50 cm) although the average length is 5–6 inches (13–15 cm). Ramie is naturally white or cream in color, has a high lustre, is extremely absorbent so it dyes well and is twice as strong as flax. Unlike flax, hemp and jute, the fiber of ramie is taken from the stalk by hand or hand-operated machine before the plant drys out and is not retted. Once the fiber has been separated it can be processed in the same way as flax. Being a very strong vegetable fiber it has many end uses which include, filter cloths, fire hose, fishing nets, upholstery fabrics, canvases of many types and when spun into very fine yarns can be used for apparel fabrics. Ramie is also known as China grass, rhea and cambric grass. In China a fabric called kityang is made from ramie. It is hand woven in plain weave and dyed blue. Kityang is made in several weights and used for apparel.

(left) Papyrus (*Cyperus papyrus*) from *Gerard's Herball*, 1636

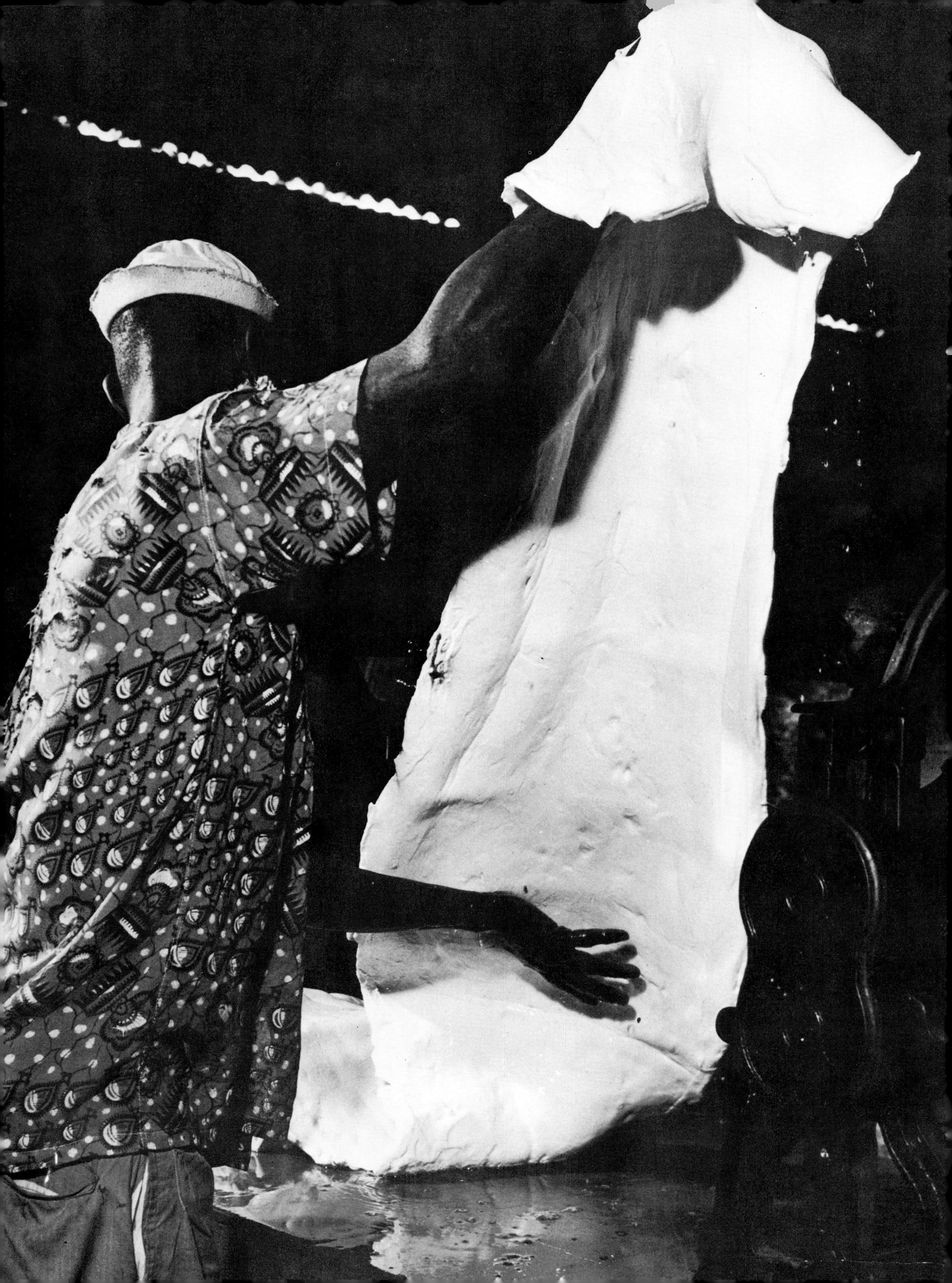

Rubber

Rubber fabric or sheeting is made from the milky white juice which comes from many species of plants and trees grown in tropical countries. Plant milk or latices (plural of latex) is also found in temperate climate plants such as the dandelion and greater celandine. Much of the tree rubber we use comes from Malaya, Indonesia and Central America. In Russia the dandelion is cultivated for the production of rubber, but the yield is poor.

Once rubber has been processed and turned into a fabric it has the unique characteristic of being totally waterproof and it also stretches. It can be used by itself or can be applied, in liquid form to other fabrics to make them waterproof. Charles Macintosh (1766–1843) was the first man to exploit the possibility of waterproofing fabric with rubber by laminating two sheets of cotton fabric together with a rubber solution made from naptha and rubber. This process was patented in 1823. The term Macintosh has been used ever since to describe any type of waterproof raincoat.

Rubber tapping in Malaysia

(opposite) Solidified rubber being rolled prior to curing by smoking in Liberia, West Africa

Sauna towels

Sauna Toweling

A great deal of flax is imported into Finland from Russia and processed into linen yarns. Linen is a popular textile material in Finland as well as other Scandinavian countries. It is strong and durable. Apart from the normal household textiles made of linen by the Finns, one of the main uses of heavy tow linen yarns is in the weaving of toweling for use in saunas. Linen absorbs moisture very well and as it dries quickly in the heat of the sauna, is cooler to the touch than other fibers. Usually sauna toweling is woven with colored yarns in stripes and is woven in 2-and-2 twill weave.

Scrim

This is an open mesh, plain-woven cloth made from jute, hemp or cotton in several weights but usually from heavy rough uneven yarns. Sometimes cheesecloth is known as scrim when it is bleached and sized. Generally it is woven from single yarns but better qualities are woven with two-ply yarns. Sometimes this fabric is used by sculptors to reinforce plaster when casting models, but usually it is more commonly used as casement curtaining.

Sisal

Sisal is a fiber which comes from the agave family of plants. The word sisal is Mayan meaning cold waters and comes from the name of the sea port of Sisal which is in the province of Yucatan in Mexico. The botanical name for sisal is *Agave sisalana*. Sisal is grown in Indonesia, East and West Africa, Haiti, Mexico and Brazil. Sisal fiber is obtained from the spear-like leaves of the plant by removing the skin or cortex by machine. It is dried in the sun and produces a white, hard, lustrous fiber measuring anything from 36–48 inches (90–120 cm) long. Sisal is resistant to salt water and therefore makes an ideal natural material from which to make rope. Sisal is also used in the production of binder twine for tying bales of hay or straw. In both these examples man-made fibers have now sometimes been substituted but in the case of binder twine sisal is preferred as it will eventually deteriorate in the field if accidentally dropped, whereas man-made fiber will not decompose and will damage machinery. Sisal is used extensively for the production of inexpensive mats and very coarse fabric for packing.

Man-Made Fibers and Mineral Fibers
History

Less than one hundred years ago in 1884 a Frenchman named Count Hilaire de Chardonnet made the first successful chemical fiber from cellulose. This nitro-cellulose process was both costly and dangerous and many of the early factories blew up but gradually other safer processes were developed. A great breakthrough came when the viscose process was developed in Britain and was patented in 1892. This new textile filament fiber was referred to as 'artificial silk' and in 1905 production of it started in Britain. By 1913 over 3 million pounds (1.4 million kg) per year were being produced. High tariffs were put on the import of artificial silk into the USA and in 1909 a British company, Samuel Courtauld, bought the US rights to produce viscose rayon in the States and by 1911, made the first commercially successful 'artificial silk' in Marcus Hook, near Chester, Pennsylvania.

The concept of imitation, or artificial natural fibers did not last for long and by the 1920s the term 'artificial silk' was dropped although even now this phrase is often heard. Until the late 1930s there were only two man-made fibers both of which were derived from natural sources, trees and cotton. Then in 1938 the latest, and truly synthetic, man-made fiber—nylon 66—was announced by Du Pont de Nemours. At about the same time research was being carried out independantly in Germany into making a similar polyamide, nylon 6. The discovery of nylon 66 and nylon 6 provided the world with a textile material which was strong, elastic, mothproof, resistant to moisture absorption and non bio-degradable (rot-proof). There was a need at this time for a soft-to-handle, man-made fiber capable of being spun into yarns from which sweaters could be knitted. Du Pont invented an acrylic fiber they called Orlon which came onto the market in 1951 in the United States. In Britain, Courtaulds produced an acrylic fiber and began selling it in the late 1950s under the trade name Courtelle. In recent years polyester has become a popular name in fabrics. It is used alone as 100 per cent polyester or blended with other fibers. Polyester fiber was invented in 1941 in Britain, manufactured by Imperial Chemical Industries Limited and was in full production in Britain under ICI's registered trade name Terylene by 1955. Commercial production of polyester fiber made by Du Pont under the trade name dacron started in 1953.

This brief history of man-made fibers is not complete without mentioning stretch fibers known in America as spandex and in Britain as elastomeric. This synthetic elastomer fiber was invented in the Du Pont laboratories in the USA. It is a polyurethane fiber which has replaced rubber for making elasticated fabrics and became commercially available in 1962.

Edwin J. Beer, one of the first research chemists in the development of viscose rayon.
He joined Samuel Courtauld in 1905

The remains of Samuel Courtauld's silk mill, now demolished, in Panfield Lane, Bocking, Essex, England

Samuel Courtauld (1793–1881), founder of the Courtauld business at Bocking in 1816.
He was born in Albany, N.Y., USA

Production

Research and development into the improvement of man-made fibers and the modification of them for new uses is going on all the time all over the world. New trade names are added to the endless list and this makes the consumer's decision-making process very difficult. Basically, however, there are only two types of man-made fibers:

Regenerated cellulose: rayon (viscose rayon) and acetate.

Synthetic polymer: acrylic, polyester, nylon (polyamide), polyethylene, polypropylene, polyurethane and polyvinylchloride (PVC).

In very basic terms man-made fibers are made by pushing plastic liquid through a nozzle, jet, or as it is usually referred to, a spinneret. As the fine streams of plastic material solidify they become continuous filaments of thread, much in the same way as the silk worm produces its two continuous filaments of silk. A single filament is known as a monofilament and many filaments are referred to as multi-filament. When man-made fibers are blended with other fibers or when they are spun into yarns by traditional spinning methods the fibers are extruded through the spinneret in multi-filament form and then chopped up into lengths similar to those of the natural fiber it is being blended with or for which it is being used as a substitute. The liquid plastic from which most man-made fibers is produced can be extruded into flat or expanded foam sheet. By using various mechanical methods sheet plastic products can be made like acetate sheet, polyester film, polypropylene foam, polyvinylchloride (PVC) sheet and celophane.

Mineral fibers for weaving and knitting into fabrics are produced from various metals and minerals. In some cases, particularly metals, they are made by drawing the material into very fine wire. Fibrous mineral rock like asbestos can be spun by traditional methods while fiberglass is produced by allowing molten glass to drop by gravity through jets, and then solidify. The following is a list of some of the mineral metal materials from which yarns can be made: aluminium, asbestos, ceramic, glass, gold, silver, stainless steel. These materials are used for making both decorative and industrial fabrics. Metallic yarns are manufactured from 100 per cent metal, plastic-coated metal, metal-coated plastic or a yarn covered by metal.

(opposite) The first viscose rayon machine built for Samuel Courtauld & Co. Limited, in 1904

(below) Birthplace of the American rayon industry, founded by Samuel Courtauld at Marcus Hook, Pennsylvania, USA

(below) Another view of the plant at Marcus Hook

Classification of Textile Fibers

- **Natural**
  - *Animal*
    - Alpaca
    - Angora Goat
    - Angora Rabbit
    - Beaver
    - Camel
    - Cow
    - Cashmere Goat
    - Chinchilla
    - Deer
    - Goat
    - Guanaco
    - Hare
    - Llama
    - Muskrat
    - Nutria
    - Opposum
    - Rabbit
    - Raccoon
    - Sheep
    - Silk
    - Vicuna
    - Yak
    - Weasel
  - *Vegetable*
    - Abaca
    - African Bowstring Hemp
    - Banana
    - Bombax
    - Coconut
    - Cotton
    - Esparto
    - Flax
    - Hemp
    - Henequen
    - Hop
    - Jute
    - Kapok
    - Kenef
    - Manilla Hemp
    - Milkweed
    - Nettle
    - New Zealand Flax
    - Papyrus
    - Pineapple
    - Pulu
    - Raffia
    - Ramie
    - Rice
    - Sisal
    - Sunn
    - Urena
    - Yucca
- **Man-made**
  - *Natural Polymer*
    - *Cellulosic*
      - Acetate
      - Cuprammonium
      - Triacetate
      - Viscose Rayon
    - *Protein*
      - Casein
  - *Synthetic Polymer*
    - *Acrylic*
      - Carbon Fiber
      - Modacrylic
    - *Olefin Fibers*
      - Polyethylene
      - Polypropylene
    - *Polyamide*
      - Nylon
    - *Polyester*
    - *Polyurethane*
      - Elastomeric
      - Spandex
    - *Polyvinyl Chloride*
      - PVC
      - Chlorofiber
  - *Non Polymer*
    - *Mineral*
      - Aluminium
      - Asbestos
      - Ceramic
      - Copper
      - Glass
      - Gold
      - Silver
      - Stainless Steel

(opposite) Part of the plant at Spondon, Derbyshire, England, for the production of ethylene used in the manufacture of acetate

Acetate

It was known how to make acetate fiber in 1865 but it was not until 1894 that the process was patented. To begin with the second man-made fiber ever to be produced was called cellulose acetate rayon, later to be referred to as acetate rayon and in recent years known simply as acetate. It was first spun commercially in England soon after World War I by British Celanese Limited who called it celanese and it was used chiefly for ladies' underwear. In December 1924 it was first spun in the USA in Cumberland, Maryland. Since then many companies throughout the world have developed the process and are are now manufacturing acetate under many trade names.

Acetate: USA Trade Marks and Makers

Celanese—made by Celanese Fiber Company, a division of Celanese Corporation. Trade names include celacloud, celacrimp, celafil, celaperm and celara.
Acele—made by Du Pont de Nemours and Co. Inc. Textile Fibers Dept.
Estron—made by Tennessee Eastman Company, a division of Eastman Kodak Company.
Sayfr—flame retardant acetate yarn made by FMC Corporation, American Viscose Division.

Acetate: British Trade Marks and Makers

Dicel—made by British Celanese Limited. Trade names include celafiber and lo-flame dicel.
Lansil—made by Lansil Limited.

Acetate, like viscose rayon, is made from cellulose base. The cellulose is obtained from wood pulp or cotton linters (short cotton fibers). Unlike viscose rayon the cellulose material is treated with acetic acid or acetic anhydride to produce the base liquid material from which the fiber is spun. The liquid acetate can be dyed (spun dyed) at this stage before spinning to produce a brilliant range of colors. Acetate fabrics have exceptionally good draping qualities. It is the one man-made fiber closely resembling silk and has a lustrous sheen. It is the ideal fiber from which satins and taffetas are made and it is also used in knitted fabrics and underwear. In conjunction with other fibers it is used in machine- and hand-knitting yarns. In fiber or tow form acetate is used for cigarette filter tips. Fabrics made from 100 per cent acetate should be washed regularly and carefully in warm suds. Rinse, squeeze and dry gently and then use only a warm iron. The dope (transparent lacquer) which is made from the cellulose acetate is also used for paints, film and fabric finishes.

Triacetate is similar to acetate but more robust in washing and wearing. Fabrics made of triacetate can be permanently pleated and are easy to wash and quick to dry. In the United States triacetate is manufactured under the trade name arnel by Celanese Fibers Company, Division of Celanese Corporation and in Britain, under the trade name tricel, by British Celanese Limited.

British celanese fashion advertisement showing a 1920s garment made from acetate fabric

(opposite above) Magnified picture to show crimped acrylic fiber used in the production of high-bulked yarn for knitting

(opposite below) One acrylic fiber magnified 4,300 times

Acrylic

Acrylic fiber, a true man-made synthetic is made entirely from mineral sources such as coal, air, water, petroleum and natural gas producing a chemical compound called polyacrylonitrile. The first garments made from acrylic fiber yarns produced by Du Pont under the trade name Orlon, were available in American stores in late 1951. Production of acrylic fiber by Courtaulds in Britain, under the trade name Courtelle, began in 1957. A whole range of acrylic fibers have been made for numerous end uses. The most common use of acrylic fiber is in sweaters but it is also being used extensively, blended with natural fibers and alone, to produce woven and knitted flat and pile fabrics. Acrylic fiber is usually produced as a cut staple, not in continuous filament form, then spun into woollen type yarns. It has many outstanding qualities making it the ideal fiber from which to make many types of fabric and garments. It can be exceptionally soft,warm to the touch and light in weight. Garments made from acrylic fiber yarns, if correctly made, can be washed easily and do not shrink or stretch. Acrylic fiber yarns are strong, hardwearing, unaffected by mildew, cannot be attacked by moths and are resistant to damage by many chemicals such as battery acid, soot and smoke. It is twice the strength of wool but not as strong as nylon.

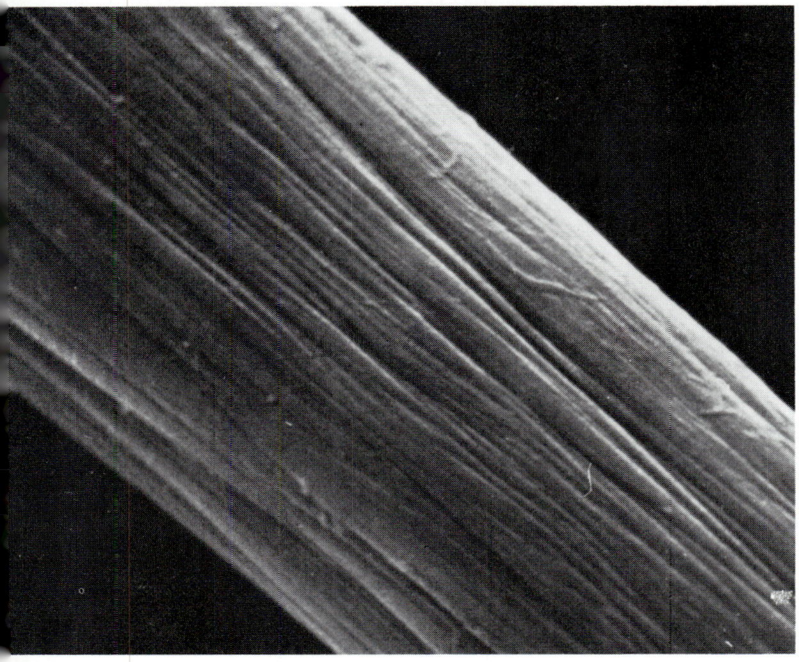

Modacrylic fiber is a modified form of acrylic fiber and has a slightly different chemical composition. It has been specially developed for fire or flame retardant fabrics used in draperies, sleepwear, firefighting clothing and fake furs. Some fake-fur is made to imitate animal fur and then there are fake-furs or fun-furs which are like no other furry fabric in the world. They can be woven on pile looms (*See* Plush, p33) but these days most fur fabrics are manufactured on special pile knitting machines. Fake-fur can imitate the pelts of many of the dying breeds of animal such as: chinchilla, coney, fox, leopard, lynx, lion, marten, mink, monkey, nutria, rabbit, sable, seal, skunk and squirrel. Fun-fur is a term originally used to overcome the exclusive, wealthy image where real fur was the symbol of affluence. Now fun-furs are enjoyed by everyone in many ways. The bright vivid colors in which it can be dyed are not only made into coats but also into toys. The popular television puppets, Fozzie Bear of 'The Muppet Show' and The Cookie Eater of 'Sesame Street' are made of fun-fur.

Acrylic: USA Trade Marks and Makers
Acrilan—made by Monsanto Co. Textiles Division.
Creslan—made by American Cyanamid Company.
Orlon—made by Du Pont de Nemours & Co. Inc. Textile Fibers Dept.
Zefran—made by Dow Badische Company.

Acrylic: Main British Trade Mark and Maker
Courtelle—made by Courtaulds Limited.

Modacrylic: USA Trade Marks and Makers
SEF—made by Monsanto Company, Textile Division.
Verel—made by Tennessee Eastman Company, Division of Eastman Kodak Company.
Zefran—made by Dow Badische Company.

Modacrylic: Main British Trade Mark and Maker
Teklan—made by Courtaulds Limited.

Acrylic and modacrylic fiber fabrics or fabrics containing either of these fibers should be washed or dry cleaned with care according to the manufacturer's instructions. For washable garments use detergent and warm water rinsing thoroughly using fabric softener in hard water areas. Do not wring or twist the garment or fabric. Remove excess moisture by rolling in a towel then lay flat to dry completely. Sturdy garments like slacks and skirts are usually machine washable but do not use the spin cycle on the washing machine. Wash and wear garments can be put through the spin cycle and tumble dried. Only use a cool iron for touch-up pressing with the iron set at 'rayon' or 'synthetic'.

Asbestos

Asbestos is a fiber which is mined like rock or coal. It is a mineral, and there are about thirty different types although only one type, chrysotile, is used in making fabrics. The word asbestos is a Greek word meaning 'will not burn'. Asbestos fiber will remain stable up to a temperature of 1,490°F (810°C). Most chrysotile asbestos comes from Quebec in Canada but there are small deposits in Columbia, Southern Rhodesia, South Africa, Turkey, United States and Venezuela. It is mined from open or underground pits and takes about twenty tons of asbestos rock to produce one ton of fiber.

The longest fibers are separated by a process called cobbing. Cobbing is done by pounding the rock with a hammer by hand. The shorter fibers are separated from the rock by crushing and screening. This is known as milling. The fibers are graded, cleaned, blended together and corded into a web. Once the web has been produced the process continues in a similar manner as for cotton or wool. A roving is produced from which the yarn is spun.

An asbestos fiber is usually quite coarse and bulky. It is used in making fire retardant fabrics and conveyor belts. For special close proximity fire fighting clothing it is used by military and civil aviation authorities, car racing tracks, and gas, coal, electricity, oil refining and petrochemical companies. The asbestos fabric is coated on the outside with aluminum pigment and usually lined with wool or a non flamable man-made fiber.

Carbon Fiber

Carbon fiber is a modified form of acrylic (polyacrylonitrile) fiber. It is as strong as glass fiber and five times stiffer. It was developed in Britain at the Royal Aircraft Establishment at Farnborough between 1936 and 1964. It is now manufactured in Britain by Courtaulds Limited under the name Grafil and under license in America by Hercules Incorporated ISD, Utah.

Carbon fibers are produced in bundles (or tons) of 5000 or 10000 filaments, each filament much finer than human hair—some are about 7 microns in diameter. It is resistant to chemicals and has good wearing qualities. As yet it is not knitted or woven but used in its fiber form sometimes laminated to woven or knitted glass fiber. One of the other great advantages of carbon fiber is that it is lightweight. This, in addition to its strength and stiffness makes it an ideal fiber for reinforcing plastics.

Carbon fiber is used in many aerospace projects, sports equipment, textile machinery, helicopter blades, rocket motors, satellite structures, boat hulls, tennis racquets, skis, ski poles, ice hockey sticks and cricket bats.

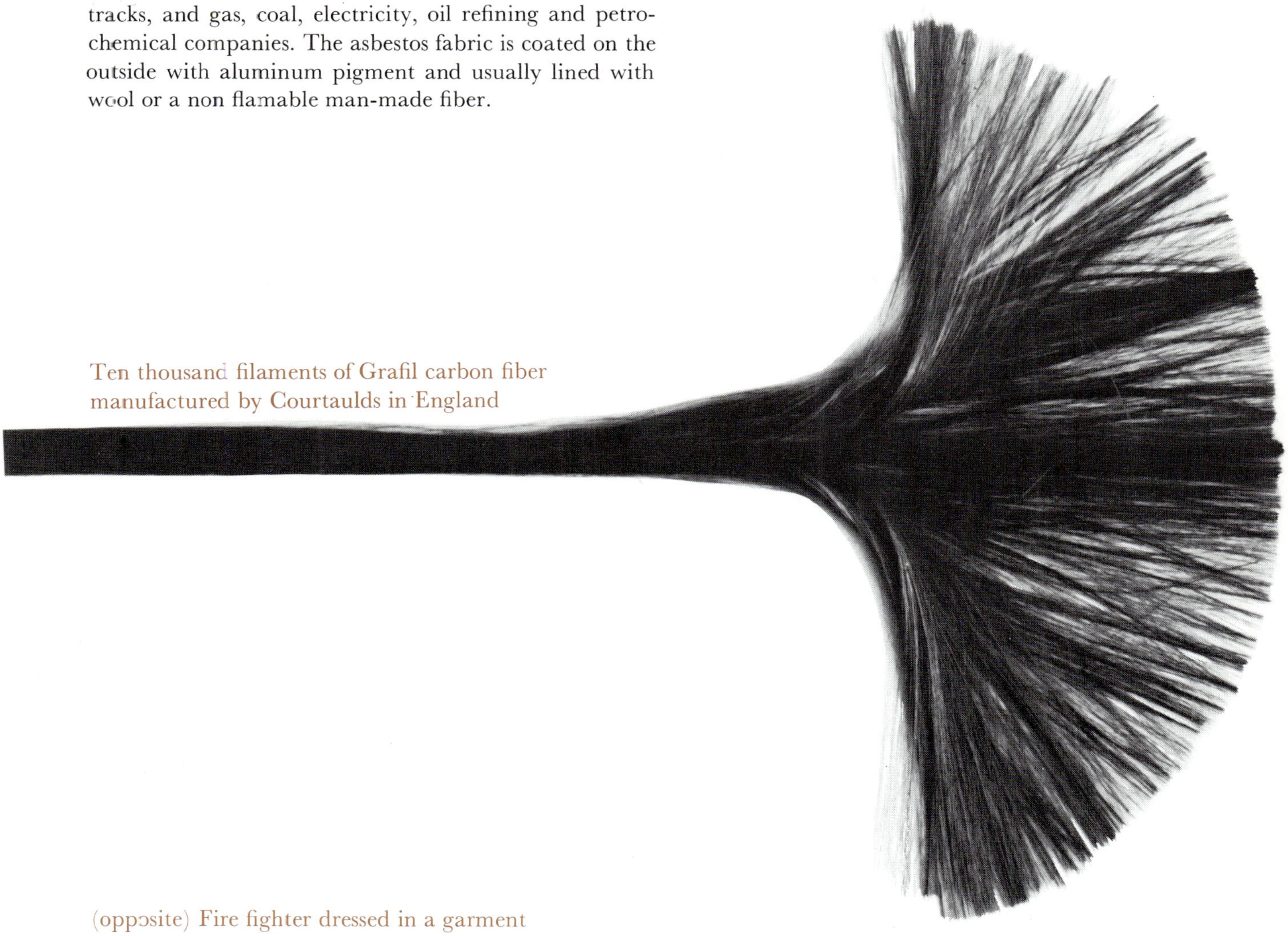

Ten thousand filaments of Grafil carbon fiber manufactured by Courtaulds in England

(opposite) Fire fighter dressed in a garment made from aluminum-coated asbestos fabric

Glass

Glass can be made into fiber, spun into yarn and made into fabric. Special glass composed of silica and various oxides is prepared and heated to a temperature of 2500°F (1365°C). The glass, once molten, is then either drawn off into fibers (known as the direct melt process) or made into marbles for easy storage and transportation. The marbles can be melted later and drawn off into fiber. The bunches of fiber can be left in straight continuous filaments, chopped up for spinning by traditional cotton or woolen processes or texturized by injecting air into the fibers.

Glass fiber, although not in the form we know today, was around in the mid-nineteenth century. A report in *L'Echo du Monde Savant*, dated the 15th February 1873, stated that the cloth of glass exhibited in the Passage de L'Opéra 'will equal in brilliancy all that is possible for the imagination to conceive; it will realize, in a word, the wonders of the enchanted palaces of the Arabian Tales'. The word fiberglas is often used to describe glass fiber. Fiberglas is the trade mark for glass fiber products made by Owens-Corning Fiberglas Corporation of North America. Owens-Corning are not, however, the exclusive maker of glass fiber but have developed a very fine glass fiber filament which is known by the trade name beta fiber. The diameter of this fiber is only 3.8 microns thick, and once bunches of these fibers have been texturized they become as soft as wool and can be used for drapes, curtains and carpets.

Comparative Size of Fibers

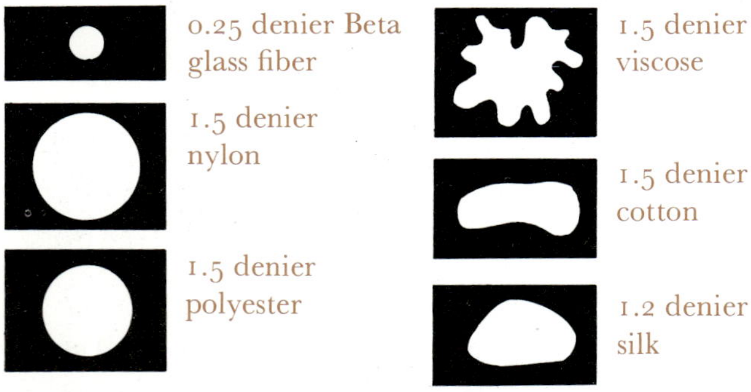

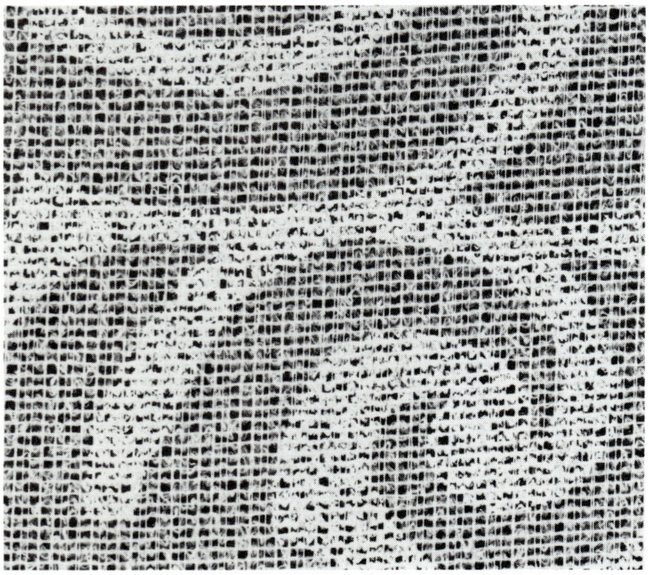

Glass Fiber: USA Makers

Ferro Corporation, Fiber Glass Division
Fiber Glass Industries Inc.
Gustin-Bacon Division, Certain-Tweed Products Corp
John-Manville Fiber Glass Inc.
Kaiser Glass Fiber Company
Modiglass Fibers, Division of Reichhold Chemicals Inc.
Oliver Glass Fiber Corporation
Owens-Corning Fiberglas Corporation
PPG Industries Inc., Fiber Glass Division
Uniglass Industries, Division of United Merchants and Manufacturers Inc.

Glass Fiber: British Makers

Marglass Limited, a company formed by Courtaulds Ltd. in Britain and United Merchants and Manufacturers Inc. in America
Fibreglass Ltd.
Deeglass Fibres Ltd.
Turner Brothers Asbestos Co. Ltd.

Glass fiber has strength, will not rot, will not burn and will not shrink or stretch making it a very useful material for certain industrial and domestic fabrics. It can be colored only after manufacture into cloth and is simple to print with pigment printing inks. Glass fiber fabrics have many applications in many military and civilian aerospace projects. It can be used for lagging pipes, insulating buildings, making insect screening and acoustical facings, for laminating as a scrim to reinforce paper or as a fabric laminated to asbestos for fire-fighting clothing. Domestically it is used for curtains, carpets, sun blinds and screens. It is woven in widths from 1–84 inches (2.5–210 cm).

In spite of its strength and non-flammability glass fiber is, like other materials, not indestructible. It does not stand up to continual abrasion, therefore curtains and drapes should be hung away from surfaces which they can rub against. Washing glass-fiber fabrics should be done carefully. Hand wash in hot water with detergent, rinse in warm water but do not wring or twist. Hang on a clothes line or shower rod to drip-dry.

In addition to pure glass fiber there is now produced a much higher heat resistant fiber known as ceramic fiber. This fiber can be spun into yarns and woven into fabric. It is a good insulation material and used in situations where heat loss must be kept to a minumum, as for instance in kilns or furnaces. Ceramic fiber is produced in the United States and in Britain by the Carborundum Company Limited under the trade name Fiberfrax.

(left) Glass-fiber curtain fabric

Metallic

Metallic yarns for weaving, knitting and embroidery are manufactured from 100 per cent metal, plastic-coated metal, metal-coated plastic or metal wound round a core yarn. Aluminium, copper, gold, silver and stainless steel are all metals which can be made into wire threads and then woven or used for embroidery. The metal is drawn through steel dies until it is fine and flexible enough to manipulate like any other continuous monofilament yarn. In the case of stainless steel yarns these are produced in very fine multi-filament bunches which can be used in carpets or for making velvet for industrial uses. Copper and stainless steel monofilaments are used for weaving screen and filter cloths for many end uses from mosquito screen and papermaking mesh to ultra fine filters in aircraft. Aluminum, gold and silver wire yarns are drawn into fine threads, some of which are made into fine spiral threads cut into short lengths and used for embroidery. One company only remains in Britain able to produce this type of material, most of which is used for making military and civilian badges of rank.

Sometimes metal wires and threads are given a coating of plastic to prevent oxidization, and metal coated plastic yarns are used extensively in making fabric (such as lamé) for apparel. Often this type of yarn is known as Lurex the trade mark of the Lurex Co. Ltd. in Britain and Dow-Badische in the United States. Although there are several other companies who produce similar yarns the word Lurex has almost become a generic term. Metal coated plastic yarns are not true metal yarns but yarns made of metalized plastic. This is done by vacuum, depositing aluminium onto one side of a transparent continuous polyester film sheet and then protecting the aluminium deposit with another fine polyester film applied either in liquid or sheet form. Gold and colored metalized polyester yarns are produced by applying transparent color to the silvery surface of the aluminium deposit before it receives its protective surface. Once the sheets of silver, gold or colored metallic film have been prepared they are slit into fine threads. In this form it is strong enough for using as weft in weaving or for embroidery but it should be supported by a fine monofilament nylon thread to give it strength for knitting or for use in the warp for weaving.

Metal wound round a core yarn usually of cotton or silk is the most traditional way of producing a metal yarn for weaving or embroidery. A polished cotton or silk thread is wound carefully with gold, silver or aluminum flattened wire to produce a flexible material. Jari gold yarns, made in India, are produced in a similar way by winding flattened silver wire round an orange dyed polished cotton core and then gold plated. Sometimes cheaper Jari gold yarns are made by coating the silver with transparent yellow lacquer.

Metallic Yarns: USA Types and Makers
Stainless steel—Brunswick Corporation
Lurex—Dow-Badische Co.
Metlon—Metlon Corporation

Metallic Yarns: British Types and Makers
Lurex—Lurex Company Limited
Metalized plastic yarns—Porth Textiles Limited
Copper and stainless steel—United Wire Limited
Gold and silver—Stephen Simpson Limited

(above) Jari gold thread made in India

Lurex fabrics

Jayne Mansfield wearing a gold lamé dress

Nylon

Nylon was the first man-made fiber to be made entirely from mineral sources and is considered to be a completely synthetic fiber. It is made from carbon and petroleum or natural gas, oxygen and nitrogen from the air and hydrogen from water. There are two basic types of nylon —nylon 66 and nylon 6. Nylon 66 was invented in the laboratories of Du Pont de Nemours in Wilmington, Delaware, USA. The official chemical name for nylon is polyhexamethyleneadipamide, referred to as polyamide, and the name nylon was made a generic term in a full-page announcement in the *New York Herald Tribune* on October 30, 1938. There has been much speculation about how nylon got its name. The Du Pont archive revealed how the name developed from suggestions like Duparooh (Du Pont pulls a rabbit out of a hat) to the speculation that it had come from NY for New York and LON for London.

The first nylon stockings were made in Wilmington, Delaware and sold to Du Pont employees in February, 1939. The following year nylons, as they were to become known, were available all over the USA, but World War II brought an abrupt halt to the civilian use of nylon in 1942 and all production went to meet military needs. It was during this period that nylon 6 was invented in Germany, quite independently from America. Research into the development of nylon resumed immediately the war was over and since then many types of nylon have been made all over the world and used for an endless number of products.

Nylon fiber and yarn is produced in many ways for making into fabrics and the method of production influences the character of the fabric. The following terms are used:

Monofilament—single, continuous, smooth, strand
Multifilament—many, continuous, smooth strands
Bulked continuous filament—many texturized, continuous, strands
Tri-lobal—bright, shiny three-leaf-clover cross-section

There are now over one hundred different types of nylon fiber manufactured for textiles. Each is available in many thicknesses and colors and there are thousands of different fabrics made from nylon alone or blended with other fibers. Nylon is extremely strong, does not absorb moisture, resists abrasion, and has an inherent elastic quality which makes it an ideal material for sails, parachutes, ropes, kites, belting, hoses, fabrics for car tyres, waterproof and showerproof fabrics as well as drip-dry and underwear cloths. The sheerest of nylon fabrics is difficult to tear.

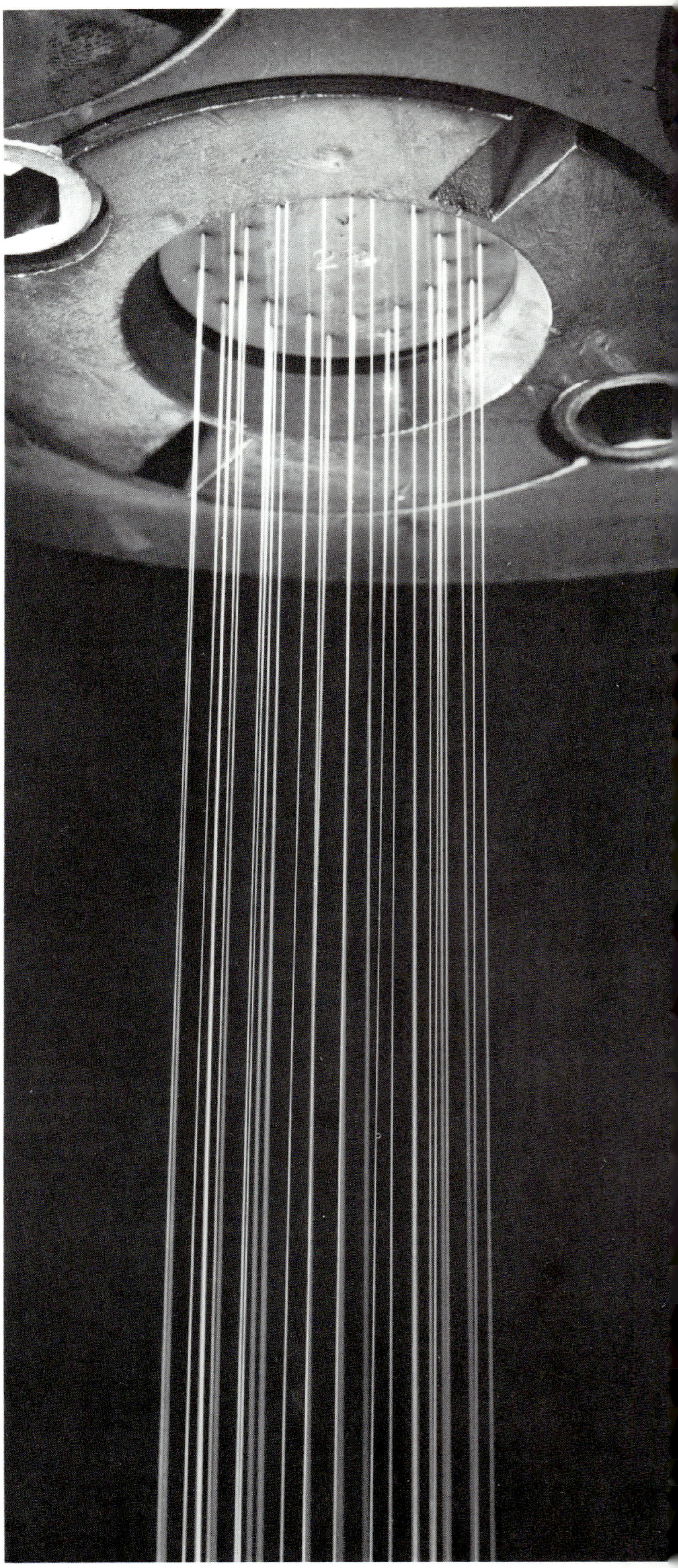

Spinneret extruding 28 filaments of 100 denier nylon (enlarged picture)

An American fireman dressed in a fire-retardant nylon uniform

Nylon: USA Trade Marks and Makers

Anzo—made by Allied Chemical Corporation
Caproian—made by Allied Chemical Corporation
Crepeset—made by American Enka Corporation
Enkalon—made by American Enka Corporation
Enkaloft—made by American Enka Corporation
Enkalure—made by American Enka Corporation
Beaunit Nylon—made by Beaunit Fibers Division, Beaunit Corporation
Shareen—made by Courtaulds Limited
Antron—made by Du Pont de Nemours & Co. Inc. Textile Fiber Dept
Cantree—made by Du Pont de Nemours & Co. Inc. Textile Fiber Dept
Cordura—made by Du Pont de Nemours & Co. Inc. Textile Fiber Dept
Nomex—made by Du Pont de Nemours & Co. Inc. Textile Fiber Dept
Qiana—made by Du Pont de Nemours & Co. Inc. Textile Fiber Dept
Cedilla—made by Fiber Industries Inc.
Astroturf—made by Monsanto Co. Textile Division
Blue 'C'—made by Monsanto Co. Textile Division
Cumuloft—made by Monsanto Co. Textile Division
Ultron—made by Monsanto Co. Textile Division
Ayrlyn—made by Rohm and Haas Co. Fibers Division

In addition to some of the names in the above list (e.g., Enkalon, Antron, Nomex, Qiana, Blue 'C' and Ultron) the following are British trade-marks and makers:

Bri-Nylon—made by ICI Fibers Limited
Celon—made by Courtaulds Limited

Most manufacturers provide washing instructions and cleaning instructions for nylon or nylon blend fabrics. If none are given the following instructions show how to treat all nylon fabrics:

1 Wash in warm water only with detergent.
2 Wash white articles only with other white articles.
3 Bleaches and optical whitening agents can be used on white articles.
4 Articles can be drip dried or low temperature tumble dried.
5 Light pressing can be done with iron set at 'rayon' or 'synthetic'.
6 Do not dry in direct heat.

Further developments have been made in nylon to make it into a high temperature resistant, flame and heat retardant fiber suitable for making fire-fighting clothing although the fabrics made from this new nylon or aramid (aromatic polyamide) in the late 1960s were intended for automobile racing and military aviation.

Olefin Fibers

Polyethylene and polypropylene are both olefin fibers and are by-products of petroleum. Polyethylene, better known as polythene, is familiar to us in sheet and bag form. Both polyethylene and polypropylene can be produced in fiber form and are used extensively throughout the textile industry. Polypropylene, invented in Italy in 1954, can be readily turned into textile fiber. Unlike other man-made fibers and because of its particular character, polypropylene is first produced in ribbon or tape form, then slit into narrower tapes, and stretched. The action of stretching the tape elongates the molecules and turns the film into long fibers. At this stage it becomes very strong and stiffer than it was originally. It is processed from then on, like jute or hemp, into string, cords, or ropes. Polypropylene is used extensively for making carpet backing and sacks, having somewhat replaced jute and hemp. Polypropylene is difficult to dye.

Polypropylene Fiber: USA Trade Marks and Makers
Herculon—Hercules Inc., Fibers and Film Department
Marvess—Phillips Fibers Corporation
Typar—Du Pont de Nemours

Polypropene Fiber: British Trade Marks and Makers
Cournova—Courtaulds Limited
Ulstron—ICI Fibers Limited

In both countries there are many other companies who make polypropylene as a direct part of the process of making cordage.

Polyethylene can be extruded in fine monofilament threads which come in a variety of colors and do not fade, or as a transparent yarn. This yarn or thread, almost as strong as nylon (polyamide), is non-absorbent and resistant to chemicals, moths and mildew. It makes an ideal material for awnings, deck chairs, nets, papermaking screens, and fly screen fabrics.

Polyethylene: USA Makers
American Thermoplastics Corporation
Indian Head Yarn and Thread Company

Polythene: British Trade Mark and Maker
Courlene—Courtaulds Limited

Deck chairs at Brighton covered with polyethylene fabric

Polypropylene cloth used for bagging and carpet backing

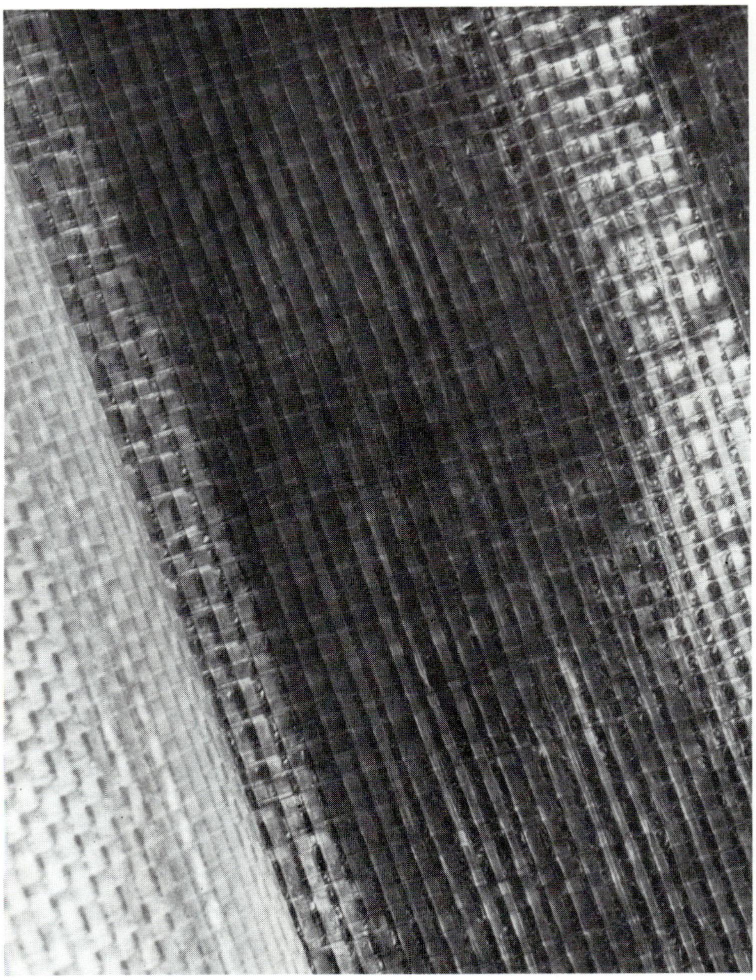

Polyester

There are hundreds of different types and sizes of polyester fibers used in the textile industry but all are made from petrochemicals (petroleum-chemicals). Although research was going on in the 1920s, it was hampered by World War II. The first polyester was in full production and being sold in American stores in 1953 and in British stores in 1955.

Polyester fiber was a British discovery and was first sold by its sole manufacturer in Britain, Imperial Chemical Industries Ltd (ICI) under the trade name terylene. At about the same time Du Pont adopted the name dacron for their polyester fiber. Polyester fiber, which is known as the work horse of the textile industry, has since the 1950s been manufactured by many chemical companies all over the world.

Polyester: USA Trade Names and Makers
Blue C—Monsanto Textiles Division
Dacron—Du Pont de Nemours
Fortrel—Celanese Corporation and ICI Ltd.
Trevira—Hystron Fibers Inc.
Zefran—Dow Chemical Company

Polyester: British Trade Names and Makers
Lirelle—Courtaulds Ltd.
Trevira—Hoechst Fibre Industries UK Ltd.
Terylene—ICI Fibres Limited

Polyester fibers, yarns and fabrics are very resilient and used either alone or blended with other fibers produce easy-care fabrics. The ideal blend of polyester fiber with cotton for shirt and dress fabrics ranges from 40 per cent polyester/60 per cent cotton to 30 per cent polyester/70 per cent cotton. It is highly resistant to abrasion and a fiber which is used for very fine fabrics as well as heavier worsted cloths. It is resistant to moths and mildew. It is, however, likely to pill and also feel clammy in hot weather.

Much use has been made of textured polyester in recent years in the double jersey Jacquard industry and it has swept the world as a fine knitted fabric for both men's and women's wear as well as stretch upholstery. It can be used in filament, for making cloths for conveyor belts, papermaker's screens, fire hose, yacht sails and protective clothing.

Washing of fabrics made with polyester yarns can be done by hand or machine. Use warm water and detergent, but do not boil. Wringing is unnecessary as fabrics and garments can be drip-dried. Some fabrics require touch-up ironing using the setting for 'rayon' or 'synthetic'. Polyester fibers as a wadding or fiberfill is a useful material for stuffing pillows, duvets, comforters, eiderdowns, sleeping bags and quilted jackets.

Polyurethane

Polyurethane is a plastic material which has had a dramatic impact on the textile industry. In one form it can be produced as a foam sheet and laminated to a knitted fabric backing. This is made in a variety of qualities and used extensively for apparel and luggage as imitation leather. As a textile fiber it is more commonly known as a 'synthetic elastomer fiber' or by the generic term elastine or as spandex in the United States and elastomeric in Britain. Spandex and elastomeric fibers are elastic threads made from bundles of multifilament polyurethane which have been fused together creating a single yarn with much more stretch than rubber of a comparable thickness.

Strands of spandex or elastomeric fiber can be wrapped with natural or non-stretch staple man-made fibers to make yarns suitable for weaving or knitting stretch fabric garments. These yarns are called corespun yarns.

Elastine yarns are ideal for use in girdles, swimwear, support hosiery and belts. They can be machine or hand washed in warm water but do not use chlorine bleach on fabrics containing this fiber as they will discolor and may be damaged. In the USA spandex fibers are manufactured by Du Pont de Nemours under the trade name Lycra. In Britain elastomeric fibers are manufactured by Courtaulds Ltd under the trade name spanzelle.

Polyvinyl Chloride

Polyvinyl chloride is commonly known as PVC. It is a plastic material and is made from basic chemicals found in salt water and petroleum. Fibers produced from this material are known as cholorofibers. The basic experiments leading to the discovery of PVC were made by a French chemist in 1840 although it was not developed for another hundred years. Research by the Dow Chemical Company began in 1939.

PVC is used in the textile industry in the following ways: continuous filament fiber (chlorofiber); continuous soft clear film (PVC sheet); continuous soft colored sheet for laminating to knitted fabric backing for artificial leathers; in liquid form for coating other plain and printed fabrics. In fiber form it can be blended with other fibers and used for curtains, rainwear, upholstery and apparel. Since it has a low melting point PVC or cloth containing PVC should be handwashed in warm water and detergent only, rinsed and drip dried.

Chlorofiber: USA Trade Marks and Makers

Saran—National Plastic Products Company
Rhovyl—Rhodia Incorporated

There are no producers of chlorofiber in Britain. Polyvinyl chloride is used extensively in Britain in sheet (PVC) form and as a coating for cotton fabrics.

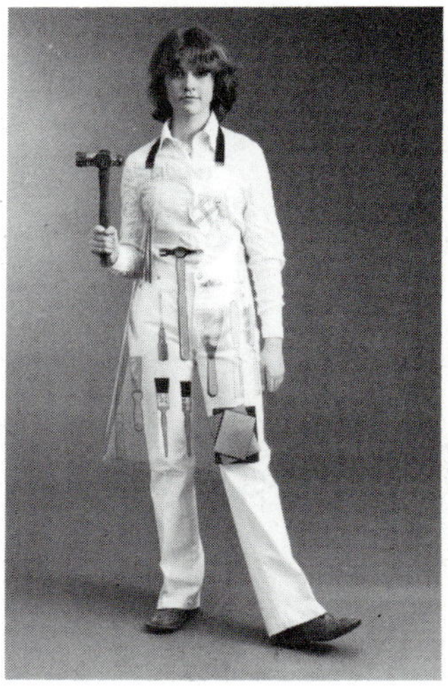

(above) Aprons made from PVC coated cotton fabric
(below) An apron made from printed transparent PVC sheet

Rayon (Viscose Rayon)

Rayon is the oldest of all the man-made fibers and was originally produced by dissolving nitro-cellulose which could then be extruded through a nozzle and made into a filament or thread. Count de Chardonnet patented his process in 1884 and began perfecting it as a fiber suitable for using as a textile thread in 1898. The process was too dangerous, since treating cotton fiber with nitric acid is a way of producing gun-cotton which is an explosive and some of the early factories were accidentally blown up. In the 1880s and 1890s further experiments were carried out to make the production of 'artificial silk' safer first by the cuprammonium process and then finally in 1892 the viscose process, developed and patented in Britain by a chemist named C. F. Cross and his partners. This process produced a viscose substance by treating wood pulp with caustic soda. and other chemicals. The first filaments of viscose were made for electric lamps and it was not until 1904 that Samuel Courtauld and Company, English silk weavers, became interested in the process and bought the patents, built a factory and by 1913 were producing over 3 million pounds (1.4 million kg) per annum in Britain.

Viscose rayon is the most versatile of all man-made fibers and capable of being modified to fit any requirements. It can be used in continuous filament form, it can be spun like cotton or wool or made into string. It is bright or dull and can be blended with any fiber, natural or man-made. Rayon is made as a very soft fiber, as soft as silk, or as hard as sisal. It can be used for underwear or capets. The viscose rayon fiber has an irregular cross section and recent developments have produced a hollow cross section fiber with the performance of cotton. It has good moisture absorbancy and dyes well although it is also available in a wide range of spun dyed colors. Rayon drapes well and can be used for all types of apparel and curtain fabrics.

Viscose rayon fabrics or fabrics containing viscose rayon wash well. It is best to use warm water only with detergent, rinse well, do not wring out and use a warm iron.

Viscose rayon: USA Trade Marks and Makers

Zantrel—American Enka Corporation
Enkaire—American Enka Corporation
Enkrome—American Enka Corporation
Briglo—American Enka Corporation
Enka—American Enka Corporation
Jetspun—American Enka Corporation
Coloray—Courtaulds North America Incorporated
Fibro—Courtaulds North America Incorporated
Viloft—Courtaulds North America Incorporated
Vincel—Courtaulds North America Incorporated
Avisco—FMC Corporation, American Viscose Division
Avron—FMC Corporation, American Viscose Division
Aviloc—FMC Corporation, American Viscose Division
Fiber 40—FMC Corporation, American Viscose Division

Viscose rayon: British Trade Marks and Makers

Vincel—Courtaulds Limited
Sarille—Courtaulds Limited
Evlan—Courtaulds Limited
Durafil—Courtaulds Limited
Vilof—Courtaulds Limited

(above) A 'box' type machine producing continuous filament viscose y
(below) Part of the machine ab

Viscose rayon filaments being formed by extrusion through a spinneret into acid

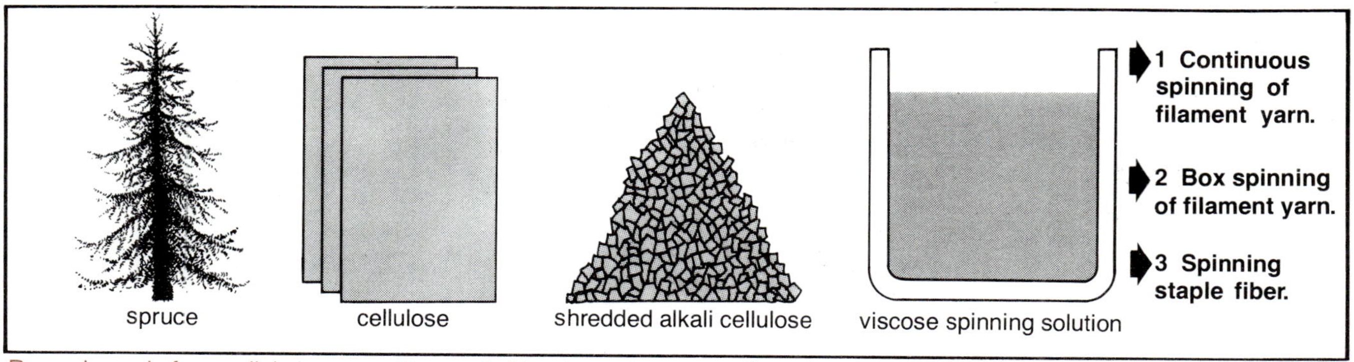

Rayon is made from cellulose, a constituent of all land-growing plant life. Spruce (from Scandinavia and Canada) and eucalyptus (from South Africa) yield much of the high-grade cellulose required for rayon.

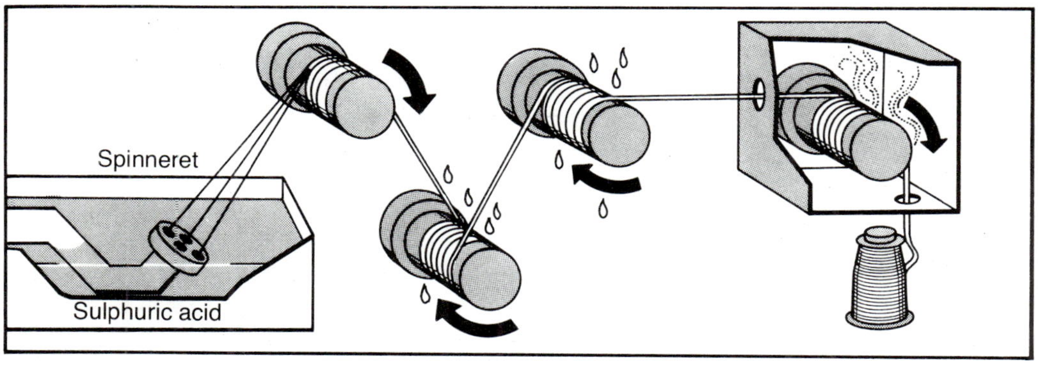

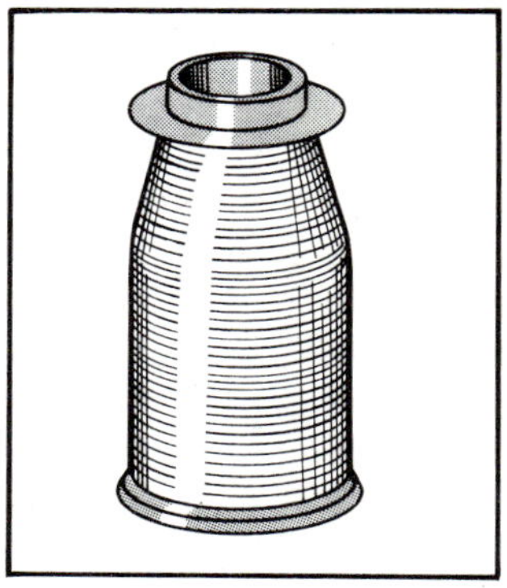

1 Continuous spinning of filament yarn. The viscose is extruded through the fine holes of a spinneret. The yarn is washed and on the final reel it is dried. The continuous filament viscose rayon yarn is given a twist and wound onto a bobbin ready for use by the weaving and knitting industries.

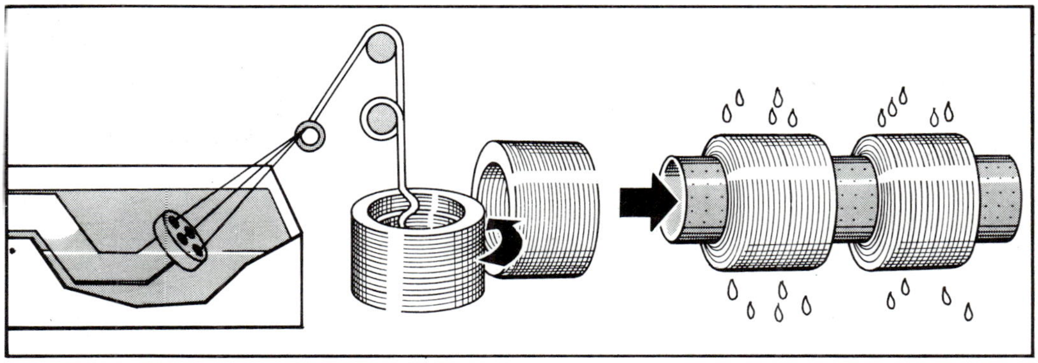

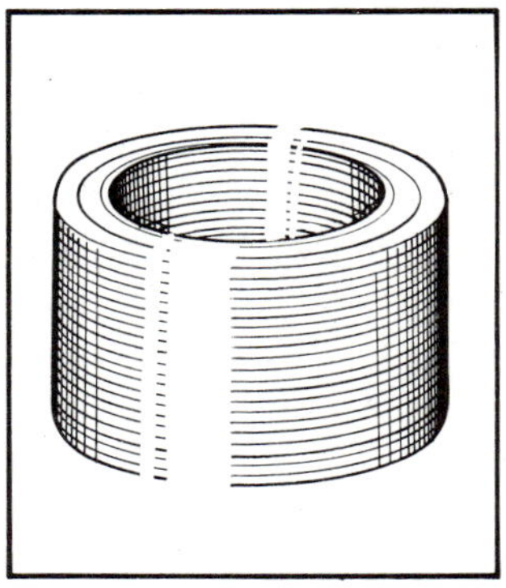

2 Box spinning of filament yarn. The yarn is extruded in the same fashion as (1) except that it is drawn round two wheels known as godets. These run at differing speeds to stretch and strengthen the yarn. The yarn is fed into the center of a revolving pot where it is given a slight twist and wound into cakes which are placed on perforated tubes and washed. The cakes are then dried ready for use in the manufacture of woven and knitted fabrics.

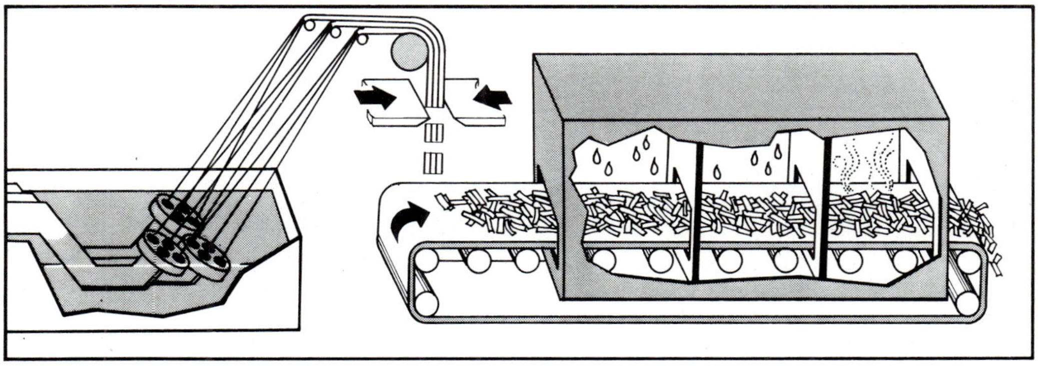

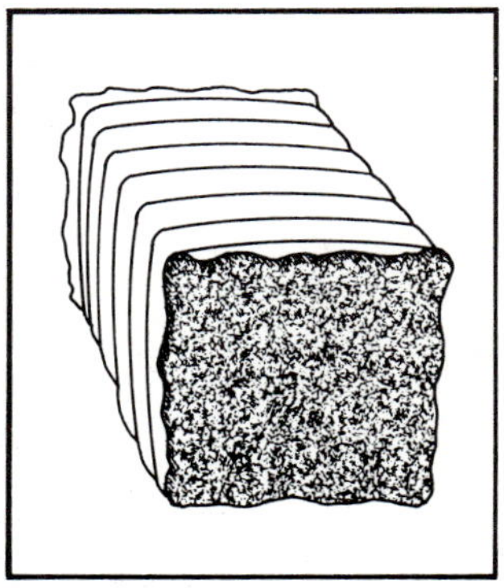

3 Spinning staple fiber. Again the yarn is extruded in the same fashion as (1) but this time the filaments from several larger spinnerets are drawn together to form a continuous tow. The tow, which consists of thousands of continuous filaments, is fed into a cutter which produces fibers of the desired staple length, e.g. $1\frac{7}{16}$in, $2\frac{1}{2}$in, 4in, 6in or 8in. The staple fiber is collected onto a conveyor belt which passes through the washing and drying compartments. The fiber is then baled ready to be spun, like cotton, into a yarn.

Textile Terms

Appliqué
Cut-out decorative fabric shapes stuck, sewn or embroidered onto a base fabric or garment.

Bleach
To remove natural or applied color or impurities from yarn or fabric by chemical treatment. Brilliant white is obtained by the application of optical bleaching agents. If chlorine bleach is used in the home be very careful with it. Follow the instructions on the bottle.

Blends
The combination of two or more different fibers in the same yarn or cloth. The fibers can differ in color or differ in fiber type.

Blistercloth
A woven or knitted fabric made from any fiber and constructed to form hollow bumps or blisters over the face of the cloth. A cloqué effect.

Bouclé
A French word to describe a curly or looped yarn. Also a fabric which has a curly or looped surface like astrakhan. (*See* Yarn, p150.)

Bonding
Fabric can be constructed by unconventional or non-traditional methods. Many of these are made by processes called bonding and are divided into three methods of production: chemical, thermal (heat) and mechanical. Fiber can be bonded to fiber, yarn to yarn, fabric to fabric, fiber to yarn, fiber to fabric and yarn to fabric. These would come under the following headings: fiber-bonded fabrics; yarn-bonded fabrics; fabric-bonded fabrics; combination-bonded fabrics. Some of the common terms used in bonded fabrics include: melding (heat); fuse bonding (heat); foam-flame bonding (heat); wet-adhesive bonding (chemical); malimo (stitch bonding); arachne (stitch bonding); rasmussen (spun bonding). Usually bonded fiber fabrics are referred to as non-woven fabrics and are chiefly used as interlinings.

Brushed
A hairy surface on a woven or knitted fabric produced by raising some of the fibers in the cloth by wire brushes or teasels. This makes the fabric softer and tends to cover up fabric structure.

Calendering
A finishing process for cloth by passing it through steam heated rollers under controlling pressure. Moiré, glazed, chased and watermarked finishes can be applied to fabrics using this method.

Appliqué comforter or quilt

(right) A teasel for raising fabric

Burns check

Ciré

Ciré is the French word for wax and is used to describe a lustrous polished effect on the surface of a fabric as if waxed. Satins finished in this way are sometimes called shoeblack satins.

Clear Finish

A woolen cloth which has been scoured and felted, raised or brushed then cropped to remove all loose and shaggy fibers from the surface.

Clip Spots

Cloth ornamented with small detached spots of either extra warp or extra weft threads, the floats of surplus thread between the spots being cut away. Examples are madras muslin or dotted Swiss.

Chamois Cloth

A woven or knitted cloth napped to imitate chamois skin. Sometimes referred to a chamois suede, chamoisetter or chamoisine.

Checks

Horizontal stripes in the weft, crossing stripes in the warp at right angles. Like tartans, plaids, and glen checks.

Chenille

A fuzzy yarn which looks like a caterpillar. Usually made of wool, cotton or man-made fibers. (*See* Yarns p150.) A fabric made from chenille yarns can also be referred to as chenille fabric.

Chevron

This term usually applies to herringbone weave effects or zig-zag patterns. (*See* Weaves p148.)

Coating

A woven or knitted fabric constructed and finished to make it suitable for coats.

Coated Fabric

Fabric which as been coated with a substance to make it longer lasting, liquid repellent or for decoration. Some substances used in coating are acrylic, melamine, rubber, resin, oil and PVC.

Cranvenette

The registered trade mark for a water repellent process for fabrics of all types.

Crêpe

Lightweight fabric with crinkled surface. The crinkled effect is obtained by the structure of the cloth, chemical application or the degree of hard twist in the yarns used in the cloth. Sometimes a crêpe effect can be achieved by embossing.

Crochet
A method of making cloth, usually by hand, using a hook-ended needle. The yarns used can vary from fine cotton to heavy worsted. A crochet effect can be obtained in knitting by hand or by machine.

Devoré
A process of printing certain chemicals onto specially made cloths to produce burnt out or sheer fabric areas. The special cloths are made from either a blend of different fibers, a combination of yarns differing in chemical content or similar yarns some of which have been chemically treated. The illustration shows a 100 per cent cotton fabric woven in India, where alternate threads in the weft have been chemically treated to resist the printed chemicals. Known as *aetzstickevei* in Germany, an animal fiber cloth is embroidered with a vegetable fiber or vice versa and either the wool is burnt out with caustic soda or the cotton with sulphuric acid leaving a lacy structure.

Dobby
A mechanism on a loom which automatically selects the warp threads according to specific weave patterns. Usually small geometric or symmetrical designs are woven on looms with this mechanism. These are known as dobby patterns.

Dog Tooth
A check pattern used in district and glen checks made by using four threads of a dark color alternating with four threads of a lighter color both in the warp and as the weft using a 2-and-2 twill weave. (*See* Houndstooth p137.)

Domestics
A general term to distinguish fabrics for use in the house—e.g., sheets, towels, blankets and washcloths—from apparel fabrics.

Double Cloth
One fabric constructed with two layers of cloth each made with its own warp and weft. The two layers are sometimes linked together by extra threads. (*See* Weave 'Double Plain' p148.)

Double Face
The front and back of certain fabrics which can be used either way round. Sometimes cloths can be used in this way.

Double Jersey
Sometimes known as double knit and if figured known as double jersey Jacquard. These fabrics are made on circular knitting machines in most fibers and most commonly produced in polyester and used for dresses, jackets and trousers. (*See* Weft Knitting p150.)

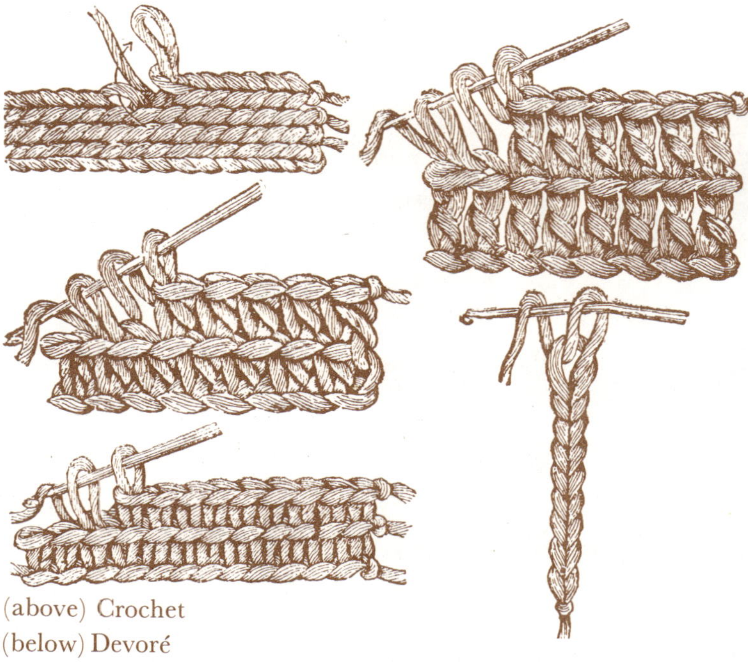

(above) Crochet
(below) Devoré

Dog tooth

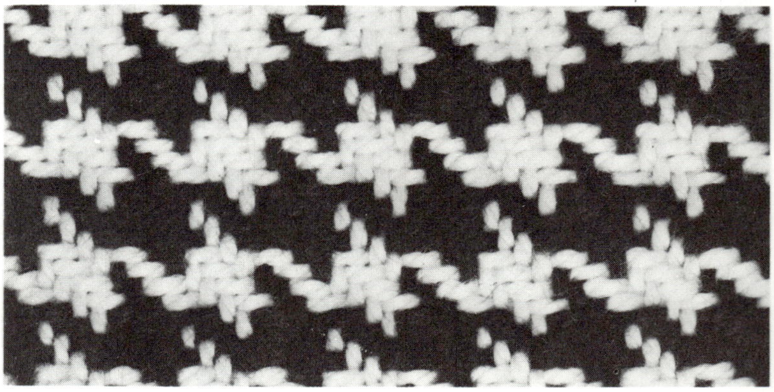

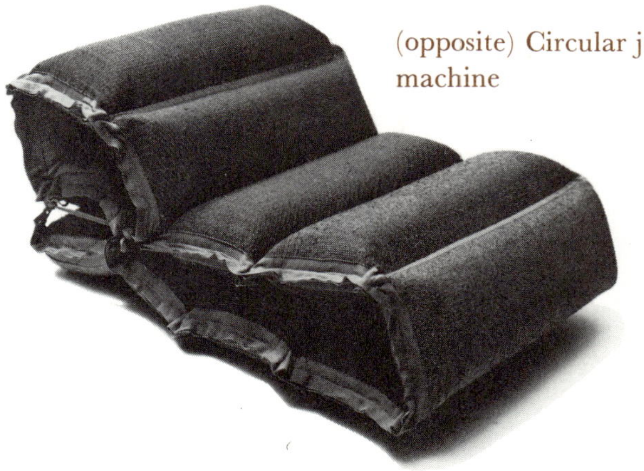

(right) A chair constructed in double cloth on the loom and stuffed

(opposite) Circular jersey knitting machine

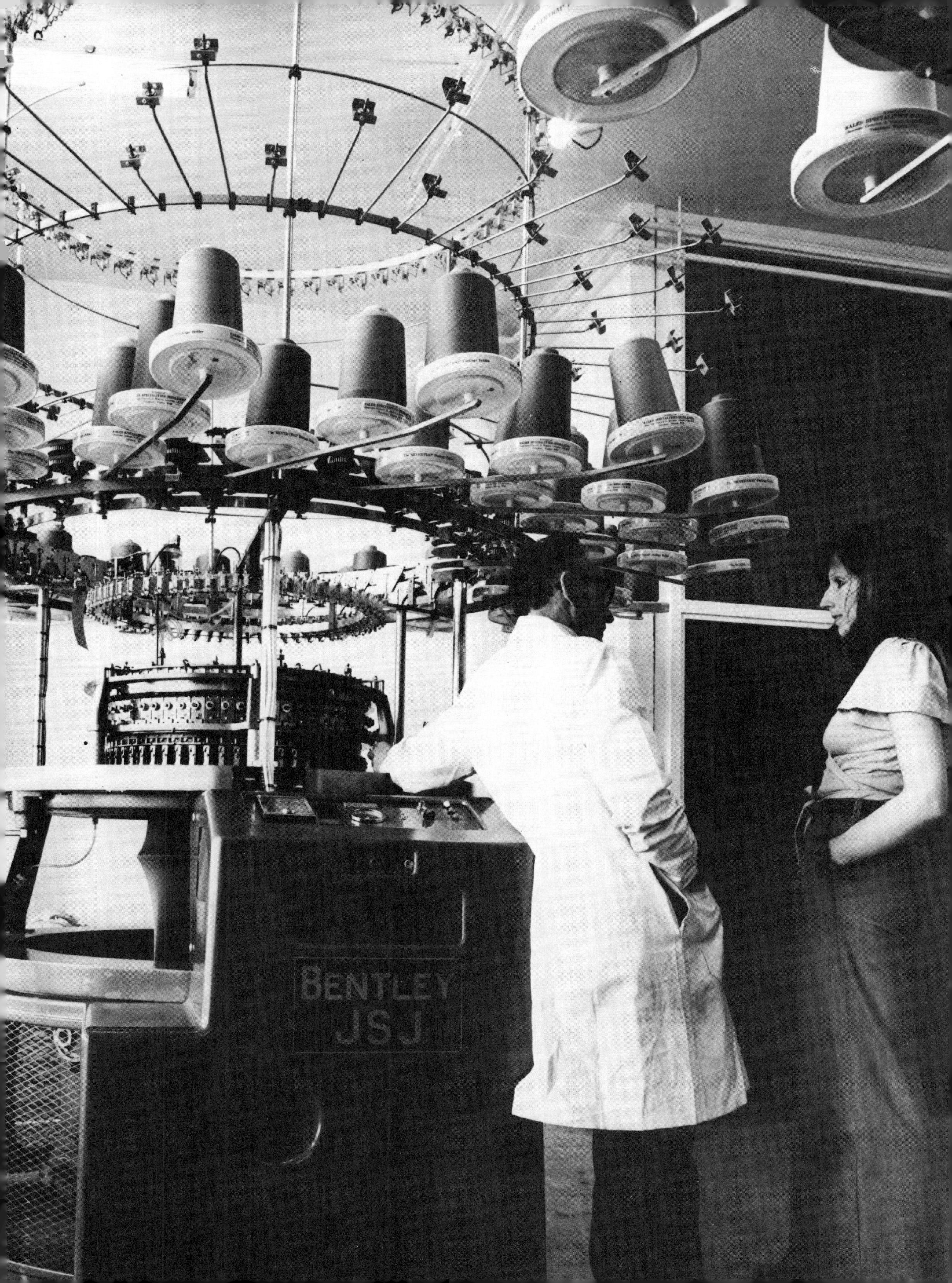
BENTLEY
JSJ

Dyeing

Dyeing is a method of putting color into fiber, yarn or fabric in liquid form. Fabrics can be dyed in an endless range of colors. The technology of dyeing is complex. Certain dyes will only dye particular fibers and these are too numerous to mention here. If you wish to do your own dyeing at home there is now a wide range of easy-to-use dyestuffs on the market. These include explicit instructions and if used properly should achieve good results.

Some of the more common dyeing methods include:

Batik
A method of resist dyeing using wax, oil, resin, paraffin, rice paste, bean paste, or mud applied to the fabric in areas whih do not require to be dyed. After dyeing the resist is washed out.

Cross-dyeing
When a fabric is made of more than one fiber and each fiber is dyed a separate color.

Dope-dyeing
When the chemical solution is colored before making it into a fiber. Also known as spun dyeing or solution dyeing.

Ikat
When either the warp or weft is tie-dyed to create a pattern.

Patola
When both the warp and weft are tie-dyed to create a pattern.

Piece-dyeing
Dyeing a finished piece of cloth.

Plangi
Similar to tie dyeing. (*See* Bandanna, p49).

Space-Dyeing
Yarn which is dyed with two or more colors usually spaced out in a random manner. This can be done by the tie-dye method similar to preparing ikat warps or wefts.

Tie-dyeing
A type of resist dyeing when areas of a cloth not to be dyed are tied or knotted to resist the dye.

Vat-dyeing
Vat-dyed fabrics are considered to be more color-fast than other dyed fabrics. Vat dye is a type of dyestuff and does not refer to the method of dyeing.

Yarn-dyeing
Yarn which is dyed before being made into a fabric.

(above) Two examples of Indonesian batik

Embossing

A surface texture or pattern in relief produced by passing a cloth under controlled heat and pressure through engraved rollers. Often the fabric has been finished in such a way as to make the embossed areas permanent.

Embroidery

Needlework done by hand or machine using a wide variety of threads to produce designs on cloth. (*See* Needlework Fabrics, p142, and Schiffli Embroidery, p144.)

Eponge

The French word for sponge is used in textiles, to describe a soft, uneven, usually loosely-woven cloth from cotton, wool or spun man-made fibers. Sometimes known as ratiné where spiral yarns have been used to create the sponge effect.

Etoffé

A collective French term used to mean all types of fabric.

Silk patola from Patan, India

(left) Indian cotton weft ikat

Fabric Care

Soiled fabrics are either washed or dry cleaned. The cleaning treatment given to each type of cloth depends on the fiber content, construction or finish of the cloth. Special finishes are now given to many cloths which make them easier and more simple to clean. It is essential to look at the fiber content and cleaning instruction label attached to most textile products or to know the exact fiber content and finish when purchasing a fabric. Always observe the washing instructions on a garment label. When in doubt about the fiber content or finish applied to a fabric, have it dry cleaned but never dry clean PVC or PVC-coated fabrics—just sponge them down.

In 1972 the Federal Trade Commission of the United States ruled that apparel and fabric sold by the yard in America must have a care label. The only exceptions are items which would be ruined by having labels attached and items selling at $3.00 or less which are completely washable. In the case of fabric only remnant lengths up to 10 yards (9 m) are exempt.

The Textile Distributors Association have produced the following fabric care labels:

Machine wash warm

Machine wash warm line dry

Machine wash warm, tumble dry, remove promptly

Machine wash warm, delicate cycle, tumble dry low, use cool iron

Machine wash warm, do not dry clean

Handwash separately use cool iron

Dry clean only

Dry clean pile fabric method only

Wipe with damp cloth only

In Britain a similar labelling system has been developed by the Home Laundering Consultative Council and this was adopted as an International Textile Care Labelling Code for Europe in 1974. Unlike the American system the European way is to use series of symbols:

For washing (by hand or machine)

For bleaching

For ironing

For dry cleaning

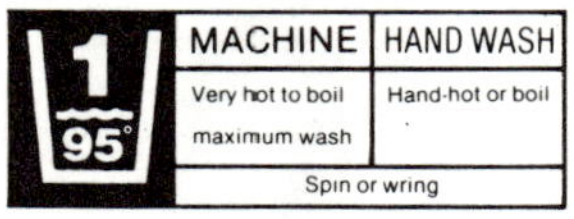

White cotton and linen articles without special finishes

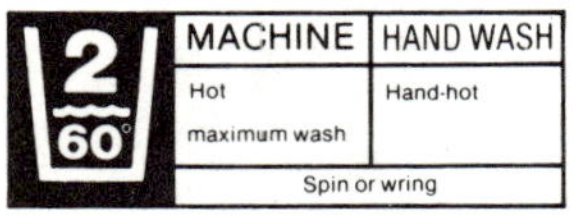

Cotton, linen or rayon articles with special finishes where colors are fast at 60°C (140°F)

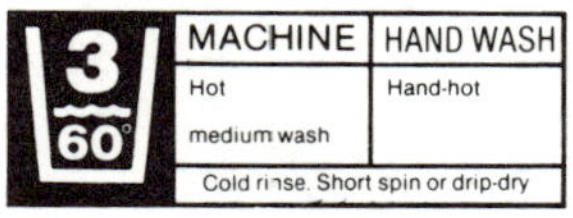

White nylon; white polyester/cotton mixtures

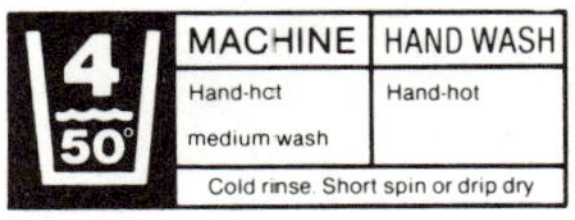

Colored nylon; polyester; cotton and rayon articles with special finishes; acrylic cotton mixtures; colored polyester/cotton mixtures

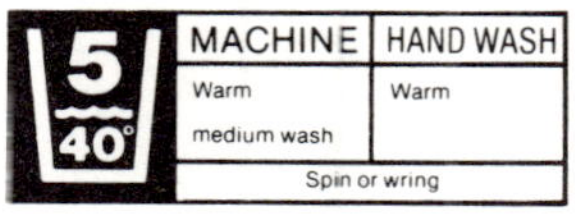

Cotton, linen or rayon articles where colors are fast at 40°C (104°F) but not at 60°C (140°F)

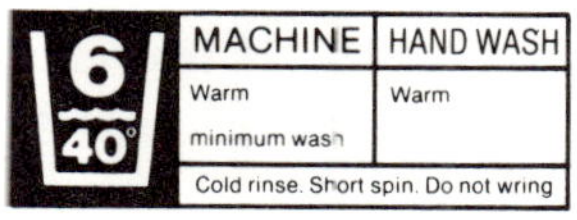

Acrylics; acetate and triacetate, including mixtures with wool; polyester/wool blends

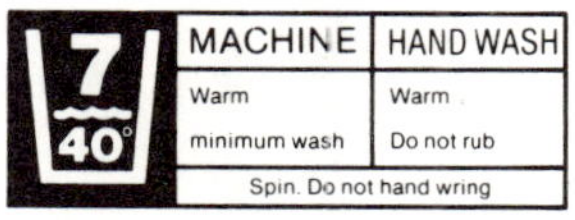

Wool, including blankets and wool mixtures with cotton or rayon; silk

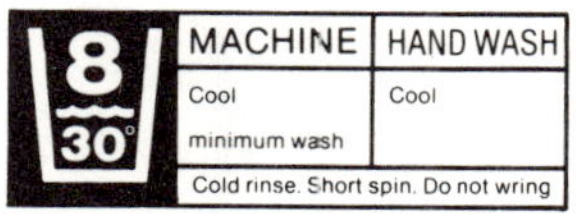

Silk and printed acetate fabrics with colors not fast at 40°C (104°F)

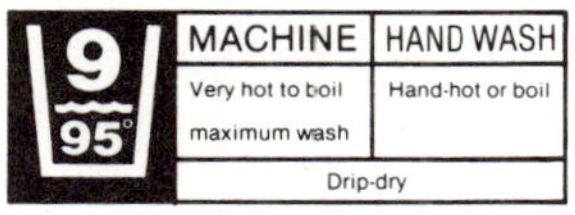

Cotton articles with special finishes capable of being boiled but requiring drip drying

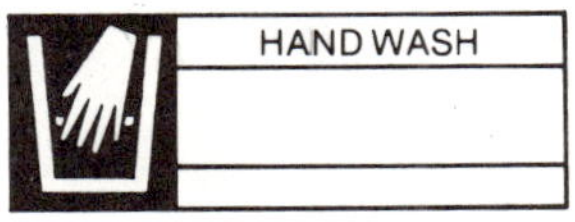

Articles which must not be machine washed. Details will vary because garment manufacturers are free to put their own written instructions on this label

Do not wash

Fabric Widths

The most common fabric widths in inches and equivalent centimeters are as follows:

25 in	65 cm	dress
27 in	70 cm	dress
32 in	80 cm	dress and non woven interlinings
36 in	90 cm	dress
40 in	100 cm	dress
42 in	105 cm	dress and furnishings
45 in	113 cm	furnishings
48 in	120 cm	furnishings and coatings
50 in	125 cm	furnishings and coatings
54 in	138 cm	furnishings, coatings and sheetings
60 in	150 cm	furnishings and sheetings
68 in	170 cm	furnishings and sheetings
72 in	180 cm	furnishings, sheetings and jersey

Face Finished Fabrics

Certain categories of fabric, usually woolens, where the face of the cloth has been raised, brushed, rubbed or treated by other processes which produce a nap and obscure the structure of the fabric.

Felt

Felt is a cloth usually made of wool although sometimes hair, cotton or man-made fibers can be added. Loose fiber is matted or compacted together by milling (*See* milled cloth, p140) with warm soapy water. (*See also* Felted Fabrics, below, and Non-woven, p143.)

Felted Fabric

A woven or knitted cloth usually made of wool which is milled (*See* milled cloth, p140) with warm soapy water to produce a solid firm fabric. The process closes the structure of the cloth and makes it impervious to rain and wind. Typical felted cloths are melton and loden. (*See* Felt, above.)

An Austrian wearing felted loden cloth (*See* p. 30)

Fiber Identifications

Only when fibers are used by themselves in a fabric or yarn and not blended with other fibers can the following identification tests be carried out. Most of the tests require the sample fabric or yarn to be burnt. So be careful. Make sure you carry out your test over a sink and hold the piece of fabric with tongs and not your fingers. Use a match to light the sample.

Wool and silk
Sizzles, self extinguishing when removed from the flame. Smells like burning hair, feathers or ammonia. Leaves a crushable black ash.

Cotton, flax, other plant fibers and viscose rayon
Burns quickly with yellow flame and continues to burn and glow after removal from flame. Smells like burning paper. Leaves soft grey ash.

Nylon
Shrinks away from the flame. Melts and then burns slowly. Smells like celery. Leaves a hard grey bead.

Polyester
Shrinks away from the flame. Melts and burns slowly giving off black smoke. Smells sweet. Leaves hard black bead.

Acetate
Melts and burns quickly and continues after removal from flame. Smells like vinegar. Leaves brittle black bead. Also disintegrates in acetone (nail polish remover).

Acrylic
Melts and burns and continues after removal from flame. Leaves hard brittle black bead. Little or no identifiable smell.

Glass
Glows but does not burn.

Polyurethane spandex or elastomeric
Becomes sticky and leaves soft fluffy black ash.

Polypropylene
Melts, shrinks and curls away from the flame. Leaves hard, brown bead.

Fireproof

Fireproof fabrics are 100 per cent fireproof such as asbestos cloth. Fire retardant, flame retardant or flameproof fabrics are treated with special chemicals to prevent fire spreading. A simple but temporary treatment to render fabrics non-flammable is to saturate them in a concentrated solution of borax, alum, phosphate or soda or a compound of titanium and antimony salts. Commercially treated fabrics can be laundered or dry cleaned under normal conditions without the loss of the flame retardant properties, but follow the washing instructions exactly on any flame-retardant treated garment to retain its effectiveness.

Hand weaving in Greece

Houndstooth

Flocking
Flock is very short wool or man-made fiber (usually $\frac{1}{32}$–$\frac{1}{8}$ in or $\frac{1}{2}$–3 mm) and can be dyed in any color. When applied to fabrics flock must be electrostaticly charged to stand upright before the tips of each fiber are applied to areas of the cloth previously printed with an adhesive. Usually flocked cloths can be washed or dry cleaned but the flock eventually wears off.

Foam-backed Cloths
Refers to any fabric laminated to any backing of polyurethane or PVC foam.

Grey Goods, Griege Goods
Woven or knitted fabric straight from the loom or knitting machine which is undyed, unbleached, unprinted or unfinished. In the case of woven fabric the term loomstate is often used. In the linen and lace trade the term brown goods is used.

Handwoven
A cloth entirely woven without any mechanical aid on a handloom where the weaver propels the shuttle across the warp by hand and changes the weave pattern by foot.

Heather Mixture
Cloth woven or knitted from yarns spun from a mixture or blend of pre-dyed fiber. Often used in Scottish woolen cloths and knitted garments.

Hosiery
A term originally used to describe knitted socks and stockings but now referring to all types of knitted garments.

Houndstooth
A check pattern used in district and glen checks made by four threads of a dark color alternating with four threads of a lighter color both in the warp and the weft using a hopsack or 2-up and 2-down weave. (*See* Dog Tooth p130.)

Intarsia
A weft-knitted pattern inlaid into a piece of weft-knitted fabric without floats making the cloth reversible.

Interlining
Stiff or semi-stiff woven or non-woven fabric used in tailoring and dressmaking. The fabric is placed between the lining and outer fabric as a stiffening. Also refers to lightweight napped fabric used for extra warmth (usually known as interlining flannel).

Interlock
A double 1 × 1 rib weft knitting construction which produces a smooth faced fabric having the wales on one side of the fabric immediately behind the wales on the other side. Used for sweaters and underwear.

Jacquard
A method of weaving elaborate motifs invented by Joseph Marie Jacquard (1752–1834) between the years 1801 and 1810. A Jacquard mechanism operated by a punched card system attached to a loom can select individual warp threads and is therefore able to weave pictures. A Jacquard mechanism has since been developed for knitting machines. Some weaving and knitting Jacquard mechanisms are now operated by computers. Designs are prepared for Jacquard weaving or knitting on squared paper known as point paper.

Jaspé
An effect achieved in weaving a cloth by using two tones of the same colored yarn in a random warping order of ones and twos. Sometimes the effect is created by twisting two single threads of similar color but contrasting tone together and using them in the warp. Sometimes referred to as jasper cloth. Jaspé silk is a French term used when either the warp is random printed or the silk contains colored slubs or nubs. Jasper is a silk cloth woven in plain weave with a black warp and white weft. Sometimes known as pepper and salt mixture.

Jersey
Jerseycloth is the name given to Milanese or tricot knitted fabrics (*See* Tricot, p147).

A jersey is a knitted garment with sleeves but usually without buttons which can be drawn down over the head. Similar to a sweater or pullover. (*See* Double Jersey, p130 and Jersey, p29.)

Joseph's Coat
A term used in weaving where the warp is made up of equal stripes of different colors and crossed by wefts of similar colors in the same order. Used to display different color and weave effects.

Kemp
Wool, particularly from mountain sheep, contains kemp or flat fiber which cannot absorb moisture and will appear to be lighter in color if dyed. Often used in tweeds.

Knitting
A method of forming a fabric by intermeshing loops of yarn by hand or machine using needles or hooks. The following are different methods: handknitting with needles, weft knitting on domestic or flat bed machines, weft knitting on circular machines (*see* Double Jersey, p130), warp knitting by interlooping warp threads, and raschel machine using the warp knitting process to produce more elaborate patterns.

(above) Jacquard loom
(right) Jacquard-woven fabric

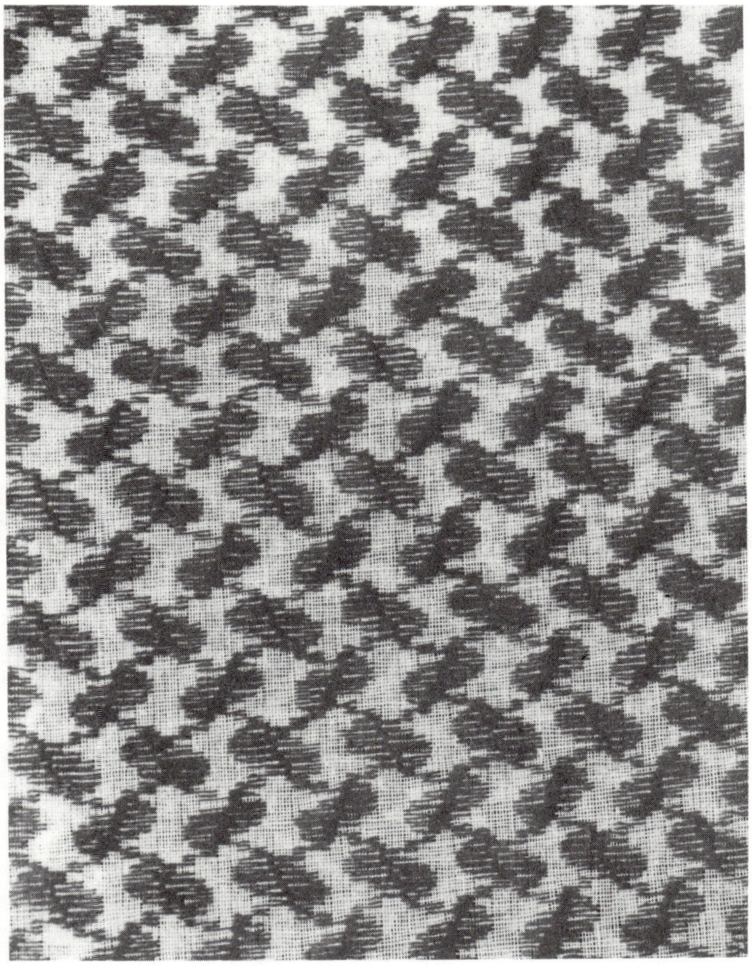

Lappet-woven fabric

Lace

The word lace comes from the Latin *laquens* meaning a noose or snare. Lace is essentially an openwork of fine thread originally made by hand. Cotton, silk or linen threads are interlaced in complex structures and patterns. When produced by hand the process is done by winding the threads around pins on hard cushions. It was not until the early nineteenth century that the Levers lace machine was invented. Cluny lace, Chantilly and Maltese lace, mosquito netting and tulle are now mass produced on the Levers machine. Lace type fabrics are frequently made on raschel knitting machines. Guipure lace is made on a schiffli embroidery machine by stitching the pattern onto a basecloth of net and cutting away the un-embroidered area Although cotton was the most common fiber used in lace manufacture man-made fibers are now used extensively.

Laminate

The joining together of two or more layers of fabric by means of an adhesive. The adhesive can be in the form of a foam or net which is melted by heat (foam flame bonding) or chemical which is sometimes heat cured. A foam itself can be laminated to a fabric. (*See* Bonding, p128.)

Lappet

Lappet weaving is done on a special loom which is able to introduce an extra warp figure or pattern into the foundation fabric. This extra figuring looks as if it has been embroidered onto the fabric.

Linings

Various fabrics used for lining apparel and curtains. Usually thinner and more stable in construction than the main fabric.

London Shrinking

This is a process by which worsted cloth is given a wet treatment, allowed to shrink and then dried without tension. Originally this process was carried on in London, England when the worsted cloth, woven in Yorkshire, bought by the tailors in London, was unrolled and left on Bermondsey Common overnight to become saturated by the dew.

Loom

A mechanism on which woven fabric is made. One of the most primitive looms is the backstrap loom. Handlooms are usually made of wood. Mechanical or so-called power looms are metal.

A Javanese backstrap loom

Macramé

The word macramé comes from the Arabic *migramah* which means an embroidered or fringed veil. It is now used to describe a coarse, knotted lacemaking technique which has been used extensively to fringe all types of fabrics. It is now a common craft technique for producing a fabric without any elaborate equipment. (*See* Narrow Fabrics, facing page.)

Mélange

A French term for mixture effect. Usually refers to a yarn spun from printed fiber to produce a mottled appearance.

Mercerize

A caustic soda treatment on cotton yarn or thread and fabric which produces a lustre, at the same time strengthening the yarn and increasing its dye affinity. Discovered by John Mercer in 1844.

Milium

A process developed by Deering Miliken & Co. Inc. in the United States for making metalized insulated fabrics. Aluminium or similar metal flakes are stuck to a fabric to allow the air still to circulate through but at the same time reflect heat and cold temperatures.

Milled Cloth

A cloth finishing process where a knitted or woven fabric (usually, but not exclusively, made of wool) is beaten in warm soapy water and at the same time shrunk.

Moth Proofing

A treatment given to a wool fabric to prevent it being destroyed by moth larvae. An untreated wool cloth can be stored with naptha or sprayed with moth repellent to prevent the cloth being destroyed.

Nap

The fibrous or hairy surface produced on the face of a fabric by brushing or raising with teasles or wire brushes. Usually obscures the construction of the fabric and makes it softer to handle.

From top to bottom:
1. Woven gift wrap ribbon
2. Woven braille name tape
3. Woven webbing
4. Russian braid
5. Knitted corking
6. Bias binding
7. Ricrac braid
8. Petersham
9. Moiré silk medal ribbon
10. Jacquard-woven braid
11. Raschel-knitted braid
12. Braiding

From top to bottom:
1. Cluny lace
2. Schiffli embroidered lace
3. Raschel-knitted lace
4. Cluny lace
5. Guipure lace
6. Levers lace
7. Broderie Anglaise (*See* p. 51)

Narrow Fabrics

Narrow fabrics are ribbons, tapes and webbing usually up to three inches wide (7.5 cm) produced by many methods including braiding, weaving, knitting, raschel, lace, embroidery, crochet, macramé and netting. Passamenterie is the general term used for all the catagories if used as trimmings. Technically a narrow fabric is one which does not exceed eighteen inches (45 cm) in width.

Braid

Although this term is used to describe many types of trimmings, braid, which comes from the Anglo-Saxon word *bregdon* meaning to move to and fro (weave), is made by interlacing or plaiting three or more threads to form a circular or flat strip. Rounded braid is produced on a maypole braiding machine. Shoe laces, cords and ropes and spaghetti braid are produced by this method. The most commonly used braid for dresses and furnishings include: Russian braid (soutache)—a simple two rib braid, president braid—similar to Russian but with three ribs, Grecian braid—closely woven cotton cord, flat braid—threads interlaced diagonally from edge to edge, folded braid—the same as flat braid but folded for edging and ricrac or Vandyke braid—similar to flat braid but wavy.

Embroidered

Embroidered narrow fabrics can look like lace or Jacquard woven cloths. The Schiffli embroidery machine produces fabric which looks like embroidered lace. The main center for this industry is St Gallen in Switzerland. (*See* Schiffli Embroidery, p144.)

Knitted

Knitted trimmings are produced in the following two main ways: weft knitting—made with a single thread as in home knitting and corking, and warp knitting—a collection of warp or lengthwise interlinked loops forming a chain stitch on a machine. Raschel is warp knitting and knitted lace is produced by this method.

Lace

Lace trimmings are made by hand or machine. (*See* Lace, p139.)

Macramé

A method of combining several threads by knotting.

Woven

Conventional woven trimmings used for dresses and furnishings include: Jacquard-figured fabrics tablet woven fabrics produced by hand, webbing—strong narrow fabric usually made of 100 per cent cotton, Petersham—a ribbon-like fabric made in plain weave with a fine warp and coarse weft used as a stiffening in dressmaking, typewriter ribbon, bandages, name tapes, woven brail name tapes and stevensongraphs, tapes for dressmaking, decorative use and tying.

Needlework Fabrics

Several types of fabric are specially made for needlework and rug making. Generally they are made of cotton or linen with varying degrees of stiffening which makes working on them easier but which washes out if necessary once the work is finished.

Linen twill
Used for traditional Jacobean or crewel embroidery.

Medium weight linen
Suitable for tablecloths and should be embroidered with stranded or twist cotton.

Sheer linen
Lightweight, fine linen for handkerchiefs to be embroidered with stranded cotton or silk.

Evenweave linen
Known sometimes as art linen. Varying weights. Used for counted or drawn work and Florentine embroidery.

Evenweave cotton
Similar uses to evenweave linen.

Hessian
A jute cloth suitable for embroidery with wool and appliqué work.

Danish hardanger
Plain weave cotton cloth used for hardanger embroidery. Also used for drawn thread work.

Calico
Lightweight cotton fabric. Use cotton threads for embroidery.

Crash
A heavy cotton fabric made with slubby yarns.

Binca, Bincarette or Ada Canvas
A stiff, mock leno-weave, open canvas in various sizes. Used for binca or cross-stitch embroidery.

Plain weave cotton cloths and canvas
Various weights are used for *gros point*, *petit point*, tent stitch, Bargello and cross-stitch.

Lockthread cloth
An open weave canvas used for large embroidery and rug making.

Felt
Used for appliqué and toy making. (*See* Felt, p135.)

Net

A very open mesh fabric produced by hand or machine in which the structure is ensured by some form of twisting or knotting of threads. Spun from any fiber, it may be produced by leno or gauze weaving, knitting, knotting or macramé or on a lace machine such as a roller-locker, Levers lace machine or Barmen lace machine. Types of net include curtain net, mosquito net, fishing net, tulle, cable net, Brussels net, Bretonne net, stirrup net.

From top to bottom:
1. Leno woven canvas for Florentine embroidery
2. Canvas for *gros point* embroidery
3. Canvas for *petit point* embroidery
4. Canvas for Bargello work
5. Canvas for Florentine work
6. Lockthread Florentine rug
7. Linen evenweave embroidery cloth
8. Open weave flax embroidery cloth
9. Mock leno woven Panama cloth for cross-stitch embroidery

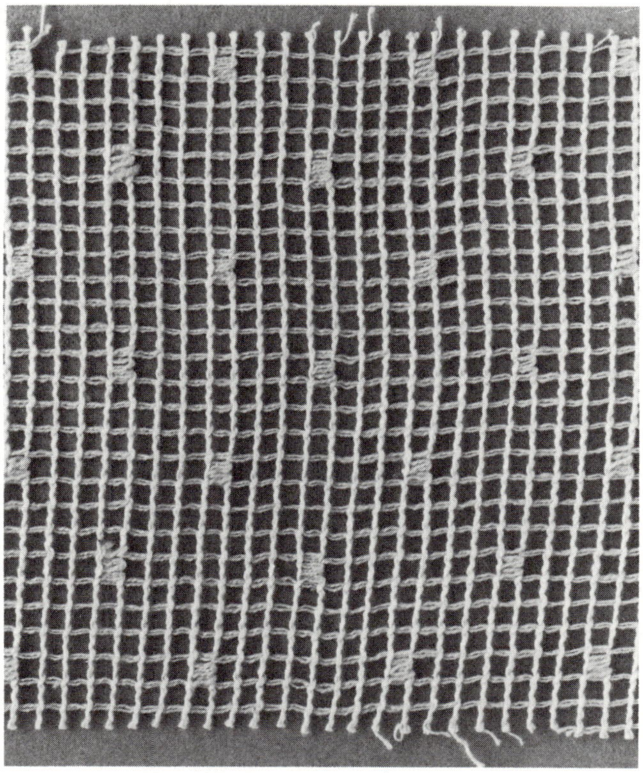

Net

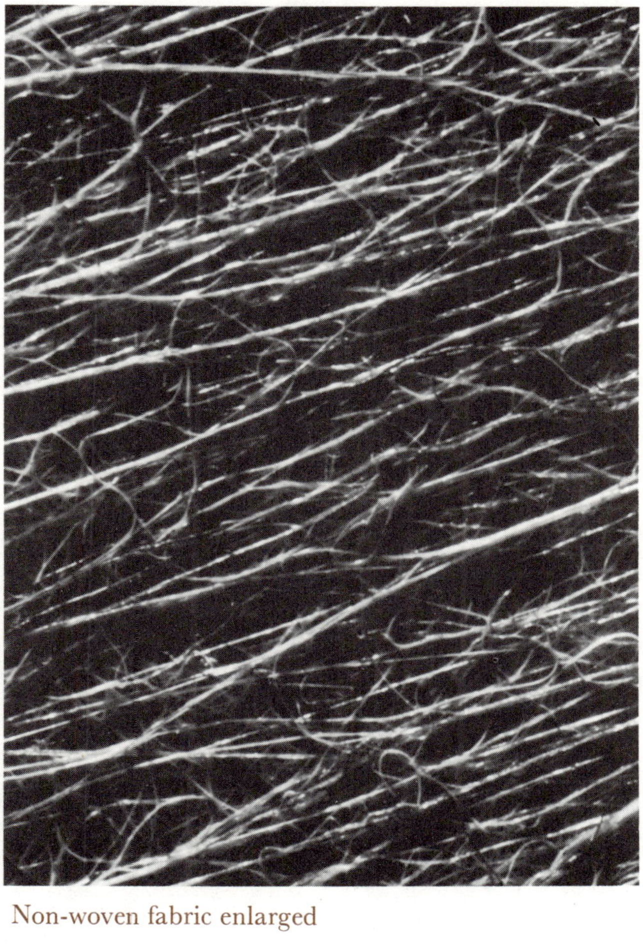

Non-woven fabric enlarged

Non-woven

This term applies to fabrics made from fibers which are bonded together by heat processing, mechanical or chemical means and which are not woven, knitted or felted. There are basically two types of non-woven fabrics: long life non-wovens made of various textile fibers by needle punching, bonding with natural and synthetic rubber and impregnating with resins; and short life non-wovens made of cellulose fibers which are disposable. There are over three hundred different non-woven products made, including interlinings, iron-on or sew-in interfacings, industrial and domestic cloths, filters and surface tissues for glass reinforced plastics and resins.

Ombre

The term applies to a woven cloth design, with stripes usually in the warp and shading from light to dark. The shaded effect is produced by using yarns dyed in various tones of the same color.

Ondulé

This is a wavy or undulating effect which can be engineered in the warp of a woven cloth by using an ondulé reed. Often the type of fabric woven with this reed is of leno construction.

Peau

Peau is French for skin. The term peau is used to describe a variety of fabrics usually a fine downy nap and include names like *peau d'ange* (angel skin)—a rayon, satin-faced fabric raised with a suede finish, *peau de cygne* (swan skin)—a fine silk, lustrous crêpe fabric similar to messaline, *peau de mouton* (sheep skin)—an imitation woven pile coat fabric, *peau de peche* (peach skin)—a fine silk and cotton fabric with a rough pile and *peau de souris* (mouse skin)—a soft silk fabric very similar to duvetyn.

Pepper and Salt

A pepper and salt effect is usually found in woolen and worsted cloth. It is created by two different colored single yarns twisted together and used in the warp and weft. A thornproof tween is a typical example of a pepper and salt effect.

Pile

The word pile comes from the Latin *pilus* meaning hair. The pile of a fabric is extra yarn or fiber which projects from the main structure of the cloth. Pile can be cut or uncut and should not be confused with the nap of a fabric (*see* Nap, p140). Typical pile fabrics include velvet, corduroy, needlecord, moquette and terry toweling.

Pleats

Pleats can be put into a fabric by pressing or steaming and by using special weaving or knitting constructions. The main types of pleat are knife, accordion and box.

Ply

This is a yarn or thread term meaning two or more threads plied or twisted together. The industrial term for ply is fold.

Printing

There are several basic methods of printing fabric and these terms are often used in conjunction with the name of the fabric—e.g., screen printed chintz or sublistatically printed polyester jersey.

Hand Methods

Block
Usually made of wood imbedded with wire nails and metal strips to form the design.

Screen
A wooden or metal frame on which a silk or polyester fabric is stretched and through which dye can be pressed with a squeezer. The screen is blocked in areas to form a pattern and to act as a stencil.

Mechanical Methods

Screen
This is similar to the hand method but the squeezer is mechanically passed from one side of the screen to the other.

Rotany screen
This is similar to flat screen printing but done with screen cylinders.

Roller
By engraved copper rollers. The engraved line of the pattern is filled with dye which is transferred onto fabric. This is a fast printing process.

Duplex
Printing by roller on both sides of the fabric so that the design coincides to give a reversible fabric.

Sublistatic
This is a method of printing fabric directly by heat from pre-printed patterned paper. Sometimes referred to as heat transfer printing.

Schiffli Embroidery

Machine embroidery onto a base net or fabric. The European center of this type of novelty embroidery is in St Gallen, Switzerland. A very large Schiffli embroidery industry exists in the United States centered in New Jersey.

Box pleating

Accordion pleating

Knife pleating

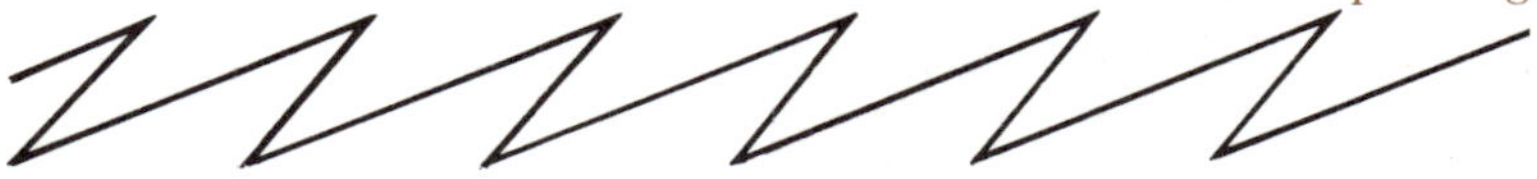

Block printing

(below) Schiffli embroidered fabric

Mechanical screen printing

(below) Roller printing

Schreiner
A special finish given to a cotton cloth which is pressed under great pressure through steel rollers which have been engraved with fine lines. The rollers flatten the threads in the cloth and at the same time leave very fine ridges across it.

Scotchguard
A registered brand name for a finish which is given to a fabric at the time of production making it more resistant to oil, water and dirt.

Selvedge
The edges of a piece of cloth.

Set, Sett
Set or sett describes the density or closeness of the yarn in the warp and the weft.

Sheer
Any thin cloth such as chiffon, batiste, voile, net or organdie where a fine yarn has been used in the warp and weft using an open, plain weave.

Sheeting
Cloth usually made of cotton or cotton and man-made fiber blends woven in plain or 2-and-2 twill weave and produced in a variety of widths from 72–120 inches (180–300 cm) for bed sheets. It is manufactured unbleached, bleached or dyed.

Shoddy
Fiber, usually wool, reconstituted from shredded rags and old yarns and re-used to spin new threads for making cloth.

Shrinkage
A reduction in the length or width of a piece of cloth either by washing or dry cleaning. Cotton and wool tend to shrink more than man-made fibers when given wet treatments.

Stitchbonding
A method of producing various types of fabric by overstitching a blanket of fiber. Sometimes referred to as stitch knitting. A wide range of cloths can be made by this process from pile fabric to fine dress fabric. There are various types of stitchbonding methods. The most well known are malimo and arachne.

(left) Arachne stitch-bonding machine

Stretch

Stretch is an important feature of certain cloths giving greater comfort. Stretch can be put into a fabric in several ways—in the construction of the cloth as in a knitted fabric, by the inclusion of stretch materials within the structure of a cloth like rubber elastic core or elastomeric core yarns in a woven fabric or by using a material with inherent stretch qualities such as rubber sheeting. Stretch fabrics should not only have the ability of stretching but should return to their original state after the release of tension.

Strié

A fine stripe or streaky effect, usually in the length of the fabric, produced by a random warp made up of threads which are dyed in a variety of tones of the same color.

Suede Finish

Suede finishes are given to woven or knitted fabrics either by raising and cropping or by embedding flock into the surface of the cloth or onto extruded plastic sheeting with adhesives.

Tape

A woven narrow fabric generally in plain weave not exceeding 4 inches (10 cm) in width with selvedges on each side. (*See* Narrow Fabrics, p141.)

Tapestry

There are three main interpretations of the term tapestry which comes from the French word *tapis* meaning carpet or covering (for a table):

1 A handwoven picture using a ribbed weave structure. The weft is usually of wool which hides the wool, cotton or linen warp. This technique is often referred to as Gobelin after the famous French tapestry workshop. Tapestry in this context has now become the generic term for many textile works of art using any material or structure.

2 A type of hand embroidery with a needle using wool thread to cover the base canvas. Often referred to as cross stitch (*point de croix*), *gros point* or needlepoint.

3 A Jacquard woven figured upholstery cloth. Constructed to produce well defined, flat and closely woven patterns.

Tebalized

A registered trade mark for a special crease or crush resistant finish applied to a variety of fabrics including pile fabrics.

Tissue

The French term used for any woven fabric. It is, however, used more often to describe lightweight woven cloths.

A fragment of woven tapestry
by the Polish artist Barbara Falkowska

Weft-knitted ribbed fabric showing two wales per rib

Tricot

The French verb *tricoter* means to knit. The term tricot has now become synonymous with fine warp knitted fabrics like milanese.

Tufting

A method of implanting a tuft of softly spun yarn (candlewick or carpet) into a backing cloth to produce a pile fabric.

Union Cloths

There are two definitions of union cloth:

1 A fabric manufactured in England from a cotton warp and shoddy weft. The cloth is heavily napped and often used as overcoating.

2 A fabric made with the warp differing to that of the weft in fiber content.

Wale

The term wale is used in knitting and weaving. A wale in knitting is one series of loops running lengthwise in a fabric. A course runs across the fabric. Wale also refers to a rib in a knitted fabric. In a woven fabric the term wale is used to describe the cords or ribs in fabrics like needlecord or corduroy.

Warp

The threads in the length of a fabric. The warp is arranged on a loom which is then crossed with the weft (*See* Weft, p150.)

Warp Knitting

The threads are looped lengthwise in a fabric. The warp on a warp knitting machine is prepared in a similar way as on a loom but there is no weft. Raschel is warp knitting.

(left) Enlargement of a cleaning cloth showing the warp knit structure and laid in bump yarn weft

Weaves

Brighton
A honeycomb weave.

Double Plain
One fabric constructed with two layers of plain-woven cloth each made with its own warp and weft. The two layers are linked together by extra threads or are interchanged.

Herringbone
A two-directional weave which produces a chevron or zig-zag pattern resembling the bones of a herring. Sometimes known as feather, arrow-head or pointed twill. Pattern is made by reversing a twill weave.

Honeycomb
A weave which creates a three-dimensional cellular structure in a cloth. Sometimes known as waffle weave. Brighton and grecian weaves are adaptations of the honeycomb.

Hopsack
Hopsack weave is sometimes called matt or basket weave. Sometimes refers to particular woolen or worsted suitings made with this weave. A square weave using a 2-and-2 or 3-and-3 interlacing structure.

Huckaback
A weave used often for making towelling having a slight three dimensional effect. Hemp, linen and cotton yarns are used to produce huckaback toweling. Sometimes known as huck or honey huck.

Leno
An open-weave structure which makes stable transparent, gauze fabrics like marquisette.

Mock leno
A weave which assimilates a leno weave, is simpler and less stable. Used for making embroidery cloths.

Plain weave or tabby
Sometimes referred to as tabby, plain weave is the most simple form of interlacing warp and weft threads in weaving.

Sateen
A weave construction which is the reverse of satin weave producing a weft faced fabric. Usually the weft is thicker than the warp.

Satin
A weave construction which is the reverse of sateen weave producing a warp faced fabric. Usually the weft is thicker than the warp.

Twill
Originally known as tweed a twill weave is characterized by diagonal lines of both warp and weft floats. Sometimes known as common twill the 2-and-2 twill is the basic weave pattern from which several other types of twill weave, stem such as 3-and-3 twill and broken twills.

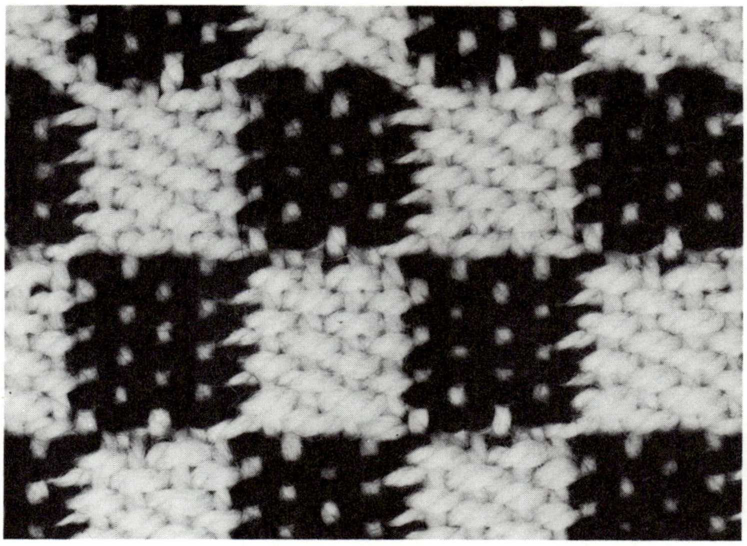

(above, left and below left) Double plain

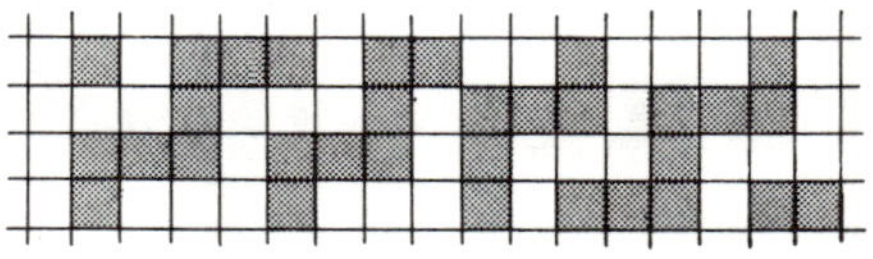

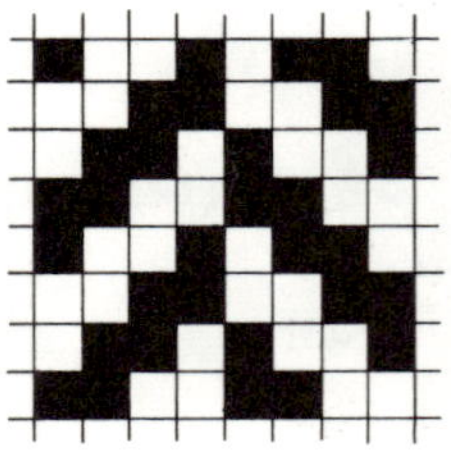

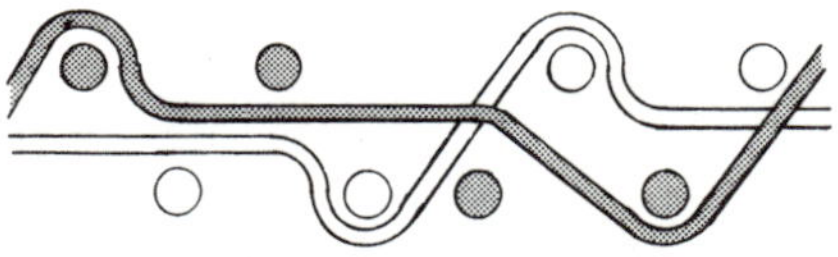

(right and above right) Herringbone

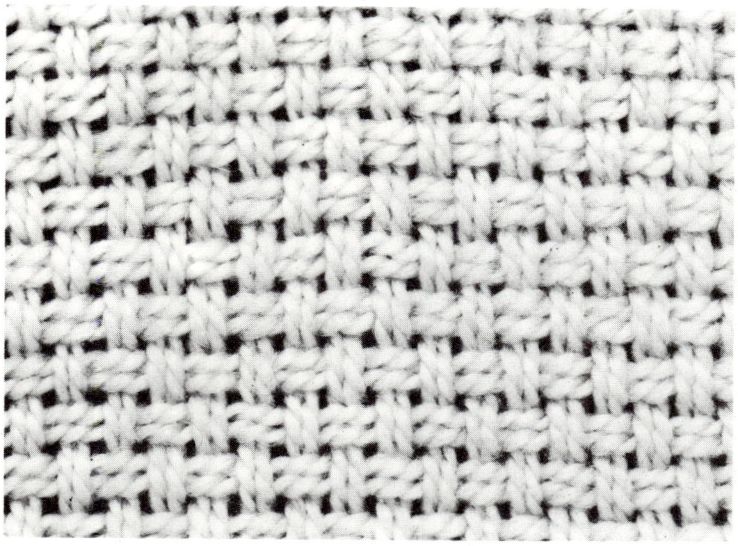

(above and right) Hopsack matt or basket

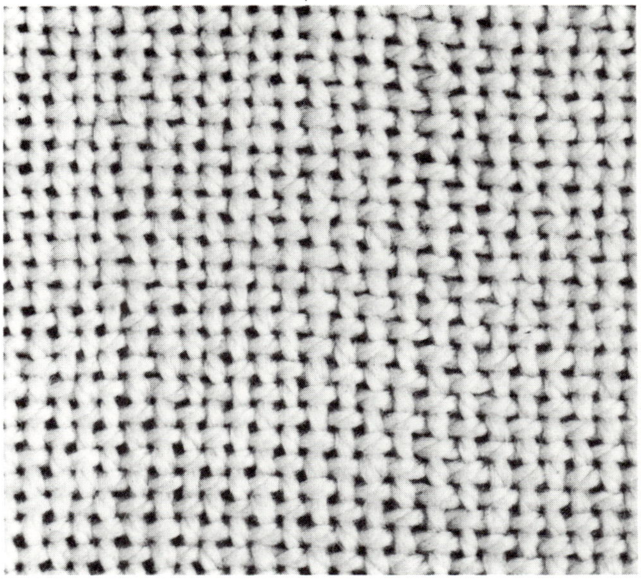

(above and right) Plain weave or tabby

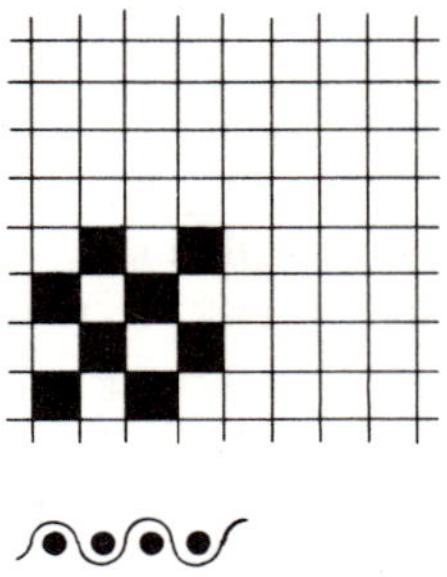

(above and right) Leno

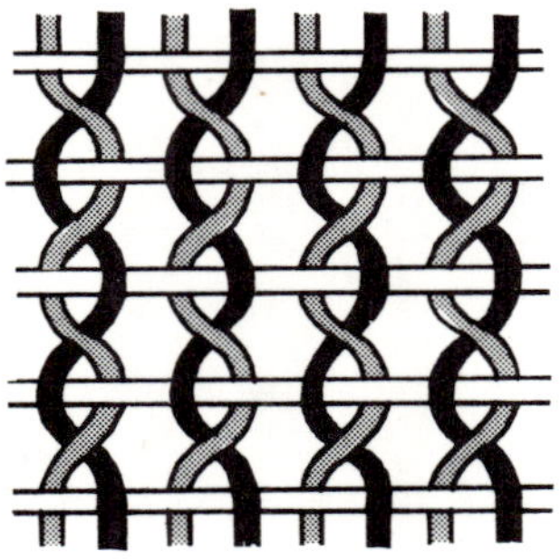

(above and right) 2-and-2 Twill

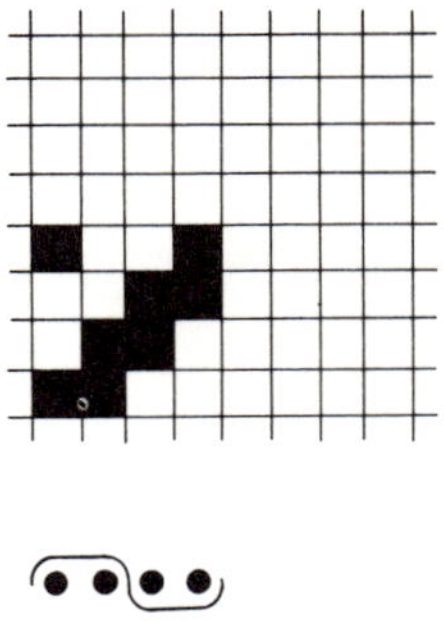

Weaving
The process of making a fabric by interlacing one set of threads (warp) at right angles to other threads (weft or filling) on a loom. The most common weaves are tabby, twill and satin.

Weft
The threads which are interlaced across the warp and make up the width of a fabric. Also known as woof. The industrial term for weft in America is filling. (*See* Warp, p147.)

Weft Knitting
The threads are looped across the fabric or garment. Hand knitting, single and double jersey are all types of weft knitting.

Yarn
The basic component of most fabric is yarn. Yarn is any form of spun-twisted or extruded natural or man-made fiber which can be interlaced in weaving or looped in knitting. It can be a blend of one or more fibers or it can be a single filament. Yarn is plied or folded when two or more yarns are twisted together. The term ply is often used in knitting yarns but usually means the size of the yarn rather than the number of components.

The earliest yarns were spun on a primitive structure called a spindle and whorl. The flax or woolen fiber was held in a loose mass on a distaff and gradually pulled off in continuous strands, a twist put in it by means of the revolving spindle to hold the fibers together and then the yarn was wound on to the spindle. The spinning wheel came later in the sixteenth century and it was not until the early eighteenth century that mechanical spinning inventions appeared. In 1737 Lewis Paul invented the roller method for preparing cotton for spinning. In 1764 James Hargreaves invented the spinning jenny and in 1769 Sir Richard Arkwright invented the roller spinning method with a spinning frame connected to water power. In 1779 Samuel Crompton invented the spinning mule. These early beginnings in mechanical spinning invented and developed by four Englishmen paved the way for all modern yarn spinning technology. The most recent development in spinning is open end spinning.

There are thousands of different yarns made in a variety of ways but all yarns are first of all spun as a single thread and multiplied to form thicker yarns or are combined by more complex methods to make fancy yarns.

Hand-knitted garments showing random effect made by using dip-dyed bouclé yarn

1 Filament
2 Single
3 2-ply
4 3-ply
5 Marl
6 Gimp
7 Snarl
8 Knop
9 Loop
10 Bouclé
11 Corkscrew
12 Slub
13 Kemp
14 Nep
15 Brushed
16 Metallic
17 Chenille

1
2
3
4
5
6
7
8
9
10
11
12
13
14
15
16
17

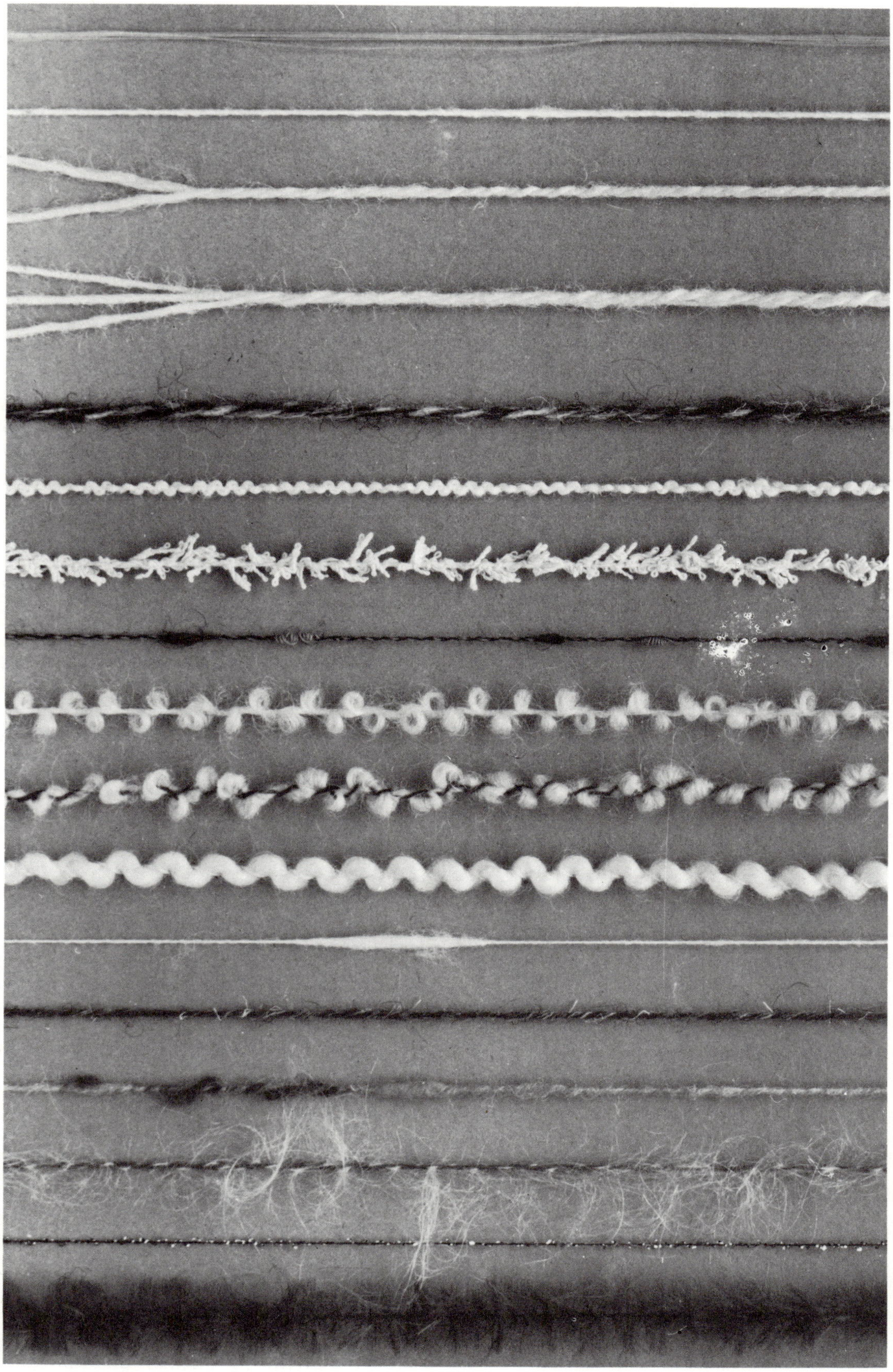

Yarns: see opposite

A Glossary of Obsolete Fabric Names

The following is a selection of names of fabrics, mostly English or French in origin, which are now no longer used. The list is by no means complete and the brief description of each cloth is in most cases all that remains. Many of these terms go back to the Middle Ages and have not been used since the nineteenth century.

Ailesham: Fine, plain-weave linen cloth
Alamode: Thin, light and glossy silk
Amabouk: Half-bleached, coarse Irish linen used for sailors shirts
Ancelia: Press fabric with hard-twist cotton warp and wool weft
Anterine: Also known as anterne. Worsted and silk or mohair and cotton
Areste: A gold cloth with elaborate patterns
Ariele: Woolen gauze
Armistice cloth: Worsted cloth, used after Boer War
Armozine: Strong corded silk
Bad: A fine linen fabric mentioned in the Bible
Baddachin: A rich, brocaded silk fabric
Ballymena: An Irish linen, hand woven
Balzarine: Cotton and worsted fabric
Bandle: A coarse, plain-weave, two-foot-wide linen hand woven in Southern Ireland
Barège: Light-weight gauze of raw silk warp and worsted weft
Barpour: Twill dress fabric of silk and wool
Bayadère: Striped mixture fabric of silk, wool or cotton
Bays: Napped woolen fabric lighter than moderate baize
Bed: Twill-woven, worsted, wide fabric
Belchester: Dress velvet
Bell-Isles: Woolen dress fabric from Norwich, England
Birdies: Plain-weave, coarse linen fabric from Kirriemuir, Scotland
Blatta: Purple silk fabric interwoven with gold
Bocking: Coarse woolen flannel-like baize
Bombazine: Light-weight fabric of silk warp with cotton, linen or woolen weft
Boratto: Silk and wool fabric similar to bombazine
Borskey: Worsted fabric
Bridgewater: Light woolen broadcloth
Brillatine: Fine cloth of silk and cashmere
Brunete: Woolen cloth from Norwich, England
Buffalo cloth: Heavy twilled woolen overcoating
Bugazeen: Calico
Burdies: Woolen fabric from Norwich
Butternut: Woolen homespun American fabric

Calamanco: Lustrous plain- or twill-woven cotton and wool cloth
Calimanco: Worsted cloth with nanon stripes
Chambertine: Light fabric of linen and wool
Côtaline: Silk and wool cloth usually black like ottoman
Cristale: White worsted cloth
Curtrike: Worsted fabric made in Flanders
Dag-swain: Coarse heavy fabric
Doily: Woolen fabric
Dowals: Coarse half-bleached linen from Daoulas, Brittany
Ducape: Heavy corded silk
Durauncer: Closely woven worsted fabric
Eolienne: Very lightweight ribbed fabric of silk warp and hard twist botany weft
Ferrandine: Lightweight cloth of silk warp and wool or cotton weft
Ferret: Silk narrow fabric
Florentine: Twill-woven silk cloth
Frocs: Coarse woolen twill made for French peasants' garments
Galloon: Narrow fabric or ribbon of silk, cotton or gold or silver tissue
Grenadine: Lightweight silk and wool mixture cloth
Grogram: Coarse fabric or silk wool and mohair
Janus cord: Black wool cotton ribbed fabric
Jonc: French linen fabric
Karamini: Light weight woolen cloth with napped surface
Kilmarnock: Coarse Scottish serge
Lahar: Soft, light cotton warp, silk weft
Linsey: Known also as Linsey-Woolsey. Coarse linen warp, woolen weft made in Linsey, Sussex, England
Little Joans: Bunting
Loughreas: Irish linen fabric from Galway, Ireland
Lutestring: Also known as lustring or lustrine; a glossy silk fabric
Lyre: Woolen cloth of good quality
Lumbard: Wool fabric
Lumberdine: Sheer black gauze
Macabre: Light weight silk and wool fabric
Malbrouk: Also known as Marlborough wool serge
Marengo: Black wool fabric shot with white, French
Marly: Light weight linen fabric
Marry-muff: Coarse fabric
Mecklenburgh: Heavy woolen cloth with floral patterns in silk
Medley: Wood fabric
Messallawny: Woolen fabric
Mocado: Pile cloth of silk and wool or linen
Moncahiard: Blade silk and wool cloth, French
Norwich Crape: Worsted and silk fabric
Orléans: Fine cotton warp and worsted weft also known as Lustre Orléans
Packing Whit: Woolen fabric
Paduasoy: Corded silk fabric
Palmyrenne: Wool and silk mixture union cloth with shot effect
Paramatta: Worsted warp and cotton or silk weft like bombazine
Philoselle: Silk fabric
Perpicuanas: Strong woolen cloth like serge
Plommet: Worsted and silk or worsted and linen
Plum Mennet: Fine, delicate wool cloth
Rashes: Twill woven silk or woolen cloth
Ripplecht: Cotton fabric
Rough Browns: Poor quality linen
Sarsenet: Fine soft silk cloth for linings
Says: Fine twill woven cloth of silk and wool
Shagreen: Silk cloth used for linings
Shalloon: Lightweight woolen cloth used for linings
Sicilienne: Silk warp with a fine cashmere weft
Silistrienne: Coarse wool and silk mixture cloth
Stament: Coarse worsted cloth
Tabaret: Alternate satin and watered silk-striped cloth
Tabby: Watered silk
Tabin: Also known as tabinet; a watered silk and wool cloth
Tamise: Soft wool cloth with some silk
Therese: Dotted gauze for hats
Tiffany: Very fine silk gauze
Tukes: Coarse linen or cotton fabric
Virli: Wool fabric
Zephiritis: Lightweight silk fabric

Bibliography

Amsden, Charles Avery, *Navaho Weaving*, Peregrine Smith Inc., 1947

Bain, Robert, *The Clans and Tartans of Scotland*, Collins 1949

Bendure, Zelma & Pfeiffer, Gladys, *America's Fabrics*, MacMillan, 1946

British Sheep Breeds, British Wool Marketing Board, London 1976

Ciba-Geigy Review, Switzerland, 1974/4, 1973/3, 1971/1

Consitt, Frances, *The London Weavers' Company*, London, 1933

A Dictionary of Textile Terms, Dan River Inc., New York, 1976

Encyclopedia of Textiles, 'American Fabrics Magazine', editors, Prentice-Hall, Inc., 1960

Fabric Forecast Magazine, London, Spring 1978

The Faithful Fibre, The Linen Thread Company, Glasgow, 1956

Gale, Elizabeth, *From Fibres to Fabrics*, London, 1972

Giles, Rosalie P., *Fabrics for Needlework*, London, 1970

Heylin, Hy B., *Cotton, Linen, Woollens, Silks*, Manchester, 1917

Hopa, Ngapare K., and Reed, A. H. and A. W., *The Art of Piupiu Making*, New Zealand, 1971

Innes, Sir Thomas of Learney, *The Tartans of the Clans and Families of Scotland*, Johnston, 1947

Ironside, Janey, *A Fashion Alphabet*, London, 1968

Irwin, John and Schwartz, P. R., *Indo-European Textile History*, Calico Museum of Textiles, India, 1966

James, Rita, *The Development of the Textile Industry in East Anglia*

Japan Textile News, January 1977

Journal of Indian Textile History, Calico Museum of Textiles, 1955, 1959, 1960, 1961

Kahlenberg, Mary Hunt, and Berlant, Anthony, *The Navajo Blanket*, New York, 1973

Kidwell, Claudia B., and Christman, Margaret C., *Suiting Everyone*, Smithsonian Institution Press, 1974

Kiewe, Heinz Edgar, *The Sacred History of Knitting*, Oxford, 1967

Kleeberg, Irene Cumming, ed., *The Butterick Fabric Handbook*, New York, 1975

Larsen, Jack Lenor, *The Dyer's Art: Ikat, Batik, Plangi*, New York, 1976

Lennox-Kerr, Peter, *The World Fibres Book*, Manchester and Atlanta, Georgia, 1972

Lipson, E., *A Short History of Wool and its Manufacture*, London, 1953

Mead, Sidney M., and Reed, A. H. and A. W., *The Art of Taaniko Weaving*, New Zealand, 1968

The 'Mercury' Dictionary of Textile Terms, 'Textile Mercury' staff

Miller, Edward, *Textile Properties and Behaviour*, London, 1968

Mortimer-Dunn, Gloria, *ABCs of Fashion and Design*, Slough, 1972

Plummer, Alfred, *The London Weavers' Company 1600–1970*, London, 1972

Robinson and Marks, *Woven Cloth Construction*, Textile Institute, London, 1967

Robinson, Stuart, *A History of Dyed Textiles*, London, 1969

The Silk Book, The Silk and Rayon Users' Association, London, 1951

Skinners British Textile Register, Thomas Skinner Directories, London, 1975

Straub, Marianne, *Hand Weaving and Cloth Design*, London, 1977

Textile Industries Magazine, December 1976, May 1977, Atlanta, Georgia

Textile Terms and Definitions, The Textile Institute, Manchester, 1970

Thomson, W. G., with revisions by Thomson, F. P. and E. S., *A History of Tapestry*, Yorkshire, 1973

Waller, Irene, *Thread: An Art Form*, London, 1973

Watson, William, *Advanced Textile Design*, London, 1954

Watson, William, *Textile Design and Colour*, London 1954

Webster's New International Dictionary, Springfield, Massachusetts, 1961

Wells, F. A., *Hollins and Viyella*, London, 1968

Wingate, Isabel B., ed., *Dictionary of Textiles*, New York, 1970

Wingate, Isabel B., *Textile Fabrics*, Prentice-Hall Inc., 1947

Acknowledgments

American Fabrics and Fashions, 24 East 38th Street, New York, New York 10016, USA
Asbestos and Rubber Co. Ltd, Waverley Street, Hull HU1 2SJ, England
Austrian Commercial Delegation, 1 Hyde Park Gate, London SW7 5ER, England
Bancroft and Sons of Halifax Ltd, Fenton Works, Halifax, England (Bunting)
Baur-Foradori, A-6021 Innsbruck, Bozner Platz 6, Austria (Loden)
Bernat Klein, Waukrigg Mill, Galashiels, TD1 1QD, Scotland (Tweed)
Bondina Limited, Greetland, Halifax, Yorkshire HX4 8NJ, England (Non-woven)
Bristol Uniforms Limited, Staple Hill, Bristol BS16 5LL, England (Asbestos clothing)
British Celanese Limited, 22/23 Hanover Square, London W1A 1BS, England (Man-made fibers)
British Man-Made Fibre Federation, 58 Whitworth Street, Manchester 1, England
British Wool Marketing Board, Oak Mills, Clayton, Bradford, Yorkshire, England
Burlington Industries Incorporated, 1345 Ave of the Americas, New York, New York 10019, USA
Bute Looms Limited, Rothesay, Isle of Bute, Scotland (Furnishing Tweed)
Calico Mills, Ahmedebad, India
Carborundum Company Limited, Rainford, St Helens, Merseyside, WA11 8LP, England (Ceramic fiber)
Cash Ltd, Kingfield Road, Coventry CV1 4DU, England (Woven name tapes)
Celanese Fibers Marketing Company, 522 Fifth Avenue, New York, New York 10036, USA (Man-made fibers)
Connemara Fabrics Limited, Kilar, County Donegal, Ireland (Tweed)
Cotton Incorporated, 1370 Avenue of the Americas, New York, New York 10019, USA
Courtaulds Limited, 18 Hanover Square, London W1A 2BB, England (Man-made fibers)
Dan River Mills Incorporated, 111 West 40th Street, New York, New York 10018, USA
Dartington Hall Tweeds Limited, Totnes, Devon, England (Tweed)
Du Pont de Nemours and Company, Wilmington, Delaware 19898, USA (Man-made fibers)
Grout and Company, Great Yarmouth, Norfolk NR31 OLW, England (Cotton crêpe bandages)
Harris Tweed Association Limited, Station Square, Inverness IV1 1LE, Scotland (Tweed)
Hollins (William) and Company Limited, Viyella House, Somercotes, Derby DE55 4JN, England
Home Laundering Consultative Council, 41/42 Dover Street, London W1X 4DS, England
I.C.I. Fibres Ltd, Bowater House, Knightsbridge, London SW1. England (Man-made fibers)
International Institute for Cotton, 17–19 Maddox Street, London W1R 9LE, England
International Wool Secretariat, Wool House, Carlton Gardens, London SW1Y 5AE, England
Irish Linen Guild, 7 Donegall Square West, Belfast BT1 6LH, Northern Ireland
Irwin (John), Victoria and Albert Museum, London SW7, England
Jacob Sheep Society, Knoll Farm, Aldington, Kent, England (Sheep)
Joshua Hoyle and Sons Limited, Summerseat, Bury, Lancashire BL9 5PP, England (Cottons)
Jute Trade Research Association, Kinnoull Road, Dundee, Scotland
Leavers Lace Association, 29/31 Lime Grove, Long Eaton, Nottingham, England
Levi Strauss, 19 South End, Kensington, London W8 5BU, England
Lewin (Janetta), Sumner House, Sumner Road, Harrow, Middlesex HA1 4BU, England (PVC aprons)
Liberty and Company Limited, Regent Street, London W1, England (Fabrics)
Magee and Company Limited, Donegal Town, County Donegal, Ireland (Tweed)
Marglass Limited, Sherborne, Dorset, England (Glass fibre)
Milliken Industrials Limited, Bury, Lancashire BL8 2AY, England (Motor tyre fabrics)
Moorhouse and Brook Limited, New Mill, Huddersfield HD7 7JZ, England (Worsted cloths)
National Association of Scottish Woollen Manufacturers, Edinburgh, Scotland
National Cotton Council of America, Memphis, Tennessee 38112, USA
National Textile Industries Corporation Limited, Dar-es-Salaam, Tanzania, East Africa
Norton and Company Limited, Nortonthorpe Mills, Scissett, Huddersfield HD8 9LA, England (Plush)
Owens-Corning Fiberglas Corporation, Toledo, Ohio, USA (Glass fiber)
Paisley Museum and Art Galleries, Paisley, Scotland
Pellon Corporation, 1120 Avenue of the Americas, New York, New York 10036, USA (Non-woven)
Peter Adams Agencies for Textiles Limited, 29 Great Pultney Street, London W1R 3DD, England
Royal College of Art, School of Textiles, London SW7 2EU, England
Sari Fabrics Limited, Sydenham Farm Industrial Estate, Leamington Spa, Warwickshire CV31 1LY, England (PVC coated aprons)
Silk Association Limited, Sovereign Way, Tonbridge, Kent TN9 1RN, England
Schlapfer and Company AG, St Gallen, Teufener Strasse 11, Switzerland (Embroidered fabrics)
Strachen and Company, Lodgemore Mills, Stroud, Gloucestershire, England (West of England wool cloths)
Tootal Fabrics Limited, PO Box 119, 45 Poland Street, Manchester M60 1NT, England (cottons)
Toye, Kenning and Spencer Limited, Bedworth, Warwickshire CV12 8QR, England (Medal ribbons)
Trimproof Limited, Trim, Ireland (Polyvinyl Chloride upholstery fabrics)
United Merchants and Manufacturers Incorporated, 1407 Broadway, New York, New York 10018. USA (All types of fabric)
United Wire Limited, Edinburgh EH5 1HT, Scotland (Woven wire cloth)
Wood (Maria), 7 Gordon Road, Shoreham by sea, Sussex, England (Calico dolls)
Wool Bureau Incorporated, 360 Lexington Avenue, New York, New York 10017, USA
World Wildlife Fund, 29 Oreville St, London EC1, England
Worshipful Company of Weavers, 1 The Sanctuary, Westminster, London SW1, England

Illustration Acknowledgments

The many museums, art galleries, firms, individuals and photographers who supplied the illustrations are kindly thanked for their cooperation and are listed below. Every effort has been made to trace the primary source of illustrations; the producers wish to apologize if in any case the acknowledgment proves to be inadequate. In no case is such inadequacy intentional and if any owner of copyright who has remained untraced will communicate with the producers a reasonable fee will be paid and the required acknowledgment made in future editions of the book.

Abbreviations used are:

RPGL The Rainbird Publishing Group Limited

JTPL John Topham Picture Library

MEPL Mary Evans Picture Library

Page

2 RPGL
6 Baker Library, Harvard Business School, Connecticut, USA
8 *Top:* Martin Hardingham
8–9 *Below:* Farmer's Weekly (John K. Wilkie), London
9 *Top:* International Wool Secretariat, (Studio Cole), London
10 *Top right:* International Wool Secretariat (Studio Cole), London
Top left: Mansell Collection, London
Top centre: Farmer's Weekly (George Weaver), London
Second from top: Farmer's Weekly, London
Centre left: Farmer's Weekly (Jack Fischer), London
Centre right: Farmer's Weekly (West Wales Press Photos Ltd.), London
Below: Farmer's Weekly (John K. Wilkie), London
11 *Top:* RPGL
Below: Farmer's Weekly (John K. Wilkie), London
12 Daily Telegraph Colour Library (G. Harrison), London
13 JTPL (Fox)
14–15 JTPL (Fox)
16 *Top:* JTPL (Fox)
Centre: RPGL
Below: RPGL
17 *Top:* JTPL (Elsa Ways)
Centre: RPGL
Below: Novosti Press Agency, London
18 *Top:* The Radio Times Hulton Picture Library, London
Below: RPGL
19 *Top:* Thurston & Co. Ltd., London
Centre: RPGL
Below: The Radio Times Hulton Picture Library, London
20 *Top:* Hamlyn Group Picture Library, London (British Museum)
Centre: National Film Archive, London
Below: Popperfoto, London
21 *Left:* US Army Photograph
Right: Royal College of Art, London (Ambassador Magazine Collection)
22 *Top:* RPGL
Below: Imperial War Museum, London (Crown Copyright)
23 *Top:* RPGL
Below: Nigel Hardingham, London
24 Central Press Photos Ltd., London
25 Patrick Eagar, London
26 *Top:* RPGL
Centre: Mansell Collection, London
Below: Hamlyn Group Picture Library, London
27 *Top:* RPGL
Centre: RPGL
Margin: Harris Tweed Association, London
Below: The Guardian (Don McPhee)
28 *Top:* RPGL
Below: Farmer's Weekly (Alex C. Cowper), London
29 *Top:* RPGL
Below: Martin Hardingham
30 *Top:* Warshaw Collection, National Museum of History and Technology, Smithsonian Institution, Washington D.C., USA
Below: MEPL
31 *Top and centre:* RPGL
Below: American Museum of Natural History, New York
32 *Top:* Renfrew District Museum and Art Gallery Service, Scotland
Centre: Biofotos (Heather Angel)
Below: Mansell Collection, London
33 *Top:* British Museum
2nd from top: RPGL
Centre: RPGL
Below: RPGL
34 Hamlyn Group Picture Library, London
35 *Top:* RPGL
Below: Farmer's Weekly (Charles Topham), London
36 RPGL
37 British Tourist Authority, London
38 *Top:* MEPL
Centre: RPGL
Below: World Wildlife Fund (William L. Franklyn/Stokes), London
39 *Top:* William Hollins & Co. Ltd.
Below: RPGL
40 RPGL
41 International Institute for Cotton, London (Brock Photography)
42 MEPL
43 International Institute for Cotton, London (Brock Photography)
44 *Top:* Martin Hardingham
Below left: Barnaby's Picture Library, London
Below right: International Institute for Cotton, London (Brock Photography)
45 International Institute for Cotton, London (Brock Photography)
46 *Top:* International Institute for Cotton, London
Below: Cotton Incorporated, USA
47 International Institute for Cotton, London (Brock Photography)
48 *Top:* Radio Times Hulton Picture Library, London
Centre: Martin Hardingham
Below: RPGL
48–49 *Centre:* Goodyear Tyre and Rubber Co. (Great Britain) Ltd., Wolverhampton
49 *Top:* Central Press Photos Ltd., London
Below: RPGL
50 RPGL
51 RPGL
52 *Top:* Pollock's Toy Museum, London
Below: RPGL
53 Radio Times Hulton Picture Library, London
54 *Top and centre:* RPGL
Below: Milk Marketing Board, Thames Ditton, Surrey
55 RPGL
56 RPGL

57 *Left:* Levi Strauss (U.K.) Ltd, London
57 *Right:* RPGL
58 *Top:* Hamlyn Group Picture Library (Jack Acheerboom)
Below: Nigel Hardingham, London
59 Martin Hardingham
60 RPGL
61 *Top:* Popperfoto, London
Below: Martin Hardingham
62 *Top:* RPGL
Centre: Martin Hardingham
Below: RPGL
63 *Top:* RPGL
Below: Mansell Collection, London
64 *Top:* Victoria and Albert Museum, London
Below: Keystone Press Agency Ltd., London
65 *Top:* Central Press Agency Ltd., London
Below: RPGL
66 RPGL
67 RPGL
68 RPGL
69 By permission of London Transport Executive
70 RPGL
71 RPGL
72 RPGL
73 National Maritime Museum, London
74 The Silk Association Ltd., Tonbridge, Kent (Tella Photography Ltd.)
75 The Silk Association Ltd., Tonbridge, Kent (Tella Photography Ltd.)
76 The Silk Association Ltd., Tonbridge, Kent (Tella Photography Ltd.)
77 The Silk Association Ltd., Tonbridge, Kent (Tella Photography Ltd.)
78 *Top:* RPGL
Below: The Silk Association Ltd., Tonbridge, Kent (Tella Photography Ltd.)
79 The Silk Association Ltd., Tonbridge, Kent (Tella Photography Ltd.)
80 *Top:* RPGL
80–81 Royal College of Art, London (Frank Thurston)
82 *Top:* RPGL
Below: Mansell Collection, London
83 *Top:* Cooper-Bridgeman Library, London
Below: The Kobal Collection Limited
85 *Left:* Hamlyn Group Picture Library (Graham Portlock)
Top right: MEPL
Below right: RPGL
86 *Top:* Photographie Giraudon, Paris
Below: RPGL
87 *Top:* Victoria and Albert Museum, London
Below: RPGL
88 Royal College of Art, London (Frank Thurston)
89 *Top:* Janet Reger, London
Below: RPGL
90 J. C. Penney Co. Inc., New York
91 The Dancing Times (J. Blake Photography), London
92 RPGL
93 New Zealand High Commission, London
94 Hamlyn Group Picture Library
95 Royal College of Art, London (Ambassador Magazine Collection)
96 Biofotos (Heather Angel)
97 RPGL
98 *Top:* Warshaw Collection, National Museum of History and Technology, Smithsonian Institute, Washington D.C.
Below: RPGL
99 RPGL
100 Hamlyn Group Picture Library
101 *Top left:* Martin Hardingham
Below left: Michael Holford (British Museum), London
Right: RPGL
102 *Top and below left:* RPGL
Right: RPGL
103 Arthur Guinness Son & Co., Ltd., Dublin
104 Paul Almasy, Paris
105 United Africa Co., Ltd., London
106 *Top:* Smithsonian Institution, Washington D.C.
Below: Royal College of Art, London (Ambassador Magazine Collection)
107 RPGL
108 John Jochimsen Ltd., London
109 *Left:* Malayian Rubber Producers Research Association, London
Right: RPGL
110 Courtaulds Ltd., London
111 Courtaulds Ltd., London
112 Courtaulds Ltd., London
113 Courtaulds Ltd., London
115 Courtaulds Ltd., London
116 *Below:* Mansell Collection, London
117 RPGL
118 Bristol Uniforms Ltd., Bristol
119 Courtaulds Ltd., London
120 RPGL
121 *Top and below left:* RPGL
Right: National Film Archive, London
122 Courtaulds Ltd., London
123 Globe Manufacturing Co., Pittsfield, New Hampshire, USA
124 *Left:* Martin Hardingham
Right: RPGL
125 RPGL
126 Courtaulds Ltd., London
128 *Top and centre:* RPGL
Below: Frank Thurston, London
129 RPGL
130 RPGL
131 Courtaulds Ltd., London
132 RPGL
133 RPGL
135 RPGL
136 RPGL
137 *Top:* Martin Hardingham
Below: RPGL
138 *Top:* Robert Hall & Sons (Bury) Ltd., England
Below: RPGL
139 *Top:* RPGL
Below: British Museum (Museum of Mankind), London
140 RPGL
141 RPGL
142 RPGL
143 RPGL
144 *Top:* RPGL
Centre: Royal College of Art (Ambassador Magazine Collection)
Below: RPGL
145 *Top:* Courtaulds Ltd., London
145 *Centre:* Courtaulds Ltd., London
145 *Below left:* Investa, Prague, Czechoslovakia
145 *Right:* RPGL
146 L. Mekowski, London
147 RPGL
148 RPGL
149 RPGL
150 John Clamp, Sussex
151 RPGL

Index